A Special Issue of
Memory

Episodic memory and healthy ageing

Edited by

Chris J. A. Moulin
University of Leeds, UK

Moshe Naveh-Benjamin
University of Missouri, USA

and

Celine Souchay
University of Leeds, UK

Psychology Press
Taylor & Francis Group
LONDON AND NEW YORK

First published 2009 by Psychology Press
27 Church Road, Hove, East Sussex, BN3 2FA

Simultaneously published in the USA and Canada
by Psychology Press
711 Third Avenue, New York, NY 10017, USA

Psychology Press is an imprint of the Taylor & Francis Group, an informa business

British Library Cataloguing in Publication Data
A catalogue record for this book is available from the British Library

ISBN 13: 978-1-84872-708-3
ISSN 0965-8211

Cover design by Design Deluxe
Typeset in India by Datapage International

Contents*

MEMORY, 2009, 17 (2), i–iv

Editorial

Moshe Naveh-Benjamin
University of Missouri, USA

Celine Souchay and Chris J. A. Moulin
University of Leeds, UK

One of the most interesting aspects of age-related changes in memory is their variability. While some memory abilities decline significantly in old age, others remain fairly constant throughout adulthood. Research in this domain has aimed, among other things, to account for the unevenness of age-related changes in memory. One important distinction is between *episodic memory*—related to a particular time and place in an individual's personal history (e.g., remembering whom you met last Friday for dinner)—and *semantic memory*, involving knowledge of general facts not related to a particular time and place (for instance, knowing that Sweden is located in Europe; see Tulving, 1972). Research shows differential age-related changes in performance on tasks tapping episodic and semantic memory. Whereas semantic memory seems to persevere into old age, episodic memory has been shown to display an appreciable decline. Furthermore, it appears that even within episodic memory, age-related decline is not homogeneous (for recent reviews, see Hoyer & Varhaeghen, 2006; Old & Naveh-Benjamin, 2008).

The articles in this special issue of *Memory* explore ageing and episodic memory in healthy adults. They provide interesting and important new findings on different aspects of episodic memory, including patterns of decline and sparing, heterogeneity in older adults' memory performance, and cognitive and non-cognitive factors that may potentially improve older adults' episodic memory performance.

PATTERNS OF DECLINE

Several of the articles explore the role of inefficient or scarce utilisation of effortful memory strategies in older adults' episodic memory deficit. The study by Clarys, Bugaiska, Tapia, and Baudouin (2009 this issue), for example, reports that older adults make fewer Remember judgements, even when they can correctly recognise something. This suggests that older adults experience their episodic memory in a different manner, with less recollection. Clarys et al. argue that such decline is part of a wider failure in executive function. The study by Shing, Werkle-Bergner, Li, and Lindenberger (2009 this issue) similarly implicates strategy utilisation in older adults' high false alarm rates in associative recognition tests, attributing them to a scarce use of recall-to-reject strategies when word pairs are used. Improper strategy utilisation is also implicated in the study by Naveh-Benjamin et al. (2009 this issue), which finds a deficit in older adults' name–face associations under intentional learning instructions, where strategies can be initiated, but not under incidental learning instructions. Decreased initiation of episodic memory strategies also seems to partially underlie the slowdown that older adults show in cognitive procedural learning (Beaunieux, Hubert, Lise Pitel, Desgranges, & Eustache, 2009 this issue). Finally, the studies by Antonova et al. (2009 this issue) suggest that different patterns of strategy usage might explain the age-related decline in

Address correspondence to: Moshe Naveh-Benjamin, Dept. of Psychological Sciences, University of Missouri, 106 McAlester Hall, Columbia, MO 65211, USA. E-mail: navehbenjaminm@missouri.edu

http://www.psypress.com/memory   DOI:10.1080/09658210802432527

allocentric spatial memory. This decline would be associated to attenuated hippocampal activation at encoding and retrieval and modified function and structure of prefrontal and parahippocampal regions.

PATTERNS OF SPARING

In contrast to these patterns of decline, the articles in this special issue of *Memory* report relatively intact episodic memory performance when such performance is based on more automatically driven processes. For example, familiarity judgements seem to show little decline with age, as reflected by a lack of age-related differences in numbers of Know judgements (Clarys et al., 2009 this issue) and in relatively intact memory for item recognition (words in the study by Shing et al., 2009 this issue, and separate names and faces in the study by Naveh-Benjamin et al., 2009 this issue). Interestingly, the sparing of familiarity-driven automatic processes, which seems to be beneficial to older adults, can sometimes be associated with a decline in other tasks. For example, the high false alarm rates shown by older adults for recombined pairs in the associative recognition tests in the Shing et al. (2009 this issue) and the Naveh-Benjamin et al. (2009 this issue) studies could be partially due to the high familiarity of the items (components). These familiar items could be mistaken as being previously seen together in pairs, resulting in older adults' high erroneous "yes" responses coupled with high confidence ratings (Shing et al., 2009 this issue; see also Souchay, Moulin, Clarys, Taconnat, & Isingrini, 2007). It is interesting to note that the above-mentioned studies appear to provide convergence between objective performance measures of episodic memory (for example, accuracy of responses), and those based on more subjective awareness (for example, K and R responses; see e.g., Tulving, 1985). Note also that Tulving's distinction between remembering and knowing suggests that these experiential states map separately onto episodic and semantic memory, emphasising that the deficit in older adults is episodic in nature; judgements about past personal events that can be made in the absence of recollection are spared.

Somewhat paradoxically, two other sparing findings in this special issue seem to reflect the processing of self-relevant information. One of these findings is related to the advantage provided when using self-referential processes, while the other reports the benefit incurred in remembering emotionally relevant information. The study by Glisky and Marquine (2009, this issue) shows that when people are asked to relate information to their own traits, older adults seem to benefit by this strategy as much as do younger adults in improving their recognition memory (see also Gutchess, Kensinger, Yoon, & Schacter, 2009 this issue[1]). This result is in line with studies showing that the relatively intact semantic memory in old age (in this case, the representation of one's self) can be used to support performance in episodic memory tasks (e.g., Naveh-Benjamin, 2000; Wingfield, Lindfield, & Kahana, 1998). As suggested by Gutchess et al. (2009 this issue), the extent to which older adults benefit from the self-reference effect would depend on the amount of cognitive resource involved. A second study reporting a relative sparing of episodic memory in old age deals with emotional information. In her contribution to this special issue, Kensinger (2009 this issue) reviews studies on age and memory for emotional materials, concluding that emotion can enhance older adults' memory, sometimes decreasing age-related differences in episodic memory. Finally, Kvavilashvili, Kornbrot, Mash, Cockburn, and Milne (2009 this issue) report that older adults (especially a young-old group) showed a relative sparing of laboratory-based prospective memory (for future events) in contrast with a decline in retrospective memory (for past events). This interesting finding deserves further investigation, as it seems to differ from previous studies and theoretical predictions regarding the vulnerability of prospective memory to ageing (e.g., Craik, 1986). The finding is in line with a recent meta-analysis on the issue (Henry, MacLeod, Phillips, & Crawford, 2004; but see also other accounts based on the type of cue, e.g., Kliegel, Phillips, & Jager, 2008).

Prospective and retrospective memory performance, as reported in the literature, may behave differently, partly due to different demands by different tasks, which can be difficult to equate or control. Overall, the relative sparing of these aspects of episodic memory in self-referential, emotional, and prospective domains could help in mapping the terrain of age-related changes in memory, while also providing potential

---

[1] Please note that the Gutchess et al. paper at the end of this book is a reprint of a paper that was originally published in 2007 in *Memory*, *15*(8), 822–837.

ways to mitigate episodic memory decline through interventions capitalising on spared memory capacities. Furthermore, as pointed out in the study by West, Dark-Freudeman, and Bagwell (2009 this issue), higher-order cognitive processes not limited to memory may also mediate memory gains, including self-efficacy and explicit goal setting.

Theoretically, the findings reported in this issue implicate both general-distal mechanisms of cognitive ageing and specific mechanisms of age-related changes in memory. The general mechanism approach is consistent with the studies by Kvavilashvili et al. (2009 this issue), Clarys et al. (2009 this issue), West et al. (2009 this issue), and Naveh-Benjamin et al. (2009 this issue), which indicate an underlying overall decline in attentional resources, executive functioning, and strategic processes. The memory-specific approach is likewise implicated in the studies by Shing et al. (2009 this issue), Naveh-Benjamin et al. (2009 this issue), and Clarys et al. (2009 this issue), which point to the role of more specific deficits in processes involving the binding of episodic elements into cohesive units, and in the retrieval of these episodes using recollective processes.

HETEROGENEITY IN OLDER ADULTS' PERFORMANCE

Although the differential pattern of performance in different tasks, materials, and types of memory discussed above can provide research and theory with important clues on memory and ageing, one important variable, sometimes ignored in experimental approaches to ageing and memory, is the finding of heterogeneity within older age groups. Two studies in this issue indicate somewhat different patterns of memory performance in young-old (ages 65–74) and old-old adults (ages 75 and above). Specifically, Glisky and Marquine (2009 this issue) report that the benefit of deep semantic processing is smaller in the oldest adults group, and Kvavilashvili et al. (2009 this issue) similarly show that prospective memory is more negatively affected in the old-old group. Such results are important for both theoretical and methodological reasons. First, they highlight questions regarding continuities and discontinuities in cognitive development in old age. Second, they emphasise the importance of defining more specifically the age samples used for older adults

in studies of memory, as this may have important implications for the pattern of results obtained.

SUMMARY

Despite their considerable variety in experimental materials (words, names, faces, spatial locations, shopping lists, and events) and methodological approaches (experimental manipulations, correlations, multivariate statistical control, cognitive–brain relationships, and dissociations), the articles in this special issue of *Memory* seem to converge on an age-related episodic memory decline. This decline is shown to be modulated by different factors, including the type of task (smaller decline for prospective memory), the type of to-be-remembered material (smaller decline for emotional materials), the demand on processing (larger decline when strategy is required), and the type of processing (smaller decline for self-referential processing). Episodic memory decline, in turn, seems to modulate performance on procedural cognitive learning, and may be related to the ability to encode and effortfully retrieve specific contextual elements and their association with focal elements (recollection and associative deficits). Future studies can assess the degree to which these age-related changes in long-term episodic memory are related to deficits that occur early in the acquisition process (involving working memory) or in retention, when information is consolidated. To provide a broader picture of memory and ageing, future studies on age-related changes in episodic memory may also explore these in relation to other memory systems and processes, including implicit memory and semantic memory. Like many avenues in memory research, theories are likely to be illuminated by neuroimaging techniques. As one better understands the effects of ageing on the brain, one should be able to point to more specific causes and consequences of episodic memory decline.

REFERENCES

Antonova, E., Parslow, D., Brammer, M., Dawson, G. R., Jackson, S. H. D., & Morris, R. G. (2009). Age-related neural activity during allocentric spatial memory. *Memory, 17*, 125–143.

Beaunieux, H., Hubert, V., Lise Pitel, A., Desgranges, B., & Eustache, F. (2009). Episodic memory deficits slow down the dynamics of cognitive procedural learning in normal ageing. *Memory, 17*, 197–207.

Clarys, D., Bugaiska, A., Tapia, G., & Baudouin, B. (2008). Ageing, remembering, and executive function. *Memory, 17*, 158–168.

Craik, F. I. M. (1986). A functional account of age differences in memory. In F. Klix & H. Hagendorf (Eds.), *Human memory and cognitive capabilities* (pp. 409–422). New York: Elsevier.

Glisky, E. L., & Marquine, M. J. (2009). Semantic and self-referential processing of positive and negative trait adjectives in older adults. *Memory, 17*, 144–157.

Gutchess, A. H., Kensinger, E. A., Yoon, C., & Schacter, D. L. (2009). Ageing and the self-reference effect in memory. *Memory, 17*, 245–260. [Originally published in 2007. Reprinted from *Memory, 15*, 822–837].

Henry, J. D., MacLeod, M. S., Phillips, L. H., & Crawford, J. R. (2004). A meta-analytic review of prospective memory and aging. *Psychology and Aging, 19*, 27–39.

Hoyer, W. J., & Verhaeghen, P. (2006). Memory aging. In J. E. Birren, K. W. Schaie, R. P. Abeles, M. Gatz, & T. A. Salthouse (Eds.), *Handbook of the psychology of aging* (pp. 209–232). New York: Academic Press.

Kensinger, E. A. (2009). How emotion affects older adults' memories for event details. *Memory, 17*, 208–219.

Kliegel, M., Phillips, L. H., & Jager, T. (2008). Adult age differences in event-based prospective memory: A meta-analysis on the role of focal versus nonfocal cues. *Psychology and Aging, 23*, 203–208.

Kvavilashvili, L., Kornbrot, D. E., Mash, V., Cockburn, J., & Milne, A. (2009). Differential effects of age on prospective and retrospective memory tasks in young, young-old, and old-old adults. *Memory, 17*, 180–196.

Naveh-Benjamin, M. (2000). Adult age differences in memory performance: Tests of an associative deficit hypothesis. *Journal of Experimental Psychology: Learning, Memory, and Cognition, 26*, 1170–1187.

Naveh-Benjamin, M., Shing, Y. L., Kilb, A., Werkle-Bergner, M., Lindenberger, U., & Li, S-C. (2009). Adult age differences in memory for name–face associations: The effects of intentional and incidental learning. *Memory, 17*, 220–232.

Old, S. R., & Naveh-Benjamin, M. (2008). Differential effects of age on item and associative measures of memory: A meta-analysis. *Psychology and Aging, 23*, 104–118.

Shing, Y. L., Werkle-Bergner, M., Li, S-C., & Lindenberger, U. (2009). Committing memory errors with high confidence: Older adults do but children don't. *Memory, 17*, 169–179.

Souchay, C., Moulin, C. J. A., Clarys, D., Taconnat, L., & Isingrini, M. (2007). Diminished episodic memory awareness in older adults: Evidence from feeling-of-knowing and recollection. *Consciousness and Cognition, 16*, 769–784.

Tulving, E. (1972). Episodic and semantic memory. In E. Tulving & W. Donaldson (Eds.), *Organization of memory*. Oxford, UK: Academic Press.

Tulving, E. (1985). Memory and consciousness. *Canadian Psychology, 26*, 1–12.

West, R. L., Dark-Freudeman, A., & Bagwell, D. K. (2009). Goals-feedback conditions and episodic memory: Mechanisms for memory gains in older and younger adults. *Memory, 17*, 233–244.

Wingfield, A., Lindfield, K. C., & Kahana, M. J. (1998). Adult age differences in the temporal characteristics of category free recall. *Psychology and Aging, 13*, 256–266.

MEMORY, 2009, 17 (2), 125–143

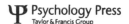

Age-related neural activity during allocentric spatial memory

E. Antonova, D. Parslow, and M. Brammer
Institute of Psychiatry, King's College London, UK

G. R. Dawson
Warneford Hospital, Headington, Oxford, UK

S. H. D. Jackson and R. G. Morris
Institute of Psychiatry, King's College London, UK

Age-related decline in allocentric (viewer-independent) spatial memory is seen across species. We employed a virtual reality analogue of the Morris Water Maze to study the effect of healthy ageing on neural activity during allocentric spatial memory using functional magnetic resonance imaging. Voxel-based morphometry was used to ascertain hippocampal volumetric integrity. A widespread neural network comprising frontal, parietal, occipital, thalamic, and cerebellar regions was activated in young and older adults, but only young adults significantly activated bilateral hippocampus and left parahippocampus, as well as right frontal pole and dorso-lateral prefrontal cortex (DLPFC) during encoding and right DLPC during retrieval. Hippocampal grey matter volume was unchanged in older adults; however, prefrontal and parahippocampal functional attenuation was accompanied by volumetric reduction. We conclude that the decline in allocentric spatial memory with age is associated with attenuated hippocampal function, as well as compromised function and structure of prefrontal and parahippocampal regions.

Age-related changes in spatial memory are observed across different species and in various procedures that essentially measure allocentric memory, the ability to represent location or position independent of bodily orientation (O'Keefe & Nadel, 1978). Significant age-related decline in spatial memory in humans has been observed using both large-scale environments and laboratory-based paradigms designed to engage allocentric spatial memory, mimicking navigational requirements of the real world (Caplan & Lipman, 1995; Moffat, Zonderman, & Resnic, 2001; Ohta, 1983; Ohta & Kirasic, 1983; Walsh, Krauss, & Reginer, 1981).

There is a strong consensus that spatial memory is dependent on hippocampal function. This is supported by lesion studies in rodents (Morris, Garrud, Rawlins, & O'Keefe, 1982), non-human primates (Lavenex, Amaral, & Lavenex, 2006), and humans (Feigenbaum & Morris, 2004; Parslow et al., 2005), as well as functional magnetic resonance imaging (fMRI) studies (e.g., Parslow et al., 2004), which implicate hippocampal involvement in allocentric, but not egocentric, spatial memory. Pronounced age-related performance deficits in allocentric spatial learning in animals have been shown to correlate with changes in cellular, pharmacological and metabolic function

Address correspondence to: Dr Elena Antonova, PO Box 78, Department of Psychology, Institute of Psychiatry, King's College London, De Crespigny Park, London SE5 8AF, UK. E-mail: e.antonova@iop.kcl.ac.uk

DOI:10.1080/09658210802077348

of the hippocampus (Barnes, 1979; Gallagher & Rapp, 1997; Rosenzweig & Barnes, 2003).

In animals the neurobiological mechanisms that support spatial memory have been widely investigated using a well-established paradigm, the Morris Water Maze task (MWT). The MWT consists of a circular pool with an underwater platform hidden by opaque water. The rodent is placed into the pool at a different location at the beginning of each trial and has to find the platform. The task requires allocentric memory, as the animal relies on distal cues around the pool for orientation and guidance. The MWT has been used extensively in rodents to demonstrate the relationship between spatial learning and hippocampal integrity (Morris et al., 1982), as well as to explore the association between ageing and spatial learning (Diana, Domenici, Scotti, Loizzo, & Sagratella, 1995; Gallagher & Rapp, 1997; Rosenzweig & Barnes, 2003). Human analogues of this task using virtual reality (VR) have also been developed and employed to study the effects of ageing. For example, Driscoll et al. (2003) found that older adults required many more trials to reach the same level of performance as young adults in a VR circular "pool" surrounded by a "square room" containing the distal cues. Older adult performance was correlated with both hippocampal volume and magnetic resonance spectroscopy measured n-acetylaspartate/creatine ratios. Moffat and Resnick (2002) used another MWT VR analogue to demonstrate age-related decline, with older adults spending less of a proportion of the distance travelled in proximity to a "hidden platform" and having to rely more on proximal cues rather than room-geometry cues. A similar age-related decline has been observed by Newman and Kaszniak (2000) using a real-space tent-like enclosure with distal cues on the interior walls. The participants had to walk to a pole within the tent and subsequently return to the pole's position from a different entry point. Older participants were impaired in finding the location of the target relative to the younger adults.

Despite the link between hippocampal dysfunction and age-related decline in allocentric spatial memory in animals, there is very little direct evidence implicating changes in hippocampal function in age-related decline in humans. Moffat, Elkins, and Resnick (2006) reported the first fMRI study employing allocentric processing of a VR environment, representing several rooms with interconnecting hallways with six common objects placed throughout. Compared with young adults, older adults showed reduced activation in neural network supporting allocentric spatial memory, including the hippocampus and parahippocampal gyrus, medial parietal lobe, and retrosplenial cortex.

The aim of the present study was to provide a more direct link between animal and human studies of age-related effect in allocentric spatial memory decline by employing a translational paradigm, a VR analogue of the MWT. This procedure, termed the Arena task, involves navigation in a circular arena, surrounded by walls adorned with abstract colour patterns. The participants start from the periphery and move towards a "pole" trying to remember the position of the pole relative to the landmarks provided by the walls. After a delay, starting from a different direction and with the pole removed they have to move to the remembered position using the spatial cues provided by the walls to determine the original pole location. Since the pole has been presented away from the walls they cannot rely on proximity to a specific visual cue, but have to integrate distances and directions from a number of cues. Notably, this procedure differs from the original MWT used with rodents in that the participants are presented with the target location from the outset, rather than having to search for it, an adaptation that reduces the use of specific search strategies, whilst measuring the same essential function. Parslow et al. (2004) have previously used the Arena task to explore the neural correlates of spatial memory in healthy adults, demonstrating posterior hippocampus and the parahippocampal gyrus activation during allocentric, but not egocentric, encoding in a group of male adults of a wide age range (19–45 years old). Additionally, the task engaged several other brain regions implicated in spatial navigation, including the parietal lobe and thalamus, broadly consistent with previous studies examining the neural network underlying spatial memory (Burgess, Maguire, & O'Keefe 2002).

It was predicted that while young adults will show significant hippocampal/parahippocampal activation, older adults would show attenuated activation. We have also applied Voxel-Based Morphometry (VBM) (Ashburner & Friston, 2000) in the same sample of young and older adults to investigate whether the attenuation in hippocampal function during spatial memory processing in healthy ageing is accompanied by its volumetric reduction.

METHOD

Participants

Two groups of right-handed healthy adults took part in the study: 10 young adults with the mean age of 23.6 years ($SD = 1.78$), range 20–26 years; and 10 older adults with the mean age of 72.14 ($SD = 5.33$), range 64–79 years. Older adults were recruited from the healthy volunteer database of the Clinical Age Research Unit at King's College London Medical School and were screened by a clinical gerontologist (SJ) using the Mini-Mental State Examination (MMSE, Kurlowicz & Wallace, 1999). All participants had higher education (years of education more than 16) and were free of any significant physical illness, with no history of neurological or psychiatric conditions. All participants gave informed consent.

Verbal, Performance and Full Scale IQ was estimated using Wechsler Abbreviated Scale of Intelligence (WASI; Wechsler, 1999). The two groups did not differ significantly in Verbal IQ (Young group mean = 117.90, $SD = 11.46$, Older group mean = 122.85, $SD = 4.22$) $p = .205$, at 5% level. The older participants had slightly higher Performance and Full Scale IQ (Performance: Young group mean = 121, $SD = 7.57$, Older group mean = 132, $SD = 12.3$) $t_{15} = -2.29$, $p = .04$ at 5% level (Full Scale: Young group mean = 121.90, $SD = 9.29$, Older group mean = 131.57, $SD = 8.16$) $t_{15} = -2.22$, $p = .04$ at 5% level. Handedness was assessed using the Edinburgh Handedness Inventory (Oldfield, 1971).

fMRI experimental task

The experimental task "Arena" is a test of spatial memory, presenting a circular arena the walls of which are rendered with abstract coloured patterns. The floor and the ceiling of the arena are grey. Short markers are distributed on the arena floor at random angles to each other and with random distance from each other to enhance the perception of motion and perspective.

An "AB" fMRI design was implemented. The full fMRI experiment consisted of six trials with a total duration of 15 minutes (2.5 minutes per trial). Each trial contained five epochs presented in the following order: encoding, retention, retrieval, first rest epoch, visual control, and a

second rest epoch. The duration of encoding, retention, retrieval, and visual epochs was 30 seconds each, with 15 seconds for each rest period. The order of the epochs in the trials and the order of the trials were held constant across participants.

During encoding a pole positioned on the top of a circular puck is presented within the participants' field of view (FOV). The participants have to navigate from the periphery of the arena to the pole using a joystick, trying to encode pole's position relative to the background wall patterns. When the participants reach the pole, the image freezes until the end of the encoding phase. During retention the participants are presented with a blank screen and asked to rehearse the location of the pole. During retrieval the pole is removed and the participants are placed in the different starting position in the periphery of the arena, having to navigate to the remembered position of the pole. The participants indicate the remembered position of the pole by pressing a button on the joystick. However, if no button has been pressed during retrieval epoch, the participant's position within the arena at the end of 30 seconds is taken as their best estimate of the pole position. Since the starting position of the retrieval phase is different from that of the encoding phase, the accurate performance on the task requires a viewer-independent knowledge of the arena environment, making demands on allocentric spatial memory. During rest epochs a blank screen is presented with no active instructions to the participants. During the visual control epoch, participants passively watch a static image with abstract coloured patterns resembling those of the arena walls (Figure 1).

A standard computer game joystick is used to navigate the arena. Tilting the joystick signals the movement around the arena; pushing forward accelerates forward movement to fixed speed; and sideways tilt allows rotation movement to the right or to the left. The movement velocity for the joystick was set constant across trials, such as to allow the participants to reach the pole no sooner than 22–26 seconds, depending on the starting position during encoding and retrieval phases.

The Arena Virtual Reality Software was programmed by Third Dimension Ltd, Sherborne, UK.

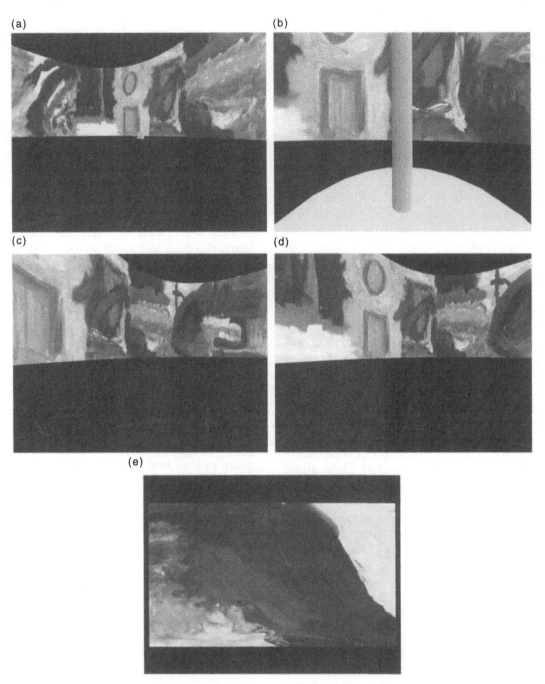

Figure 1. Snapshots of the ARENA task representing: (a) a close-up of a view from the encoding starting position showing target location (the pole); (b) a close-up of a view from the encoding finishing position; (c) retrieval starting position for one of the trials; (d) retrieval finish position for a particular participant; and (e) visual control.

Task training

Each participant completed a training session. The task was presented via a standard computer screen. The experimenter introduced the task using a version with no time constraints, which participants used until fully confident with the task. In addition participants completed one trial with the same time constraints as an experimental trial. Training and experimental trials shared identical arena environment (i.e., identical wall patterns), but differed in the pole locations and the starting positions for encoding and retrieval phases. All participants were able to understand the task requirements at the end of the training period.

Apparatus

A Dell computer with a Pentium III processor was used during the fMRI experiment: 450-MHz microprocessor, 64-MB RAM, an 8-MB 3D AGP graphics card. The images were displayed via a Proxima 55100 projector onto a perspex screen at the foot of the scanning table.

Function MRI data acquisition

Gradient recalled echoplanar MRI data were acquired using a GE Signa 1.5 Tesla system (General Electric) retrofitted with advanced NMR hardware using a standard head coil. Hundred $T2^*$-weighted images depicting the Blood Oxygenation Level Dependent (BOLD) contrast (Ogawa, Lee, Kay, & Tank, 1990) were acquired at each of 43 noncontiguous near-axial planes (3 mm thick, 0.3-mm slice skip) parallel to the intercommissural (anterior commissure–posterior commissure) line; echo time (TE) = 40 ms, repetition time (TR) = 3 s, flip angle = 90 degrees, number of signal averages = 1.

Structural MRI data acquisition

Structural MRI images of the whole brain in SPGR format using a standard 3D $T1^*$- weighted sequence were acquired for each participant.

Data analysis

fMRI experimental study

Individual maps. First, data were processed to remove low-frequency signal changes and motion-related artefacts (Bullmore et al., 1999). The responses at each voxel were then analysed by regressing the corrected time-series data on a linear model produced by convolving each contrast vector to be studied with two Poisson functions parameterising haemodynamic delays of 4 and 8 seconds (Friston, Josephs, Rees, & Turner, 1998). Following fitting, a statistic describing the standardised power of response was derived by calculating the ratio between the sum of squares due to the model fit and the residual sum of squares (SSQ ratio). Significant values of this statistic were identified by comparison with its null distribution computed by repeating the fitting procedure 20 times at each voxel after wavelet-based permutation of the time series. This procedure preserves the noise structure of the time-series during the permutation process and gives good control of Type I error rates (Bullmore et al., 2001). The voxel-wise SSQ ratios were calculated for each participant from the observed data producing individual maps contrasting experimental and control conditions versus rest.

Group maps. To derive group-level statistics, the observed and randomised SSQ ratio individual maps were transformed into standard space (Talairach & Tournoux, 1988) by a two-stage process (Brammer et al., 1997) using spatial transformations computed for each participant's high-resolution structural scan. A generic brain activation map (GBAM) was produced for each experimental and control conditions versus rest by using the permutation-based inference method described by Brammer et al. (1997) extended to cluster-level analysis as described by Bullmore et al. (1999). The latter method allows the expectation of false positive clusters to be set at the whole brain level at any desired level. For the present study the expectation of false positive clusters was set to < 1 per brain. To achieve this, thresholds of 0.05 and 0.001 were used at voxel and cluster levels respectively.

Analysis of variance (ANOVA). Randomisation-based tests for voxel-wise and cluster-wise differences were performed on individual statistics maps (SSQ ratio) in standard space. First the difference between the mean SSQ ratio values in each group was calculated at each voxel. The mean ratio was then recalculated reiteratively at each voxel following random permutation of group membership. The latter operation yields the distribution of mean differences under the null hypothesis of no effect of group membership. Voxel-wise maps of significant group differences at any desired level of type I error can then be obtained using the appropriate threshold from the null distribution. Using identical permutations at each voxel (to preserve spatial correlations) this method was then extended to yield cluster-level as described above with the expectation of false positive clusters set to < 1 over the whole brain.

Analysis of residual variance. The effect of normal ageing on the properties of fMRI signal is currently poorly understood. D'Esposito, Zarahn, Aguirre, and Rypma (1999) investigated the effect of normal ageing on the coupling of neural activity to the BOLD response and found that young adults had a slightly greater signal-to-noise ratio per voxel than the older adults, which was attributed to a greater level of noise per voxel in the older adults. We performed ANOVA comparing the residual variance in young and older groups to ascertain that the difference in the activation of hippocampal/parahippocampal region by young and older adults was not due to greater "noise" in the older group. The significance thresholds of 0.05 and 0.001 were used at voxel and cluster levels respectively.

Structural MRI analysis

Structural images were converted into ANA-LYZE format (ANALYZE software, BRU, Mayo Foundation, Rochester, MN) and pre-processed using SPM2 (Wellcome Department of Cognitive Neurology, London; http://www.fil.ion.ucl.ac.uk/spm), running in MATLAB 6.1 (MathWorks, Natick, MA). The images were pre-processed following the optimised VBM protocol, as developed, validated and described in detail by Good et al. (2001). Study-specific templates of the whole brain and grey matter, white matter, and cerebro-spinal fluid compartments were created, with the images of all participants contributing. The images were re-sliced to $1 \times 1 \times 1$ mm voxel size during spatial normalisation to minimise the partial volume effect, ensuring accurate segmentation. Normalised grey matter segments were modulated with Jacobian determinants to "restore" the original volume altered as the result of non-linear spatial normalisation and smoothed with isotropic Gaussian kernel of 12mm at FWHM to make the data conform to the Gaussian filed model, which underlies statistical inferences as implemented in SPM2. The significance threshold for regionally specific differences between the groups was set at $p < .05$ corrected for multiple comparisons.

The Montreal Neurological Institute (MNI) x, y, z coordinates of significant voxels were converted to Talairach and Tournoux space using a non-linear transform (Brett, 1999). The voxel locations were identified using the Talairach and Tournoux atlas (Talaraich & Tournoux 1988) and the Talairach Daemon software (Lancaster et al., 2000).

RESULTS

fMRI study

Behavioural performance

The behavioural measure of Arena performance is the displacement error, which represents the distance (in arbitrary units) from the recalled position of the pole during retrieval to the actual position of the pole as presented during encoding. The behavioural performance for each group was estimated over three blocks, each containing six trials, to achieve a more reliable measure of spatial memory. Older participants were significantly less accurate in recalling the exact position of the pole presented during encoding (Young group: Mean displacement error = 12.25, $SD =$ 5.915; Older group: Mean displacement error = 21.27, $SD = 5.38$), $t_{17} = -3.542$, $p = .003$).

fMRI group analysis

Encoding versus rest. Both young and old participants activated a widespread neural network during encoding relative to rest, including prefrontal, insular, sensory-motor, lateral temporal, lateral and medial posterior, left and right parietal, visual, and cerebellar regions, as well as the thalamus and the putamen (Table 1 & 2; Figure 2 & 4).

The young group showed activations in the bilateral hippocampus and in the left parahippocampal gyrus, but this was not observed in older adults (Figure 3). Other differences between the groups included activation of right anterior frontal pole (BA 10) and dorsolateral prefrontal cortex (DLPFC, BA 9/46) in young participants, and of the corpus striatum in older participants.

Retrieval versus rest. During retrieval the activation pattern in the neocortex and the cerebellum was similar to that of the encoding phase in both groups, whereas activation of the thalamus and the putamen was only seen in young participants. As during encoding, only young participants showed significant activation of the medial temporal lobe structures, including right hippocampus and left parahippocampal gyrus. In addition, young participants showed activation of the right DLPFC (BA9). In contrast, the older participants activated the anterior-medial cingulate gyrus (BA 24) (Table 1 & 2 and Figures 2 & 4).

TABLE 1
Brain regions activated in young participants during encoding and retrieval

Brain region	Encoding Maxima voxel x	y	z	No. of voxels	Side		Retrieval Maxima voxel x	y	z	No. of voxels	Side	Brodmann Area
Frontal	25	41	20	6	R	10	–			–	–	–
	36	33	23	11	R	46	–	–	–	–		
	36	41	30	10	R	9	47	33	30	10	R	9
	54	15	16	17	R	44	54	15	16	21	R	44
	−43	0	13	11	L	32	–			–	–	–
	43	11	13	7	R	32	43	15	7	8	R	32
Sensory–motor	51	7	20	30	R	6	51	7	20	28	R	6
	−22	−7	56	23	L	6	−25	−19	56	41	L	6
	25	−11	50	16	R	4	25	−11	50	7	R	4
	−40	0	30	11	L	4	–			–	–	–
	–			–	–		−36	−44	40	32	L	1
	–			–	–	–	40	−41	40	20	R	1
Medial temporal	25	−30	−3	3	R	Hippocampus	32	−37	−3	8	R	Hippocampus
	−36	−52	0	2	L	Hippocampus	43	−44	−3	3	R	Hippocampus
	−18	−26	−7	3	L	28	−18	−26	−7	12	L	28
Lateral temporal	−36	−48	20	6	L	42	32	−48	−7	29	R	37
	43	−59	0	8	R	37	−51	−56	−3	4	L	37
	32	−44	−10	4	R	36	32	−44	−10	6	R	36
	−51	−41	20	6	L	22	−25	−41	−7	4	L	36
Parietal	–			–	–	–	54	−33	33	27	R	40
	−58	−26	26	24	L	40	−32	−44	43	19	L	40
	–			–	–	–	32	−70	23	36	R	39
	–			–	–	–	−32	−34	33	41	L	31
	14	−44	40	13	R	31	11	−44	40	10	R	31
	–			–	–	–	14	−44	20	9	L	27
	22	−9	0	12	R	27	–	–	–	–		
	−22	−0	0	5	L	27	−22	−19	0	20	L	27
	−18	−70	43	59	L	7	22	−74	43	97	R	7
	22	−70	46	54	R	7	−14	−63	53	49	L	7
Visual	−14	−78	36	62	L	19	−14	−78	36	57	L	19
	14	−78	40	45	R	19	25	−74	30	50	R	19
	−25	−85	−3	51	L	18	14	−93	−3	82	R	18
	29	−85	−3	48	R	18	−25	−85	3	40	L	18
	−18	−93	−7	120	L	17	−11	−93	−13	132	L	17
Cerebellum	−11	−89	−16	82	L	–	−11	−89	−16	112	L	–
	18	−78	−20	22	R	–	18	−81	−20	56	R	–
Thalamus	−18	−22	16	18	L	–	−7	−15	7	22	L	–
	22	−30	3	11	R	–	11	−19	7	12	R	–
Basal Ganglia	−22	−15	0	16	L	Putamen	22	−22	3	8	R	Putamen
	−14	−19	−3	13	L	Putamen	–			–	–	–

Only the largest clusters for each area are listed.

Visual control versus rest. Both young and older participants showed activation of the visual cortex during visual control condition as contrasted with rest, with both groups activating striate (BA 17) and peristriate (BA 18) areas bilaterally, with only older participants showing activation in bilateral parastriate cortex (BA 19).

In addition, both groups showed bilateral activation of the frontal eye fields (BA 8), medial frontal lobe (BA 32), and premotor cortex and supplementary motor area (SMA) (BA 6). Further, the young group activated right and the older group bilateral frontal pole (BA 10), DLPFC (BA 9) and anterior cingulate cortex

TABLE 2
Brain regions activated in older participants during encoding and retrieval

Brain region	Encoding						Retrieval					
	Maxima voxel			No. of voxels	Side	Brodmann Area	Maxima voxel			No. of voxels	Side	Brodmann Area
	x	y	z				x	y	z			
Frontal	51	4	26	15	R	44	–			–	–	–
	–			–	–	–	−32	4	26	8	L	44
	−32	−30	20	6	L	32	−32	−33	7	4	L	32
	47	7	13	4	R	32	43	−19	16	5	R	32
	–			–	–	–	−4	−22	43	14	L	24
	–			–	–	–	1	−11	46	7	R	24
Sensory–motor	47	4	30	18	R	6	0	−15	50	15	R	6
	−25	−11	53	14	L	6	−4	−19	53	14	L	6
	−40	−26	53	13	L	4	−29	−33	53	38	L	4
	25	−7	46	8	R	4	–			–	–	–
	54	−15	26	6	R	1	32	−41	40	26	R	1
	–			–	–	–	−29	−30	46	10	L	1
Lateral Temporal	40	−67	3	22	R	37	47	−52	−10	17	R	37
	−40	−67	3	10	L	37	−40	−70	3	28	L	37
	25	−44	−13	26	R	36	–	–	–	–		
	–			–	–	–	47	−26	20	11	R	42
	–			–	–	–	32	−67	13	28	R	22
	–			–	–	–	−36	−30	16	6	L	22
Parietal	−47	−30	30	29	L	40	−29	−37	56	36	L	40
	58	−19	20	11	R	40	40	−44	46	9	R	40
	47	−59	10	25	R	39	36	−52	33	15	R	39
	−25	−70	13	28	L	31	−22	−52	36	59	L	31
	11	−22	0	4	R	27	–			–	–	–
	–	–	–	–	−14	−30	0	4		27	L	
	22	−67	36	98	R	7	14	−63	43	92	R	7
	−7	−74	43	84	L	7	−4	−74	40	60	L	7
	–			–	–	–	−7	52	7	7	L	30
	–			–	–	–	0	−52	10	4	R	30
	–			–	–	–	0	−56	16	9	R	23
Visual	22	−74	33	115	R	19	36	−70	7	41	R	19
	−25	−78	7	28	L	19	−18	−70	33	96	L	19
	−25	−85	−3	50	L	18	−22	−81	13	59	L	18
	29	−78	13	27	R	18	18	−89	−3	114	R	18
	18	−89	−10	73	R	17	18	−89	−10	89	R	17
	−14	−89	−3	5	L	17	−11	−89	3	4	L	17
Brain Stem	4	−22	−7	9	R	Nucleus Ruber	–			–	–	–
Cerebellum	−22	−81	−13	39	L	–	−18	−85	−16	41	L	–
	7	−63	−43	9	R	–	22	−81	−16	32	R	–
Thalamus	−14	−15	10	29	L	–	−11	−19	10	30	L	–
	14	−11	10	12	R	–	–	–	–	–		
Basal Ganglia	−25	−4	13	16	L	Putamen	–			–	–	–
	−14	−15	20	13	L	Caudate Nucleus	–			–	–	–

Only the largest clusters for each area are listed.

(a)

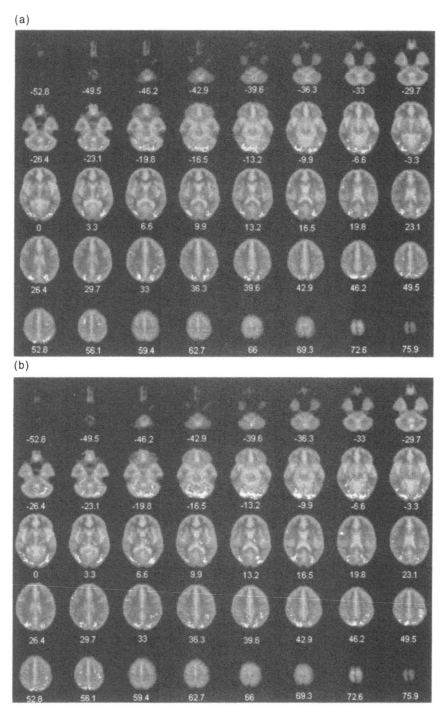

(b)

Figure 2.   Brain regions activated in young participants during (a) encoding and (b) retrieval (*p* <.001). Left side of the image corresponds to the right side of the brain. The slices are designated by z coordinates of Talairach and Tournoux (1988).

(BA 24), whereas the older group activated right and the young group activated bilateral cerebellum (BA 71). Finally, both groups activated Broca's area (BA 44) and only older group activated corpus striatum (BA 68). (Data are not shown.)

Analysis of variance (ANOVA)

Encoding. The group comparison of activations during encoding revealed significantly stronger activation of the *right* medial parietal and occipital lobes in young participants, and significantly

(a)   (b)

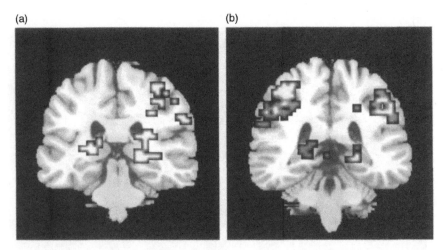

Figure 3. Coronal images showing right hippocampal activation in young participants during (a) encoding (y = −30) and (b) retrieval (y = −37). The right side of the images corresponds to the right side of the brain.

stronger activation of the *left* medial parietal and occipital lobes in older participants (Table 3; Figure 5).

Retrieval. Older participants showed significantly stronger activation of the left post-cingulate gyrus, right precuneus, bilateral visual cortex, and bilateral cerebellum during retrieval (Table 4; Figure 6). There were no areas of significantly stronger activation in young relative to older participants.

Analysis of covariance (ANCOVA)

Given significant differences in PIQ between young and older participants, we performed ANCOVA for encoding and retrieval taking PIQ as a covariate. The results were essentially unchanged, and therefore are not reported or discussed further.

We also performed ANCOVA for encoding and retrieval taking the behavioural variable (mean displacement error) to investigate which between-group differences could be attributable to between-group behavioural difference. In young adults covarying for performance abolished the right-sided activation during encoding. In older adults, left-sided activation in the primary visual cortex (BA 18) survived correction for behavioural performance (largest cluster size 57 voxels, centred at x = 14, y = −70, z = 40) during encoding. During retrieval only the cluster in the right visual cortex has survived in older males, cluster size 32 voxels, centred at x = 4, y = −78, z = −16.

Analysis of residual variance

There was no significant difference in the median residual variance in the hippocampal/parahippocampal region between young and older adults.

Voxel-based morphometry

The young group exhibited greater grey matter volume in a number of brain regions, including bilateral superior frontal gyrus, bilateral precentral gyrus, left post-central gyrus, bilateral parahippocampal gyrus, left caudate nucleus, right thalamus, and bilateral cerebellum (Table 5; Figure 7). There were no hippocampal volume differences between the groups. There were no areas of greater grey matter volume in older participants compared with young.

DISCUSSION

In the young adults, allocentric spatial memory processing was associated with the activation of the hippocampus and related mesiotemporal regions, including the perirhinal cortex. The activation at encoding was bilateral accompanied by left parahippocampal activation, while the latter extended to the right side in the previous study (Parslow et al., 2004). The mesiotemporal regions in young adults were also activated during retrieval, including right hippocampus and left parahippocampal gyrus. We did not observe significant activation of hippocampal-parahippocampal region in older adults either during

(a)

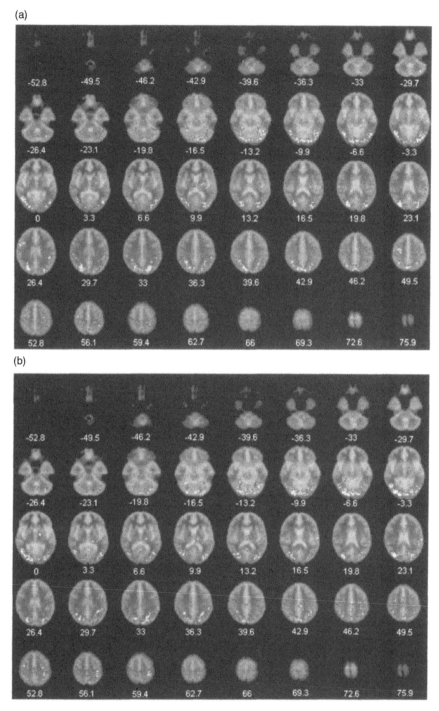

(b)

Figure 4. Brain regions activated in older participants during (a) encoding and (b) retrieval ($p <.001$). Left side of the image corresponds to the right side of the brain. The slices are designated by z coordinates of Talairach and Tournoux (1988).

encoding or retrieval, and this could not be explained by greater "noise" in this group. In the young adults the task has also activated a network of cortical and sub-cortical regions implicated in allocentric spatial memory, including the thalamus and parietal regions, during both encoding and retrieval. The older adults showed

similar activation pattern, but lacked activation of the frontal pole (BA 10) and dorsolateral pre-frontal cortex (DLPFC, BA 9/46) observed in younger adults. The young adults showed greater *right* parietal and visual cortex activation than the older adults, whereas the older adults showed greater *left* parietal and visual cortex activation

TABLE 3
Brain regions of significantly greater activation during encoding in young participants relative to older participants

| | | | | Encoding | | |
| Brain region | \x | \y | \z | No. of voxels | Side | Brodmann Area |
	Maxima voxel					
Parietal	29	−67	23	5	R	39
	29	−52	26	2	R	31
	25	−63	33	2	R	7
Visual	29	−63	30	11	R	19
	29	−70	20	10	R	19
	25	−78	16	5	R	19
	29	−67	26	3	R	19
	25	−67	26	2	R	19
	25	−78	23	1	R	19
	29	−70	13	3	R	18
	22	−74	13	3	R	17

$p < .001$. There were no significantly greater activated areas in young participants relative to older ones during retrieval.

than the young adults during encoding. The VBM analysis revealed that while there were widespread reductions of the grey matter volume in older adults, the hippocampus was not affected.

The attenuation of hippocampal function in older adults was accompanied by poorer performance on the Arena task. The impaired spatial memory of the older adults is in agreement with previous studies using human analogues of the Morris Water Maze (Driscoll et al., 2003; Driscoll, Hamilton, Yeo, Brooks, & Sutherland, 2005; Moffat et al., 2000). In these studies the performance of the older adults seems to indicate a use of proximal cue guidance rather than cognitive mapping, in which the direction of multiple cues is used to determine position, in search for a hidden platform. In the current version of the MWT VR analogue developed specifically for fMRI, there is no "search" component, as the

remembered location (a pole) is made visible at the start of each trial, excluding the possibility of specific search strategies being used by the participants to aid performance. Therefore poorer performance of older adults in the present study is unlikely to be explained by the lack of strategy formation or implementation.

In the current study the bilateral hippocampal activation in young adults was found during both encoding and retrieval, whereas this was limited to encoding in the previous study using Arena paradigm (Parslow et al., 2004). An inclusion of adults over the age of 35 in Parslow et al. sample (age range 18 − 45 years) might have "diluted" hippocampal activation during retrieval. In the present study the attenuation of hippocampal and perirhinal activity with age was observed for both encoding and retrieval; however, the difference between the groups was not strong enough to

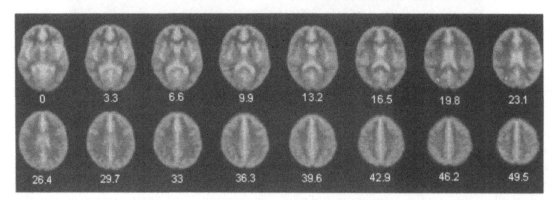

Figure 5. Brain regions activated significantly more strongly in young participants relative to older participants during encoding, using ANOVA group contrast ($p < .001$). Left side of the image corresponds to the right side of the brain. The slices are designated by z coordinates of Talairach and Tournoux (1988).

TABLE 4
Brain regions of significantly greater activation during encoding and retrieval in older participants relative to young participants

| | Encoding | | | | | | Retrieval | | | | | |
| | Maxima voxel | | | | | | Maxima voxel | | | | | |
Brain region	x	y	z	No. of voxels	Side	Brodmann Area	x	y	z	No. of voxels	Side	Brodmann Area
Parietal	−25	−70	16	9	L	31	−14	−63	20	7	L	31
	−25	−63	23	1	L	31	–	–	–	–	–	–
	−18	−74	36	9	L	7	–	–	–	–	–	–
	−14	−67	46	8	L	7	–	–	–	–	–	–
	−14	−67	43	5	L	7	–	–	–	–	–	–
	−14	−70	40	4	L	7	–	–	–	–	–	–
	−14	−63	50	3	L	7	–	–	–	–	–	–
	−14	−67	33	1	L	7	–	–	–	–	–	–
	–	–	–	–	11	−74	40	9	R	7	–	–
Visual	−18	−74	30	11	L	19	11	−78	33	9	R	19
	−22	−70	33	5	L	19	−36	−78	3	3	L	19
	−18	−67	26	11	L	18	14	−78	−10	10	R	18
	−18	−70	23	10	L	18	−22	−74	16	6	L	18
	−22	−78	20	7	L	18	18	−70	26	4	R	18
	−29	−74	13	4	L	18	0	−85	−7	5	R	17
Cerebellum	–		–	–	–	–	−11	−81	−16	17	L	–
	–		–	–	–	–	4	−78	−16	12	R	–

$p < .001.$

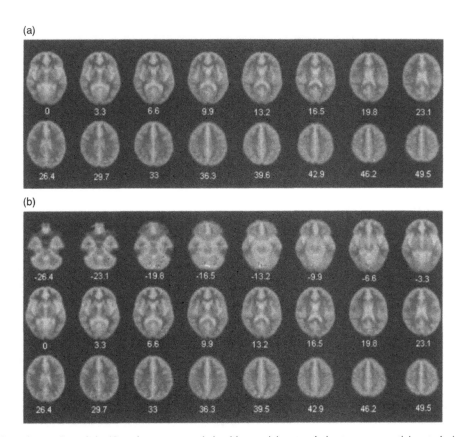

Figure 6. Brain regions activated significantly more strongly in older participants relative to young participants during (a) encoding and (b) retrieval, using ANOVA group contrast ($p < .001$). Left side of the image corresponds to the right side of the brain. The slices are designated by z coordinates of Talairach and Tournoux (1988).

TABLE 5
Brain regions of greater grey matter volume in young adults relative to older adults

Brain region	Maxima voxel			Side	Brodmann Area	T value	P value corrected (family-wise error)
	x	y	z				
Superior frontal gyrus	−12	52	−13	L	10	7.25	0.012
	−24	64	−7	L	10	6.89	0.02
	15	48	−14	R	10	7.15	0.014
	15	55	−9	R	10	6.87	0.021
Precentral gyrus	46	−12	41	R	4	8	0.004
	−45	−18	37	L	4	7.63	0.007
Postcentral gyrus	−51	−25	47	L	2	8.53	0.002
	−59	−18	37	L	3	7.9	0.005
Parahippocampal gyrus	−30	−53	−6	L	19	8.35	0.003
	−24	−57	−5	L	19	7.74	0.006
	39	−34	−10	R	36	8.33	0.003
	22	−57	−4	R	19	6.76	0.024
Caudate nucleus	−3	4	3	L	–	8.03	0.004
Thalamus	2	−2	9	R	–	7.72	0.006
Cerebellum	−22	−58	−24	L	–	7.86	0.005
	3	−73	−11	R	–	7.66	0.007
	39	−68	−18	R	–	7.36	0.01
	27	−56	−22	R	–	7.31	0.011
	26	−48	−23	R	–	6.59	0.031

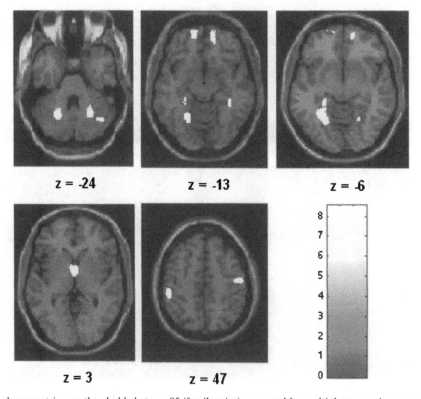

Figure 7.   Statistical parametric map thresholded at $p < .05$ (family-wise) corrected for multiple comparisons overlaid on axial slices to show all significant clusters of greater grey matter volume in young adults compared with older adults. The left side of the image corresponds to the left side of the brain.

differentiate them in the between-group analysis of variance. Hippocampal activations normally observed in fMRI studies have small effect size, affecting the power of between-group analysis.

Despite the attenuated hippocampal function, there was no detectable loss of hippocampal volume in older adults. The volumetric integrity of hippocampus in the ageing brain is consistent with previous studies using VBM (e.g. Good et al., 2001; Maguire & Frith, 2003). The lack of association between hippocampal loss of performance and volume has been found in other studies exploring age-related effects on episodic memory (for review, Van Petten, 2004). Hippocampal volume decrease does not seem to have been demonstrated convincingly across studies and those studies that have correlated volume and age did not yield significant results (Van Petten, 2004). Furthermore, the studies that have demonstrated significant hippocampal volume reduction using longitudinal design have failed to demonstrate its association with memory performance (Cohen, Small, Lalonde, Friz, & Sunderland, 2001; Rodrigue & Raz, 2004). The preservation of hippocampal volume in the ageing brain suggests that more subtle changes might be driving the loss of function. One possibility that has been suggested is a reduction in hippocampal neurogenesis, which correlates with MWT performance in ageing rats (Drapeau et al., 2003), or neuropharmacological changes such as loss of cholinergic modulation of hippocampal function (Furey, Pietrini, Alexander, Schapiro, and Horwitz, 2000). Alternatively, the attenuation of hippocampal function with age might be related to the degeneration of its cortical connections and/or of functionally related structures.

In addition to hippocampal activation, the young adults activated left parahippocampal gyrus during both encoding and retrieval. The boundaries between hippocampus and parahippocampal gyrus are difficult to determine given the spatial resolution of fMRI in combination with Talairach mapping. Nevertheless, this is in keeping with studies that have supported the role of the parahippocampal region in spatial memory through representation of spatial layout (Brewer, Zhao, Desmond, Glover, & Gabrieli, 1998; Kirschhoff, Wagner, Maril, & Stern, 2000; Weis, Klaver, Reul, Elger, & Fernandez, 2004) and the geometric analysis of spatial scenes (Burgess et al., 2002; Epstein & Kanwisher, 1998). Furthermore, spatial view and place cells are found in this region in non-human primates

(Nishijo, Ono, Eifuku & Tamura, 1997). Meulenbroek, Petersson, Voermans, Weber, and Fernandez (2004), using fMRI, have previously demonstrated reduced parahippocampal activity in older adults relative to young in egocentric route learning task. Our study extends their finding to allocentric spatial memory, as well as demonstrating reduced grey matter volume of parahippocampal gyrus in older adults. The degeneration of parahippocampal function and structure might have more direct (or earlier) involvement in ageing-related decline in spatial memory.

The Arena task activated a range of brain structures implicated in allocentric spatial memory alongside the mesiotemporal lobe. These included the parietal cortex (Burgess et al., 2001), the thalamus (Goodridge & Taube, 1997; Wiener & Taube, 2005), and the cerebellum (Lalonde & Strazielle, 2003; Rondi-Reig & Burguiere, 2005). Interactions between the parietal and the mesiotemporal areas are likely to support the processing of allocentric spatial representations. One possibility is that visuo-spatial and self-motion cues are initially processes by the associative parietal cortex in an egocentric frame of reference, with the subsequent transfer of these egocentric representations into an allocentric cognitive map by the hippocampus (Save & Poucet, 2000a). Alternatively, the allocentric representation might be progressively derived from the egocentric representations in the parietal cortex itself, with the allocentric representation than being transferred into a long-term storage by the hippocampus (Save & Poucet, 2000b). Burgess et al. (2001) have proposed that the posterior parietal lobe has the specific role in recoding body-centred representations into view-independent ones.

The between-group analysis of variance has revealed dissociation in the activation of right and left visual/parietal cortices during encoding, such that young adults activated right hemisphere and older adults activated the left hemisphere significantly more strongly. This different locus of activation may reflect different modes of representing spatial information by young and older adults. Kosslyn and colleagues (Kosslyn, Chabris, Marsolek, & Koenig, 1992; Kosslyn et al., 1989) provided evidence for two types of spatial information processing: categorical or relative (e.g. above–below) and coordinate or metric (e.g. near–far). Empirical evidence suggests that these qualitatively different computations are processed in separate neural systems, with the left hemisphere having an advantage for making judgements requiring categorical spatial relations, presumably as they are language-based; while the right hemisphere having an advantage for making judgements requiring coordinate spatial relations (e.g., Hellige & Michimata, 1989; Kosslyn, 1987; Kosslyn et al., 1989; Okubo & Michimata, 2002). Both types of information could be used to encode the pole's position within the virtual arena. In fact, a combination of both types of representations would yield the most accurate performance: categorical information would aid encoding of the pole's position relative to the landmarks provided by the walls, whereas co-ordinate information would aid encoding the pole's distance from the arena walls. From the pattern of the observed activation it appears that young adults may have made greater use of coordinate processing to encode the pole's posi-tion, which resulted in more accurate perfor-mance compared with older adults who appear to have relied on left-hemisphere-based catego-rical processing, yielding poorer performance accuracy. The analysis of covariance seems to confirm the association between these activations and the behavioural performance. Thus, covary-ing for performance accuracy has abolished the right-sided visual cortex activation during encod-ing in young adults, suggesting that right-hemi-sphere-based coordinate processing during encoding is related to the accuracy of locating the pole's position during retrieval. Left-sided visual cortex activation in older adults during encoding was not related to the accuracy of performance; however, the left-sided activation during retrieval did, indicating that reliance on categorical processing during retrieval is asso-ciated with less accurate performance.

In keeping with this notion, Bruyer, Scailquin, and Coibion (1997) have reported a detrimental effect of ageing on coordinate spatial relation processing on the measures of performance accuracy in a perceptual task. Our results further support the idea that coordinate representation of spatial information might be compromised in healthy ageing. A simple possibility is that the relative loss of right parietal lobe activity with ageing reflects accelerated functional loss in the right hemisphere, as indicated by the right hemi-ageing hypothesis. This hypothesis was originally based on the finding that performance on spatial tasks tends to decline more rapidly with age than performance on verbal tasks (Goldstein &

Shelley, 1981). However, this difference may be due to the spatial tests used being more sensitive, since when task complexity is matched the difference disappears (Elias & Kinsbourne, 1974). Studies comparing hemisphere function using dichotic listening have produced mixed results (see review by Dolcos, Rice, & Cabeza, 2002), suggesting that the effect may be task related. Alternatively, some structures in the right hemisphere might age more quickly than others (Gerhardstein, Peterson, & Rapcsak, 1998). How-ever, the current study did not observe a differ-entially greater grey matter volume reduction of the right hemisphere in the older group, and there is no evidence for this from other volumetric studies (Raz et al., 2004). Another alternative is that reliance on categorical representations might be a strategic switch by cognitive systems in the presence of compromised hippocampus-based allocentric spatial processing and/or fine-grained coordinate representations.

The between-group comparison of the retrie-val has revealed no significantly stronger activa-tions in young adults and significantly stronger bilateral activations of the visual and parietal cortices in older adults. The reduced lateralisation of brain activation during cognitive performance with ageing, particularly in the prefrontal cortex (PFC) (for review, see Cabeza, 2001) has become known as the HAROLD (Hemispheric Asymme-try Reduction in Older Adults) Model (Cabeza, 2002). This effect is observed for both encoding and retrieval of verbal information, with the findings for retrieval being more consistent (e.g., Backman et al., 1997; Cabeza et al., 1997; Madden et al., 1999). Our results further support this effect during retrieval, and extend it to the to the posterior regions of the brain during the processing of non-verbal stimuli.

The young adults activated the frontal anterior pole (BA 10) and the right DLPFC (BA 9/46) during both encoding and retrieval. These areas are known to be associated with maintenance and manipulation of memory representations (Smith & Jonides, 1997). These areas of activation were not seen in older adults, with the lack of frontal pole activation being accompanied by its reduced grey matter volume. The under-recruitment of PFC has been previously observed in the studies of ageing on verbal memory decline and was interpreted as lack of self-initiated effective strategies in problem solving (Cabeza et al., 1997; Grady et al., 1995; Logan, Sanders, Snyder, Morris, & Buckner, 2002). Age-related decline in allocentric memory might, therefore, occur due to a functional and structural degeneration of dorsolateral–mesiotemporal network. However, this is a tentative conclusion since we have not performed co-activation correlation between the prefrontal cortex and the mesiotemporal lobe structures in the present study. Our future work will extend to age-related functional connectivity of brain regions supporting allocentric spatial memory. Finally, both young and older adults activated ventro-lateral PFC (VLPFC, BA 44), with young adults showing right hemisphere activation during both encoding and retrieval, whereas older participants activated right VLPFC during encoding and left VLPFC during retrieval. Whereas the DLPFC is thought to be involved in spatial processing, the VLPFC is suggested to be involved in processing the features and identity of objects (Romanski, 2004).

In conclusion, the Morris Water Maze analogue procedure, the Arena task, has been used in conjunction with fMRI to demonstrate age-related decline in brain neural activity associated with allocentric memory. Although the older adults did not have reduced hippocampal volume they had attenuated hippocampal activation, both at encoding and retrieval, and this was accompanied by a decrease in performance accuracy. In addition, an intriguing crossover interaction between age and parietal lobe activation was observed, suggestive of a "switch" from coordinate to categorical processing of spatial information with age. The findings are consistent with previous work using human MWT analogue tasks in ageing showing an age-related decline in spatial memory, with this study using fMRI measurement showing this is related to loss of hippocampal activity.

REFERENCES

Ashburner, J., & Friston, K. J. (2000). Voxel-based morphometry – the methods. *Neuroimage, 11*, 805–821.

Backman, L., Almkvist, O., Andersson, J., Nordberg, A., Windblad, B., Rineck, R., et al. (1997). Brain activation in young and older adults during implicit and explicit retrieval. *Journal of Cognitive Neuroscience, 9*(3), 378–391.

Barnes, C. A. (1979). Memory deficits associated with senescence: A neurophysiological and behavioral study in the rat. *Journal of Comparative Physiology and Psychology, 93*, 74–104.

Brammer, M. J., Bullmore, E. T., Simmons, A., Williams, S. C., Grasby, P. M., Howard, R. J., et al. (1997). Generic brain activation mapping in functional magnetic resonance imaging: A nonparametric approach. *Magnetic Resonance Imaging, 15*, 763–770.

Brett, M. (1999). The MNI brain and the Talairach atlas. MRC Cognition and Brain Sciences Unit (http://www.mrc-cbu.cam.ac.uk/Imaging/mnispace. html)

Brewer, J. B., Zhao, Z., Desmond, J. E., Glover, G. H., & Gabrieli, J. D. (1998). Making memories: Brain activity that predicts how well visual experience will be remembered. *Science, 281*, 1185–1187.

Bruyer, R., Scailquin, J. C., & Coibion, P. (1997). Dissociation between categorical and coordinate spatial computations: Modulation by cerebral hemispheres, task properties, mode of response, and age. *Brain and Cognition, 33*, 245–277.

Bullmore, E., Long, C., Suckling, J., Fadili, J., Calvert, G., Zelaya, F., et al. (2001). Colored noise and computational inference in neurophysiological (fMRI) time series analysis: Resampling methods in time and wavelet domains. *Human Brain Mapping, 12*, 61–78.

Bullmore, E. T., Brammer, M. J., Rabe-Hesketh, S., Curtis, V. A., Morris, R. G., Williams, S. C., et al. (1999). Methods for diagnosis and treatment of stimulus-correlated motion in generic brain activation studies using fMRI. *Human Brain Mapping, 7*, 38–48.

Burgess, N., Maguire, E. A., & O'Keefe, J. (2002). The human hippocampus and spatial and episodic memory. *Neuron, 35*, 625–641.

Burgess, N., Maguire, E. A., Spiers, H. J., & O'Keefe, J. (2001). A temporoparietal and prefrontal network for retrieving the spatial context of lifelike events. *Neuroimage, 14*, 439–453.

Cabeza, R. (2001). Cognitive neuroscience of ageing: Contributions of functional neuroimaging. *Scandinavian Journal of Psychology, 42*(3), 277–286.

Cabeza, R. (2002). Hemispheric asymmetry reduction in older adults: The HAROLD model. *Psychology of Ageing, 17*(1), 85–100.

Cabeza, R., Grady, C. L., Nyberg, L., McIntosh, A. R., Tulving, E., Kapur, S., et al. (1997). Age-related differences in neural activity during memory encoding and retrieval: A positron emission tomography study. *Journal of Neuroscience, 17*(1), 391–400.

Caplan, L. J., & Lipman, P. D. (1995). Age and gender differences in the effectiveness of map-like learning aids in memory for routes. *The Journals of Gerontology. Series B, Psychological Sciences and Social Sciences, 50*(3), 126–133.

Cohen, R. M., Small, C., Lalonde, F., Friz, J., & Sunderland, T. (2001). Effect of apolipoprotein E genotype on hippocampal volume loss in ageing healthy women. *Neurology, 57*, 2223–2228.

D'Esposito, M., Zarahn, E., Aguirre, G. K., & Rypma, B. (1999). The effect of normal ageing on the coupling of neural activity to the bold hemodynamic response. *Neuroimage, 10*, 6–14.

Diana, G., Domenici, M. R., Scotti, d. C., Loizzo, A., & Sagratella, S. (1995). Reduced hippocampal CA1

Ca(2+)-induced long-term potentiation is associated with age-dependent impairment of spatial learning. *Brain Research, 686*, 107–110.

Dolcos, F., Rice, H. J., & Cabeza, R. (2002). Hemispheric asymmetry and ageing: Right hemisphere decline or asymmetry reduction. *Neuroscience Biobehavioral Reviews, 26*, 819–825.

Drapeau, E., Mayo, W., Aurousseau, C., Le Moal, M., Piazza, P. V., & Abrous, D. N. (2003). Spatial memory performances of aged rats in the water maze predict levels of hippocampal neurogenesis. *The Proceedings of the National Academy of Sciences of the United States of America, 100*, 14385–14390.

Driscoll, I., Hamilton, D. A., Petropoulos, H., Yeo, R. A., Brooks, W. M., Baumgartner, R. N., et al. (2003). The ageing hippocampus: Cognitive, biochemical and structural findings. *Cerebral Cortex, 13*, 1344–1351.

Driscoll, I., Hamilton, D. A., Yeo, R. A., Brooks, W. M., & Sutherland, R. J. (2005). Virtual navigation in humans: The impact of age, sex, and hormones on place learning. *Hormones and Behavior, 47*, 326–335.

Elias, M. F., & Kinsbourne, M. (1974). Age and sex differences in the processing of verbal and nonverbal stimuli. *Journal of Gerontology, 29*, 162–171.

Epstein, R., & Kanwisher, N. (1998). A cortical representation of the local visual environment. *Nature, 392*, 598–601.

Feigenbaum, J. D., & Morris, R. G. (2004). Allocentric versus egocentric spatial memory after unilateral temporal lobectomy in humans. *Neuropsychology, 18*, 462–472.

Friston, K. J., Josephs, O., Rees, G., & Turner, R. (1998). Nonlinear event-related responses in fMRI. *Magnetic Resonance in Medicine, 39*, 41–52.

Furey, M. L., Pietrini, P., Alexander, G. E., Schapiro, M. B., & Horwitz, B. (2000). Cholinergic enhancement improves performance on working memory by modulating the functional activity in distinct brain regions: A positron emission tomography regional cerebral blood flow study in healthy humans. *Brain Research Bulletin, 51*, 213–218.

Gallagher, M., & Rapp, P. R. (1997). The use of animal models to study the effects of ageing on cognition. *Annual Review of Psychology, 48*, 339–370.

Gerhardstein, P., Peterson, M. A., & Rapcsak, S. Z. (1998). Age-related hemispheric asymmetry in object discrimination. *Journal of Clinical and Experimental Neuropsychology, 20*, 174–185.

Goldstein, G., & Shelly, C. (1981). Does the right hemisphere age more rapidly than the left? *Journal of Clinical Neuropsychology, 3*, 65–78.

Good, C. D., Johnsrude, I. S., Ashburner, J., Henson, R. N., Friston, K. J., & Frackowiak, R. S. (2001). A voxel-based morphometric study of ageing in 465 normal adult human brains. *Neuroimage, 14*, 21–36.

Goodridge, J. P., & Taube, J. S. (1997). Interaction between the postsubiculum and anterior thalamus in the generation of head direction cell activity. *Journal of Neuroscience, 17*, 9315–9330.

Grady, C. L., McIntosh, A. R., Horwitz, B., Maisog, J. M., Ungerleider, L. G., Mentis, M. J., et al. (1995).

Age-related reductions in human recognition memory due to impaired encoding. *Science, 269*, 218–221.

Hellige, J. B., & Michimata, C. (1989). Categorization versus distance: Hemispheric differences for processing spatial information. *Memory and Cognition, 17*, 770–776.

Kirchhoff, B. A., Wagner, A. D., Maril, A., & Stern, C. E. (2000). Prefrontal–temporal circuitry for episodic encoding and subsequent memory. *Journal of Neuroscience, 20*, 6173–6180.

Kosslyn, S. M. (1987). Seeing and imagining in the cerebral hemispheres: A computational approach. *Psychological Review, 94*, 148–175.

Kosslyn, S. M., Chabris, C. F., Marsolek, C. J., & Koenig, O. (1992). Categorical versus coordinate spatial relations: Computational analyses and computer simulations. *Journal of Experimental Psychology: Human Perception and Performance, 18*, 562–577.

Kosslyn, S. M., Koenig, O., Barrett, A., Cave, C. B., Tang, J., & Gabrieli, J. D. (1989). Evidence for two types of spatial representations: Hemispheric specialization for categorical and coordinate relations. *Journal of Experimental Psychology: Human Perception and Performance, 15*, 723–735.

Kurlowicz, L., & Wallace, M. (1999). The Mini-Mental State Examination (MMSE). *Journal of Gerontological Nursing, 25*(5), 8–9.

Lalonde, R., & Strazielle, C. (2003). The effects of cerebellar damage on maze learning in animals. *Cerebellum, 2*, 300–309.

Lancaster, J. L., Woldorff, M. G., Pasrons, L. M., Liotti, M., Freitas, C.S., Rainey, L., et al. (2000). Automated Talairach atlas labels for functional brain mapping. *Human Brain Mapping, 10*, 120–131.

Lavenex, P. B., Amaral, D. G., & Lavenex, P. (2006). Hippocampal lesion prevents spatial relational learning in adult macaque monkeys. *Journal of Neuroscience, 26*(17), 4546–4658.

Logan, J. M., Sanders, A. L., Snyder, A. Z., Morris, J. C., & Buckner, R. L (2002). Under-recruitment and nonselective recruitment: Dissociable neural mechanisms associated with ageing. *Neuron, 33*(5), 827–840.

Madden, D. J., Gottlob, L. R., Denny, L. L., Turkington, T. G., Provezale, J. M., Hawk, T. C., et al. (1999). Ageing and recognition memory: Changes in regional cerebral blood flow associated with components of reaction time distributions. *Journal of Cognitive Neuroscience, 11*(5), 511–520.

Maguire, E. A., & Frith, C. D. (2003). Ageing affects the engagement of the hippocampus during autobiographical memory retrieval. *Brain, 126*, 1511–1523.

Moffat, S. D., Elkins, W., & Resnick, S. M. (2006). Age differences in the neural systems supporting human allocentric spatial navigation. *Neurobiology of Ageing, 27*, 965–972.

Moffat, S. D., & Resnick, S. M. (2002). Effects of age on virtual environment place navigation and allocentric cognitive mapping. *Behavioral Neuroscience, 116*, 851–859.

Moffat, S. D., Zonderman, A. B., Harman, S. M., Blackman, M. R., Kawas, C., & Resnick, S. M.

(2000). The relationship between longitudinal declines in dehydroepiandrosterone sulfate concentrations and cognitive performance in older men. *Archives of Internal Medicine, 160,* 2193–2198.

Moffat, S. D., Zonderman, A.B., & Resnick, S. M. (2001). Age differences in spatial memory in a virtual environment navigation task. *Neurobiology of Ageing, 22,* 787–796.

Morris, R. G., Garrud, P., Rawlins, J. N., & O'Keefe, J. (1982). Place navigation impaired in rats with hippocampal lesions. *Nature, 297,* 681–683.

Mulenbroek, O., Petersson, K. M., Voermans, N., Weber, B., & Fernandez, G. (2004). Age differences in neural correlates of route encoding and route recognition. *Neuroimage, 22,* 1503–1514.

Newman, M. C., & Kaszniak, A. W. (2000). Spatial memory and ageing: Performance on a human analogue of the Morris water maze. *Ageing, Neuropsychology, and Cognition, 7*(2), 86–93.

Nishijo, H., Ono, T., Eifuku, S., & Tamura, R. (1997). The relationship between monkey hippocampus place-related neural activity and action in space. *Neuroscience Letters, 226,* 57–60.

Ogawa, S., Lee, T. M., Kay, A. R., & Tank, D. W. (1990). Brain magnetic resonance imaging with contrast dependent on blood oxygenation. *The Proceedings of the National Academy of Sciences of the United States of America, 87,* 9868–9872.

Ohta, R. J. (1983). Spatial orientation in the elderly: The current status of understanding. In H. L. Pick Jr. & L. P. Acredolo (Eds.), *Spatial orientation: Theory, research, and application* (pp. 105–124). New York: Plenum Press.

Ohta, R. J., & Kirasic, K. C. (1983). The investigation of environmental learning in the elderly. In G. D. Rowles & R. J. Ohta (Eds.), *Ageing and milieu* (pp. 83–95). New York: Academic Press.

O'Keefe, J., & Nadel, L. (1978). *The hippocampus as a cognitive map.* Oxford, UK: Clarendon Press.

Okubo, M., & Michimata, C. (2002). Hemispheric processing of categorical and coordinate spatial relations in the absence of low spatial frequencies. *Journal of Cognitive Neuroscience, 14,* 291–297.

Oldfield, R. C. (1971). The assessment and analysis of handedness: The Edinburgh inventory. *Neuropsychologia, 9,* 97–113.

Parslow, D. M., Morris, R. G., Fleminger, S., Rahman, Q., Abrahams, S., & Recce, M. (2005). Allocentric spatial memory in humans with hippocampal lesions. *Acta Psychologica, 118,* 123–147.

Parslow, D. M., Rose, D., Brooks, B., Fleminger, S., Gray, J. A., Giampietro, V., et al. (2004). Allocentric spatial memory activation of the hippocampal formation measured with fMRI. *Neuropsychology, 18,* 450–461.

Raz, N., Gunning-Dixon, F., Head, D., Rodrigue, K. M., Williamson, A., & Acker, J. D. (2004). Ageing, sexual dimorphism, and hemispheric asymmetry of the cerebral cortex: Replicability of regional differences in volume. *Neurobiology of Ageing, 25,* 377–396.

Rodrigue, K. M., & Raz, N. (2004). Shrinkage of the entorhinal cortex over five years predicts memory performance in healthy adults. *Journal of Neuroscience, 24,* 956–963.

Romanski, L. M. (2004). Domain specificity in the primate prefrontal cortex. *Cognitive Affective Behavioral Neuroscience, 4,* 421–429.

Rondi-Reig, L., & Burguiere, E. (2005). Is the cerebellum ready for navigation? *Progress in Brain Research, 148,* 199–212.

Rosenzweig, E. S., & Barnes, C. A. (2003). Impact of ageing on hippocampal function: Plasticity, network dynamics, and cognition. *Progress in Neurobiology, 69,* 143–179.

Save, E., & Poucet, B. (2000a). Hippocampal–parietal cortical interactions in spatial cognition. *Hippocampus, 10,* 491–499.

Save, E., & Poucet, B. (2000b). Involvement of the hippocampus and associative parietal cortex in the use of proximal and distal landmarks for navigation. *Behavioral Brain Research, 109,* 195–206.

Smith, E. E., & Jonides, J. (1997). Working memory: A view from neuroimaging. *Cognitive Psychology, 33,* 5–42.

Talairach, J., & Tournoux, P. (1988). *Coplanar stereotactic atlas of the human brain.* Stuttgart, Germany: Thieme.

Van Petten, C. (2004). Relationship between hippocampal volume and memory ability in healthy individuals across the lifespan: Review and meta-analysis. *Neuropsychologia, 42,* 1394–1413.

Walsh, D. A., Krauss, I. K., & Reginer, V. A. (1981). Spatial ability, environmental knowledge, and environmental use: The elderly. In L. S. Liben & A. H. Patterson Newcombe (Eds.), *Spatial representation and behavior across the life span: Theory and application* (pp. 321–357). New York: Academic Press.

Wechsler, D. (1999). *Wechsler Abbreviated Scale of Intelligence (WASI) manual.* San Antonio, TX: The Psychological Corporation.

Weis, S., Klaver, P., Reul, J., Elger, C. E., & Fernandez, G. (2004). Temporal and cerebellar brain regions that support both declarative memory formation and retrieval. *Cerebral Cortex, 14,* 256–267.

Wiener, S. I., & Taube, J. S. (2005). *Head direction cells and the neural mechanism of spatial orientation.* Cambridge, MA: MIT Press.

MEMORY, 2009, 17 (2), 144–157

Semantic and self-referential processing of positive and negative trait adjectives in older adults

Elizabeth L. Glisky and Maria J. Marquine

University of Arizona, Tucson, AZ, USA

The beneficial effects of self-referential processing on memory have been demonstrated in numerous experiments with younger adults but have rarely been studied in older individuals. In the present study we tested young people, younger-older adults, and older-older adults in a self-reference paradigm, and compared self-referential processing to general semantic processing. Findings indicated that older adults over the age of 75 and those with below average episodic memory function showed a decreased benefit from both semantic and self-referential processing relative to a structural baseline condition. However, these effects appeared to be confined to the shared semantic processes for the two conditions, leaving the added advantage for self-referential processing unaffected These results suggest that reference to the self engages qualitatively different processes compared to general semantic processing. These processes seem relatively impervious to age and to declining memory and executive function, suggesting that they might provide a particularly useful way for older adults to improve their memories.

Numerous studies in young adults have demonstrated that the processing of information in relation to the self enhances memory relative to semantic processing or processing in relation to another person—what has been termed the "self-reference effect" (SRE; for review, see Symons & Johnson, 1997). Although this effect has been found reliably across different materials, modalities, and a variety of conditions, some exceptions have emerged—for example, processing in reference to an intimate other often produces an equally beneficial effect—and these have prompted a variety of different interpretations of the phenomenon. In the seminal paper on the SRE, Rogers, Kuiper, and Kirker (1977) proposed that the self functioned as a "superordinate schema" to assist in the encoding, processing, interpretation, and retrieval of personal information. The advantage for self-referential (SR) processing was not just attributable to more semantic processing but instead reflected access to a qualitatively different, well-developed structure—the self schema—that would allow extensive elaboration of stimuli and multiple routes for retrieval. Other researchers, however, have challenged this view and suggested that the benefit of SR processing is not a result of any special mnemonic properties of the self per se, but instead is simply a consequence of ordinary memory mechanisms, namely the greater elaboration and organisation of information that occurs when processing is in reference to the self (e.g., Klein & Kihlstrom, 1986; Klein & Loftus, 1988). This view postulates that if processing is elaborate and organisational, such as might also occur when one considers whether or not an adjective describes one's mother for example, memory should be equally enhanced in these conditions. A related view (e.g., Bower & Gilligan, 1979) suggests that the crucial element is the existence

Address correspondence to: Elizabeth L. Glisky PhD, Department of Psychology, 1503 E. University Blvd., University of Arizona, Tucson, AZ 85721, USA. E-mail: glisky@u.arizona.edu

This research was supported by a pilot project grant from the Arizona Alzheimer's Disease Core Center, National Institute on Aging, and by National Institute on Aging Grant AG14792. We thank Katrin Walther for assistance with data processing and analysis, and Casey Catlin, Carolyn Langlois, and Tiffany Lupton-Stegall for help in data collection.

DOI:10.1080/09658210802077405

of a well-differentiated information structure. Here again the key comparison is not self versus non-self but well-known person versus other kinds of semantic information.

Another explanation that has been suggested concerns the affective component of SR judgements (Miall, 1986). Considerable evidence attests to the power of emotion to enhance memory (e.g., Bradley, Greenwald, Petry, & Lang, 1992; Davidson, McFarland, & Glisky, 2006; Kensinger & Corkin, 2003; Reisberg & Heuer, 2003). Because SR processing may typically evoke emotion, this too might be a contributor to the memory benefits associated with the SRE. A related idea is that any evaluative judgement, such as deciding whether a certain trait is desirable, will enhance memory, and there is evidence to support this view as well (Ferguson, Rule, & Carlson, 1983; Gutchess, Kensinger, Yoon, & Schacter, 2007).

The debate concerning whether the self is special has also extended to studies examining the neural correlates of SR processing, with some studies proposing specific neural circuitry associated with the processing of self-relevant information, and others suggesting that these brain circuits may support something broader than self processing, for example, person processing or processing of emotional information (for review, see Gillihan & Farah, 2005). The brain regions that have most often been associated with SR processing include cortical midline structures both in frontal (e.g., Amodio & Frith, 2006; Craik et al., 1999; Fossati et al., 2003; Macrae, Moran, Heatherton, Banfield, & Kelley, 2004; Northoff et al., 2006; Schmitz & Johnson, 2006) and parietal cortex (Lou et al., 2004; Northoff et al., 2006; Schmitz & Johnson, 2006). These same regions, however, are often activated in "other" processing and in the processing of emotion (Amodio & Frith, 2006; Ochsner et al., 2004), and so have not provided solid evidence concerning the special status of the self (see Gillihan & Farah, 2005).

In contrast to SR processing, deep semantic processing that is not self-relevant has been shown to activate left inferior prefrontal cortex and lateral temporal cortex (for review, see Cabeza & Nyberg, 1997; Gabrieli et al., 1996; Kapur et al., 1994; Schmitz & Johnson, 2006; Wagner, 2002) rather than medial structures. In addition, studies that have contrasted self-referent and other-referent judgements have often found these same lateral brain structures activated in both tasks, suggesting that access to

general semantic information occurs when judgements about either the self or other are made (Craik et al., 1999; Kelley, 2002).

The neuroimaging studies, like the behavioural studies, have not been able to adjudicate between the two most popular interpretations of the SRE: (a) the self has special mnemonic properties or (b) processing in relation to the self simply allows information to be encoded more elaborately. One possible interpretation of existing findings is that processing of stimuli such as trait adjectives requires access to semantic memory structures for any orienting task related to meaning. Thus SR, other-referential, and general semantic tasks should all activate the left inferior prefrontal and lateral temporal brain regions that are associated with deep semantic processing. Additional judgements about the relation of the stimulus to the self or an intimate other would require access to more specific schemata.

In an attempt to provide information relevant to this issue and with a goal of discovering ways to enhance memory in brain-injured individuals, we tested a group of memory-impaired neurological patients in a SR paradigm (Marquine & Glisky, 2005) in which we looked at recognition of trait adjectives following SR processing, general semantic processing, and a baseline structural level of processing. We found that despite general memory deficits, most patients could benefit from either semantic processing or self-referential processing, or both. Of particular interest was the finding that the size of the SRE was correlated with prefrontal function in patients although the semantic processing effect was not, consistent with the notion that the SRE depends not just on more elaborate semantic processes but on qualitatively different processes associated with the self. In addition, some patients showed greater benefits for semantic than SR processing, providing further evidence that the two tasks involved qualitatively different processes.

Virtually all of the studies on the SRE, both behavioural and neuroimaging, have involved younger adults only. In an early study of older adults (mean age = 67 years), Mueller, Wonderlich, and Dugan (1986) found, in a recall test, that older people exhibited a SRE for trait adjectives (relative to an other-reference condition) that was of approximately the same size as that found in younger adults, although their overall level of performance was somewhat lower. A similar finding was recently reported by Gutchess et al. (2007) in recognition memory. Thus, SR processing appears to be intact in older adults. The Gutchess et al. study also provided preliminary evidence concerning individual differences in the SRE, demonstrating that older adults who performed poorly on speed of processing measures benefited less from SR processing than faster performers. The authors proposed that processing speed reflected the availability of cognitive resources, and that those older adults with fewer resources were less able to benefit from SR processing. However, the processing speed measure in their study was also related to age and education, and in prior studies has been found to be correlated with memory and executive function (Park et al., 2002). Thus, the implications of this finding with respect to the mechanisms underlying the SRE remain uncertain.

We were interested in exploring further whether the benefits of SR processing might accrue to a particular subset of older adults, namely those with good executive function, consistent with our previous findings that the SRE was correlated with prefrontal function in memory-impaired patients. Evidence from both cognitive neuropsychological and neuroimaging studies of older adults suggests that normal ageing is associated with declining function in prefrontal cortex (for reviews, see Park & Gutchess, 2005; Raz, 2000, 2005), although there is considerable variability. One might hypothesise, then, that older adults with reduced executive function may benefit less from SR processing to the extent that it depends on prefrontal brain regions. Older people also show relatively intact emotional processing and emotion regulation (Mather & Knight, 2005; Reminger, Kaszniak, & Dalby, 2000; Williams et al., 2006), processes that have been associated with medial frontal brain structures, and exhibit preserved memory enhancement effects for emotional stimuli (Davidson et al., 2006; Denburg, Buchanan, Tranel, & Adolphs, 2003). To the extent that SR processing involves emotional components, older adults should show normal benefits, particularly for positively valenced self traits. Consistent with theories of socioemotional selectivity (Carstensen, Fung, & Charles, 2003), considerable recent evidence points to a positivity effect in older adults, whereby positive emotional experiences and stimuli are remembered better than negative (Charles, Mather, & Carstensen, 2003; Mather & Carstenson, 2005). Thus, if emotion plays a specific role in the SRE, benefits for older adults may be greater for positive than negative traits.

Many people also experience more general memory declines as they get older such that episodic memory is increasingly impaired with advancing years (for reviews, see Glisky, 2007; Kester, Benjamin, Castel, & Craik, 2002; Zacks, Hasher, & Li, 2000), although again there is substantial variability. It may be that if basic memory function is compromised, older adults will be less likely to benefit from mnemonic strategies, including SR processing (see Glisky & Glisky, 2008). Evidence consistent with this view comes from studies that have found that, although instructions to process information semantically generally improve memory in older adults, the age deficit is not always eliminated (Craik, 2002). One interpretation of this finding is that some older people may have deficits in semantic processing, which results in less semantically elaborated or less distinctive memory traces. If this were the case, one might expect to see impairments in episodic memory in older people following both semantic and SR processing. On the other hand, if the self has special mnemonic properties over and above the elaborative and organisational properties associated with semantic processing, and the self-representation remains intact in older people, SR processing may still provide a benefit.

In the present study we used a recognition task to investigate the effects of deep semantic processing and SR processing in young adults and two groups of older adults: a younger-older group, aged 66–75 years, and an older-older group, aged 76–91 years. All older participants had been characterised according to neuropsychological tests as above or below average on executive function and memory function. Most studies of memory and ageing have not distinguished between younger-older and older-older groups, focusing instead on the younger cohort. However, recent evidence from longitudinal studies (Rönnlund, Nyberg, Bäckman, & Nilsson, 2005) suggests that although episodic memory impairments in older adults appear to begin, on average, around the age of 60 and decline sharply thereafter, significant declines in semantic memory may not occur until beyond the age of 75. Thus, if semantic memory deficits play a role in episodic memory by reducing the degree of elaboration or distinctiveness of memory traces, these effects are more likely to be observed in the older-older group.

A number of hypotheses were tested in the present study. First, on the basis of previous research (Gutchess et al., 2007; Mueller et al.,

1986), we expected that our younger-older adult group (of similar age to participants in previous studies) would benefit from both semantic and SR processing, with SR processing being the superior of the two. We speculated, however, that our older-older adults might show a reduced ability to benefit from semantic and SR processing because of semantic processing deficits. Second, we predicted that the beneficial effect of SR processing might be dependent on good executive function (Marquine & Glisky, 2005). Third, we considered that there might also be an effect of basic memory ability, namely that those with poor memory function might benefit less than those with good memory function. Fourth, consistent with Carstensen and colleagues' findings of a positivity effect in older adults, we expected that older people might show better memory for positive trait adjectives than negative trait adjectives across all conditions, an effect that might be enhanced in the SR condition.

METHOD

Participants

A total of 48 older adults between the ages of 66 and 91 years participated in the study. Older adults were recruited from our laboratory pool of healthy, community-dwelling adults, with no history of neurological problems or current psychiatric illness or alcohol or substance abuse. Each individual in the pool had completed a battery of neuropsychological tests within 2 years of experimental testing. Two groups of tests have been identified through factor analysis, one representing executive functions associated with the frontal lobes (the FL factor), and the other representing memory functions associated with the medial temporal lobes (the MTL factor) (Glisky, Polster, & Routhieaux, 1995; Glisky, Rubin, & Davidson, 2001; Glisky & Kong, in press).

The tests contributing to the FL factor include number of completed categories on the modified Wisconsin Card Sorting Test (WCST; Hart, Kwentus, Wade, & Taylor, 1988), the total number of words generated in a word fluency test, using initial letters F, A, and S (Spreen & Benton, 1977), the Mental Arithmetic subtest from the Wechsler Adult Intelligence Scale–Revised (WAIS-R; Wechsler, 1981), and Mental Control, and Backward Digit Span from the Wechsler Memory Scale–Third Edition (WMS-III; Wechsler, 1997).

The group of tests comprising the MTL factor include Logical Memory I first recall, Faces I and Verbal Paired Associates I from the WMS-III (Wechsler, 1997), Visual Paired Associates II from the Wechsler Memory Scale–Revised (WMS-R; Wechsler, 1987), and the Long-Delay Cued Recall measure from the California Verbal Learning Test (CVLT; Delis, Kramer, Kaplan, & Ober, 1987).

Based on their neuropsychological testing performance, individuals in the pool had been assigned two scores, one representing executive function, and the other memory function. The composite scores for each individual represent average z scores for those tests loading on each factor, after variance attributable to age was removed, relative to a 227-member normative group (see Glisky & Kong, in press). For the present study older adults were selected on the basis of their neuropsychological test performance as high (i.e., above the mean) or low (i.e., below the mean) on the two composite measures. FL factor scores ranged from –1.59 to +1.64, and MTL scores ranged from –1.68 to +1.12, Characteristics of participants as a function of FL and MTL group are presented in Table 1. One-way between-participants analyses of variance (ANOVAs) indicated that the high and low FL groups differed significantly on their composite FL scores, but not on their MTL scores, while MTL groups differed significantly on their composite MTL scores, but not on FL scores. There were also no differences between groups on age, education, and raw scores from the Vocabulary subtest of the Wechsler Abbreviated Scale of Intelligence (WASI; Wechsler, 1999). The probability of a Type I error was set at .05 for all statistical comparisons.

Older adults were divided post-hoc into two subgroups on the basis of their age. Because previous research has shown that older adults do not begin to show declines in semantic memory until over the age of 75 (Rönnlund et al., 2005), that age was chosen as an appropriate point at which to divide the older group. A total of 25 older adults between the ages of 66 and 75 years old (age $M = 71.4$ years, $SD = 2.72$; education $M = 15.88$, $SD = 2.24$) comprised the younger-older group, and 23 older adults between ages 76 and 91 years old (age $M = 80.9$, $SD = 4.08$; education $M = 15.61$, $SD = 2.57$) comprised the older-older group. A between-participants ANOVA on years of education, FL and MTL scores revealed that these age groups did not differ significantly on any of these variables (all $Fs \leq 0.15$, $ps \geq .69$).

TABLE 1
Characteristics of older adults as a function of MTL and FL group

	MTL function				FL function			
	Low (n =24)		High (n =24)		Low (n =24)		High (n =24)	
Variable	M	SD	M	SD	M	SD	M	SD
Age	75.5	5.9	76.5	5.9	75.4	6.4	76.6	5.4
Education	16.0	2.4	15.5	2.4	15.1	2.1	16.4	2.6
Vocabulary[a]	66.4	6.9	68.2	6.0	65.6	6.4	68.9	6.3
MTL Score[b]	−.63	.43	.62	.24	−.06	.79	.05	.66
FL Score[b]	−.00	.79	.05	.93	−.73	.42	.78	.36

MTL = medial temporal lobe; FL = frontal lobe.
[a] Raw scores from the Wechsler Abbreviated Scale of Intelligence (Wechsler, 1999). [b] z scores (see text).

A total of 48 young adults between the ages of 18 and 27 (age $M = 19.73$, $SD = 2.00$; education $M = 12.54$, $SD = 1.05$) were recruited from undergraduate psychology classes at the University of Arizona.

Materials

Four lists of trait adjectives were created: three target lists of 24 words each to be presented during the learning phase, and one distractor list of 72 words to be used for recognition testing. Each of the three target lists constituted a block within a continuous 72-item study list, bounded by two primacy and two recency buffers. Words were selected from a pool of normalised personality trait adjectives (Anderson, 1968). Trait words were all moderate to highly meaningful with meaningfulness ratings ranging from 326 to 386 ($M = 358$). The three target lists were equated for word length, (i.e., mean number of letters = 8) and valence, such that each list was composed of half positive and half negative traits. In Anderson's (1968) list, words were ordered according to their likeability ratings. In the present study a word was considered positive if it was one of the first 252 words listed in the list and negative if it had a ranking between 253 and 555. The mean ranking for positive words was 97 and the mean ranking for negative words was 391. The distractor list was matched on the same variables to the group of three target lists.

Procedure

Participants were assessed individually, and gave informed consent before participating in experimental procedures. There were two parts to the study, an incidental learning phase and an immediate recognition memory test phase. During the learning phase, the participants' task was to answer a question about each of the target words. Each list was encoded under one of three conditions: SR, semantic, and structural encoding. In the SR encoding task participants judged whether trait adjectives were self-descriptive by answering the question "Does this word describe you?" In the semantic encoding task participants made valence judgements on a semantic dimension, answering the question "Is the dictionary definition of this word positive?" Under the structural encoding task participants were asked, "Is this word typed in upper case letters?"

Participants were presented with 72 words, consisting of the three target lists blocked by encoding task. Presentation was blocked by condition for two reasons: First, the constant switching between tasks might adversely affect performance in older people and second, a pilot study suggested that carry-over effects might occur in mixed lists, particularly in older adults. However, order of encoding tasks was counterbalanced so that each task appeared in each ordinal position an equal number of times, and across participants, target lists appeared equally often in each of the three conditions. Word order was randomised within each list, and each participant received a different random order.

Participants were seated in front of a computer where the procedure was explained to them. On each trial one of the questions defining the learning task (e.g. "Does this word describe you?") was presented on the computer screen for 2 s, after which an adjective appeared for 4 s, and participants made a yes/no response by pressing one of two keys on the computer keyboard. A blank screen was then displayed for 1 s and the next trial appeared automatically.

Following the study phase, there was a 2-minute interval in which people engaged in an unrelated distractor task, and then a yes–no recognition memory test was given. The recognition test consisted of 144 words, half targets and half distractors, randomly mixed (i.e., not blocked by condition), which were presented one at a time on the computer screen. Participants indicated whether each word was old or new. Each item remained on the screen until participants pressed one of two keys to indicate if they recognised the word as one that had been previously presented.

RESULTS

Recognition and age

Mean false alarm rates across the three age groups differed significantly: young adults = .10, younger-older adults = .14, and older-older adults = .20, $F(2, 93) = 11.8$, $p < .001$, $\eta_p^2 = .20$. All recognition memory results are therefore shown and analysed in terms of hits minus false alarms ("corrected recognition") unless otherwise noted. Figure 1 shows the mean proportion of items correctly recognised for each encoding condition (structural, semantic, and SR) as a function of age (i.e., young, younger-older and older-older adults). A 3×3 mixed model ANOVA revealed a main effect of encoding task, $F(2, 186) = 289.27$, $p < .001$, $\eta_p^2 = .76$, a main effect of age group, $F(2, 93) = 14.05$, $p < .001$, $\eta_p^2 = .23$, and a significant interaction, $F(4, 186) = 2.69$, $p < .05$, $\eta_p^2 = .06$. Analysis of the simple main effects of condition indicated that SR encoding led to

significantly better recognition than semantic encoding, which in turn produced better recognition than structural encoding (all $ps < .001$) across all age groups. Analysis of the simple main effects of age indicated that age groups did not differ in the baseline structural condition, $F(2, 93) = 2.02$, $p > .10$, but differed in both the semantic, $F(2, 93) = 10.89$, $p < .001$ and SR conditions, $F(2, 93) = 15.53$, $p < .001$. Subsequent pairwise comparisons indicated that the younger-older group was not significantly different from the young group ($ps > .05$), and both outperformed the older-older group in the semantic and SR conditions ($ps < .005$).

Recognition and neuropsychological groups

Figure 2 presents the recognition results across encoding tasks for the high and low FL and MTL groups along with the young data. A 3 (task) $\times$ 3 (group) mixed ANOVA comparing young adults and the two FL groups showed a main effect of encoding task, $F(2, 186) = 283.40$, $p < .001$, $\eta_p^2 = .75$, a main effect of group, $F(1, 93) = 8.77$, $p < .001$, $\eta_p^2 = .16$, but no interaction $F(4, 186) = 1.28$, $p = .28$. Subsequent comparisons indicated no differences between the high and low FL groups ($p = .59$), and both groups performed more poorly than the young group ($p < .01$). The ANOVA comparing young adults and the two MTL groups provided a somewhat different outcome: Although there was a significant main effect of encoding task, $F(2, 186) = 301.59$, $p < .001$, $\eta_p^2 = .76$, and a main effect of group, $F(2, 93) = 12.19$, $p < .001$, $\eta_p^2 = .21$, there was also a significant interaction, $F(4, 186) = 4.35$, $p < .01$, $\eta_p^2 = .09$. An

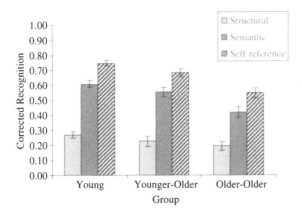

Figure 1. Corrected recognition (hits minus false alarms) as a function of age group and encoding task (Mean+SE)

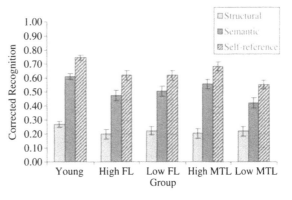

Figure 2. Corrected recognition (hits minus false alarms) as a function of FL group, MTL group and encoding task (Mean + SE)

analysis of the simple main effects of group indicated no differences in the structural encoding condition, $F(2, 93) = 1.82$, $p > .10$, but differences in the semantic, $F(2, 93) = 10.87$, $p < .001$, and SR conditions, $F(2, 93) = 14.88$, $p < .001$. Subsequent pairwise comparisons indicated that the young and high MTL groups did not differ and both were superior to the low MTL group ($ps < .05$).

Semantic & SR effects as a function of age and MTL group

To explore further the beneficial effects of semantic and SR processing in relation to age and memory function among the older adults, we performed a 2 (younger-older vs. older-older adults) × 2 (high vs low MTL group) × 2 (semantic vs SR processing) mixed ANOVA on the SR and levels of processing (LOP) effects (subtracting the structural baseline). These data are presented in Table 2. The analysis indicated that there were three main effects but no interactions: Younger-older adults recognised more trait adjectives than older-older adults, $F(1, 44) = 5.10$, $p < .05$, $\eta_p^2 = .10$, the high-MTL older group recognised more than the low-MTL group, $F(1, 44) = 9.30$, $p < .01$, $\eta_p^2 = .18$, and SR processing resulted in better memory performance than semantic processing, $F(1, 44) = 44.35$, $p < .001$, $\eta_p^2 = .50$.

In all of the analyses thus far the SRE has been significantly greater than the LOP effect and both have been assessed relative to the structural baseline condition. To the extent that both tasks require basic semantic processing, the specific contribution of SR processing might better be evaluated in terms of the additional benefit of SR

relative to the semantic processing condition. A visual inspection of Figures 1 and 2 suggests that the advantage of SR over semantic processing is constant across all groups, whereas the LOP effect varies across age and MTL function as described above. This pattern can be seen clearly in Table 3. A 2 × 2 ANOVA assessing the effect of age (younger-older vs older-older adults) and MTL on the effect specific to SR processing relative to the semantic condition (SR-Semantic) confirmed the observation that the additional benefit for SR processing was equivalent across age and MTL groups (all $Fs \leq 1$).

To test whether the reduced LOP effect in the older-older adults might be attributable to semantic processing deficits, we examined whether this group was impaired relative to the younger-older group in category fluency (e.g., Benton, Hamsher, & Sivan, 1994), a task requiring the generation of instances from three different categories (animals, fruits or vegetables, and names) each within a 1-minute interval. As predicted, the older-older group ($M = 50.1$, $SD = 10.8$) scored significantly lower than the younger-older group ($M = 59.8$, $SD = 13.1$) on the measure of category fluency, $t (46) = 2.77$, $p = .008$.

Recognition as a function of item valence

Table 4 shows the proportion of positive and negative study items that were given "yes" responses on the recognition test for each of the three age groups. Preliminary analyses indicated that valence did not interact with task and so results are collapsed across the three encoding conditions. A 3 (age) × 2 (valence) ANOVA on correctly identified items (i.e., hits) indicated a

TABLE 2
Levels of processing (LOP) effect and self-reference effect (SRE) relative to a structural processing baseline

	Age group	
MTL group	Younger-older	Older-older
	LOP	
High[a]	.43 (.14)	.28 (.17)
Low	.23 (.27)[b]	.17 (.13)[c]
	SRE	
High[a]	.57 (.16)	.39 (.17)
Low	.35 (.25)[b]	.31 (.06)[c]

The values represent mean proportions (SDs).
MTL = medial temporal lobe. [a]$n = 12$; [b]$n = 13$; [c]$n = 11$.

TABLE 3
Levels of processing (LOP) effect relevant to the structural baseline and the additional benefit of self-referential processing (SR-semantic)

Group	n	LOP	SR-semantic
Young	48	.34 (.16)	.14 (.16)
Younger-older	25	.33 (.23)	.13 (.13)
Older-older	23	.23 (.16)	.13 (.13)
High MTL	24	.35 (.17)	.13 (.12)
Low MTL	24	.20 (.21)	.13 (.14)

Values represent mean proportions (SDs). LOP = semantic minus structural condition; SR-Semantic = self-reference minus semantic condition; MTL = medial temporal lobe.

TABLE 4
Mean proportions (*SD*s) of hits and false alarms (FAs) across age groups as a function of valence

| Age group | Hits | | FAs | | Hits – FAs | |
	Positive	Negative	Positive	Negative	Positive	Negative
Young	.65 (.02)	.62 (.02)	.15 (.09)	.04 (.04)	.50 (.11)	.57 (.13)
Younger-older	.68 (.03)	.56 (.03)	.21 (.09)	.07 (.08)	.48 (.11)	.49 (.16)
Older-older	.70 (.03)	.49 (.03)	.30 (.17)	.10 (.11)	.40 (.14)	.39 (.21)

main effect of valence, $F(1, 93) = 84.8$, $p < .001$, $\eta_p^2 = .48$, such that positive items were recognised more often than negative items. However, this effect interacted with age, $F(2, 93) = 16.05$, $p < .001$, $\eta_p^2 = .26$. Analysis of the simple main effects indicated that the differences between positive and negative items occurred for all age groups. However, there were no differences across age groups for positively valenced items, $F(2, 93) = 1.07$, $p = .35$, but there was a significant difference across age groups for negatively valenced items, $F(2, 93) = 6.15$, $p = .003$, such that the older-older adults recognised significantly fewer negative adjectives than did the young adult group ($p = .001$) and marginally fewer negative items than the younger-older adults ($p = .07$). A similar analysis of false alarm rates showed a main effect of age, $F(2, 93) = 11.8$, $p < .001$, $\eta_p^2 = .20$, a main effect of valence, $F(1, 93) = 164.36$, $p < .001$, $\eta_p^2 = .64$, and an interaction, $F(2, 93) = 5.36$, $p = .006$, $\eta_p^2 = .10$. Overall, false alarm rates were higher for positively valenced distractor items than negative items and the number of false alarms to positive items increased significantly with age (all $ps < .03$). False alarm rates for negative items were also significantly higher in the older-older group relative to the young group ($p = .02$), but overall, false alarm rates to negative items were quite low. For both hits and false alarms, the difference in the number of "yes" responses between positive and negative items increased with age. Interestingly, as can be seen in Table 4, when false alarms were subtracted from hits, the recognition memory benefit for positive items disappeared. A 3 × 2 ANOVA on the corrected recognition scores indicated no main effect of valence, a main effect of age, $F(2, 93) = 11.9$, $p < .001$, $\eta_p^2 = .20$, and a marginally significant interaction, $F(2, 93) = 2.73$, $p = .07$, $\eta_p^2 = .06$. Only the young group showed a difference in memory as a function of valence, with negative items being recognised significantly more often than positive items, $t(47) = 3.96$, $p < .001$. Both older groups showed equivalent mem-

ory for positive and negative items in corrected recognition. There were no differences in recognition of positive and negative adjectives as a function of neuropsychological groups.

Recognition as a function of encoding response

In order to explore whether people were more likely to remember trait adjectives that they endorsed, we computed the proportion of correctly identified items that were answered affirmatively and negatively during learning across the three conditions (see Table 5), and conducted a 3 (age group) × 3 (encoding task) × 2 (encoding response: "yes" or "no") ANOVA on recognition hits. The key aspects of this analysis concern the effects of response and the interactions of response with the other variables. The analysis showed a significant main effect of response $F(1, 93) = 32.30$, $p < .001$, $\eta_p^2 = .26$, such that those items that were given "yes" responses during the encoding tasks were subsequently remembered better than those given "no" responses. However, this effect interacted both with task, $F(2, 186) = 16.16$, $p < .001$, $\eta_p^2 = .15$ and age group, $F(2, 93) = 3.25$, $p < .05$, $\eta_p^2 = .07$. Subsequent analysis of the response by task interaction indicated that the advantages for semantic and SR processing occurred for both "yes" and "no" encoding responses, but the advantages were slightly larger for items that had received "yes" responses. In addition, performance in the structural condition did not differ as a function of response, but "yes" responses were remembered better than "no" responses in both the semantic and SR conditions, $t(95) = 3.86$ and 6.17 respectively, $ps < .001$). Given that there were no differences in the structural condition, we re-analysed the data for the semantic and SR conditions only. In this analysis, task did not interact with response, indicating that the yes/no effect was equivalent across the

TABLE 5
Mean proportions (SDs) of recognition hits as a function of study response

Group	Structural		Semantic		Self-reference	
	Yes	No	Yes	No	Yes	No
Young	.36 (.16)	.37 (.19)	.72 (.18)	.68 (.19)	.88 (.13)	.80 (.22)
Younger-older	.34 (.22)	.39 (.22)	.73 (.16)	.64 (.20)	.91 (.09)	.73 (.22)
Older-older	.42 (.24)	.41 (.23)	.70 (.21)	.52 (.23)	.83 (.19)	.67 (.21)
High MTL	.34 (.20)	.36 (.21)	.75 (.12)	.63 (.17)	.91 (.13)	.73 (.16)
Low MTL	.42 (.26)	.44 (.23)	.67 (.22)	.54 (.25)	.84 (.17)	.66 (.26)

MTL = medial temporal lobe.

semantic and SR encoding tasks, and that the advantage of SR relative to LOP was statistically equivalent for the "yes" and "no" responses. However, the response by age group interaction persisted, $F(2, 93) = 4.92$, $p = .009$, $\eta_p^2 = .10$. Further analyses indicated that there were no age differences for "yes" responses, $F(2, 93) = 1.06$, ns, but significant age differences for "no" responses, $F(2, 93) = 5.67$, $p = .005$, such that the older-older adults were impaired relative to young adults, $t(69) = 3.33$, $p = .001$, in recognition of items that had received "no" responses to the semantic and SR encoding questions. Recognition performance for items receiving "yes" and "no" responses for the MTL groups are also shown at the bottom of Table 5. Analyses of these data showed a similar task by response interaction, but no interaction between response and group.

DISCUSSION

The present study replicated previous findings showing that older adults exhibit a normal SRE in memory for trait adjectives, and extended the study of SRE in older adults in several ways. First, the experiment reported here used a recognition test and compared SR processing to semantic processing rather than to processing with respect to other people, showing that the effect in older adults is robust not only across testing formats but also across different comparison conditions (but see Gutchess et al., 2007, Experiment 3 for an exception). Second, the effects of semantic and SR processing were examined in several sub-groups of older adults, including those over age 75, and those with varying levels of basic memory and executive functioning. Findings were consistent with the idea that the advantage provided by access to a self-representation (or perhaps a well-known person representation) is only partly

affected by the same variables that affect semantic processing. Specifically, older age (i.e., over 75) and reduced episodic memory function affected the ability to benefit from semantic processing, but did not influence the additional benefit gained from SR processing. If one assumes that the semantic processing necessary to decide whether an adjective represents a positive or negative attribute is shared by the semantic and SR processing conditions, then variables that affect semantic processing should also affect SR processing, as was shown when each effect was assessed relative to a structural processing baseline. However, when the SRE was assessed relative to the LOP effect, these same variables had no additional impact on the size of the SRE. Although it is possible that the additional benefit of SR processing reflects additional semantic or more elaborate processing, we think it more likely that SR processing results in memory traces that are qualitatively different from those that are elaborated semantically, enriched by SR information or a self-schema that is relatively resistant to ageing. This interpretation is consistent with neuroimaging studies indicating that semantic and SR encoding processes activate similar regions of left inferior prefrontal cortex and lateral temporal cortex (Craik et al., 1999; Kelley, 2002), but SR judgements additionally activate midline brain structures. Further, these midline structures appear less susceptible to the effects of normal ageing (Salat et al., 2004). A qualitative distinction is also more consistent with previous findings in brain-damaged patients (Marquine & Glisky, 2005), showing better memory for SR processing in some patients but for semantic processing in others.

Previous studies with older adults (Gutchess et al., 2007; Mueller et al., 1986) tested relatively young groups of older participants (mean age = 69–71 and 67 yrs respectively). Thus it seemed possible that the failure to find age-related deficits in the SRE in those studies may have been attributable to the young age of the older adults. In the present study we divided our older adults into a younger-older group with a mean age of 71 yrs and an older-older group with a mean age of 81 yrs. When compared to a common baseline, both the LOP effect and the SRE were preserved in the younger-older group but showed impairments in the older-older group. We speculate that this reduced benefit in the oldest group might be attributable to declining semantic processing abilities with advancing years. This view was supported by the finding of lower levels of category (i.e., semantic) fluency in the older-older adults relative to the younger-older group, despite the fact that the two groups were matched for education. However, although age had a negative effect on general semantic processing, the additional SR processing benefit was not reduced in the older-older group attesting to the robustness of the effect even into very old age.

We had expected, on the basis of findings from neuroimaging studies and our previous work with brain-injured patients (Marquine & Glisky, 2005), that SR processing would engage prefrontal brain regions, and that the SRE would be dependent on executive function. However, we found no differences between the high and low FL groups in the extent to which they benefited from either semantic or SR processing. This outcome may reflect the complexity of the frontal lobes and the diversity of functions associated with them, and suggests that, to the extent that the SRE depends on the FLs, it relies on regions different from those that support the tasks in our FL factor. Although the precise functions associated with the FL factor are still undetermined, we have suggested elsewhere (Glisky & Kong, in press; Glisky et al., 2001) that they may involve the initiation of processing activities that serve to integrate and manipulate multiple components of an experience in working memory, tasks that engage primarily dorsolateral prefrontal brain regions. SR processing, on the other hand, has been associated with medial prefrontal brain structures and may therefore not depend on the functions associated with our FL factor. Brain-injured patients in our previous study tended to have diffuse lesions affecting broad areas of prefrontal and temporal cortex, which may have accounted for the correlation of the SRE with executive function in those individuals.

Although we did not find an effect of executive function in this study, it may be that processes associated with the FL factor would be important if specific encoding instructions were not provided and recall tests given. Craik (1986, 2005) has argued that age-related deficits in memory are reduced as environmental support is increased. This may be particularly important for those with declining executive function, who may fail to initiate the deep semantic or self-referential processes that enhance memory, unless instructed to do so. However, when orienting tasks cue those processes, the frontal lobes may not be needed. In addition, trait adjectives may lend themselves rather naturally to SR processing, and this may further obviate the need for frontal involvement.

The ability to benefit from semantic and SR processing, however, seemed to be at least partly dependent on basic memory function. Older people with below average scores on the MTL factor showed reduced LOP and SR effects relative to baseline. This effect was independent of age, and may reflect reduced consolidation or binding problems in people with poor memory function. This finding thus places boundary conditions on levels of processing and SR benefits. If memory deficits stem from fundamental problems in binding or memory storage, providing deep semantic or SR encoding strategies may have limited benefit.

Two other findings are worth mentioning: Items given positive responses during semantic and SR encoding were more likely to be recognised later. This yes/no effect has been observed before in levels of processing studies (Craik & Tulving, 1975) and has been interpreted in terms of the greater or richer elaboration made possible by items that fit the orienting questions compared to those that do not. It has also been observed in previous SRE studies (e.g., Kuiper & Rogers, 1979) where it was interpreted as evidence that the self functions as a schema. A possible explanation for the advantage of SR processing over semantic processing could therefore be the greater number of "yes" responses in the SR condition than in the semantic condition. This occurs because "yes" and "no" responses are distributed approximately equally in the semantic condition but not in the SR condition where people tend to endorse as self-referent more positive than negative adjectives. However, although there were more "yes" responses in the SR condition than in the semantic condition, the SRE relative to the LOP effect was equivalent for "yes" and "no" responses, suggesting that this difference could not account for the SR advantage.

It was also found that the yes/no effect was exaggerated in the older-older adults, who had significantly more difficulty than young adults recognising items that had received "no" responses during encoding. These "no" items, which did not match the orienting question, may have been particularly difficult for the older-older adults to elaborate semantically because of semantic processing difficulties. Thus, the memory traces for these items may have been of poor quality and thereby less likely to be retrieved. However, this same problem did not occur in the low MTL group, which showed equivalent deficits for items receiving "yes" and "no" responses, suggesting that the problem for the low MTL individuals was not primarily one of semantic processing.

The last finding of interest concerns the effect of valence. Considerable evidence has suggested a positivity bias in older adults, such that positive stimuli are more likely to be remembered than negative stimuli (Mather & Carstensen, 2005). This outcome has been interpreted in terms of socioemotional selectivity theory (Carstensen et al., 2003), whereby as people age they tend to optimise their experiences by attending more to positive than to negative events. This effect was evident in the present experiment. For all groups, positive items had higher hit rates than negative items, but with increasing age there was a significant reduction in the hit rate for negative items, but no age differences in the hit rate for positive items. However, false alarm rates for positive items were also significantly higher than for negative items, and this effect too increased with age. These findings are consistent with the, notion that as people get older, they pay increasing attention to positive experiences. However, as evidenced by the corrected recognition scores (hits minus false alarms), this does not necessarily result in overall better recognition memory for positive than negative items. In fact, the high false alarm rates for positive items suggest that discriminating positive targets from positive lures is particularly difficult for older adults, possibly because these encodings appear less distinctive against a background of similar positive events. Thus, although positive stimuli may attract greater attention from older adults, this information is not necessarily processed more deeply. This idea is

consistent with recent findings from a study by Kensinger, Garoff-Eaton, and Schacter (2007), who found that older adults but not younger had enhanced recognition for the gist of positive stimuli compared to neutral stimuli—in this case pictures of objects—but no better memory for the details. This finding suggests that positive stimuli are encoded rather generically, lacking the level of detail necessary for them to be distinguished from positively valenced lures. Thus, the advantage of increased attention to positive events at encoding in older adults may be offset by the lack of discriminating detail available at retrieval. Negative items, on the other hand, may not attract the same attention during encoding, but appear to be encoded more specifically (Kensinger et al., 2007), making them more discriminable at time of test. These two offsetting processes may result in no differences in recognition memory for positive and negative adjectives in older adults, when hits are corrected for false alarms. The advantage for negative stimuli in young adults, on the other hand, may be attributable both to an attentional bias during encoding and to a more detailed memory trace, which is readily discriminable from similar lures at retrieval.

Two final points: One concerns the suggestion in the literature (Mather & Carstensen, 2005) that the positivity effect might depend on encoding tasks and be greater when processing is personally relevant and emotionally important. We did not obtain that result in this study. The valence effects were virtually identical across conditions, suggesting that the stimuli themselves carried the effect, which was not enhanced by SR processing. Second, given that more positive than negative items were endorsed in the SR condition, could this account for the valence effect? Although we could not test this directly because of missing data for several individuals (i.e., they did not endorse any negative items), again the finding that the valence effects were equivalent across all conditions, whereas the endorsement effects differed across conditions, argues against this possibility.

Although not conclusive, the present study adds further support to the view that the self is special, at least relative to general semantic processing. It may also be that other people, particularly those well-known to the individual (e.g., one's mother or spouse), would provide similar advantages for memory because of the extent of personal knowledge known about them. This hypothesis was not tested in the present study although it has been supported in past studies (e.g., Bower & Gilligan, 1979; Czienskowski & Giljohann, 2002; Keenan & Baillet, 1980). Further, it appears that the SRE remains intact well into the upper years of life, even in the face of declining executive and memory functions, suggesting that self-referential processing may provide a particularly useful way for older adults to improve their memories.

REFERENCES

Amodio, D. M., & Frith, C. D. (2006). Meeting of minds: The medial frontal cortex and social cognition. *Nature Reviews Neuroscience*, 7, 268–277.

Anderson, N. H. (1968). Likeableness ratings of 555 personality-trait words. *Journal of Personality and Social Psychology*, 9, 272–279.

Benton, A. L., Hamsher, K., de, S., & Sivan, A. B. (1994). *Multilingual Aphasia Examination* (3rd ed). San Antonio, TX: Psychological Corporation.

Bower, G. H., & Gilligan, S. G. (1979). Remembering information related to one's self. *Journal of Research in Personality*, 13, 420–432.

Bradley, M. M., Greenwald, M. K., Petry, M. C., & Lang, P. J. (1992). Remembering pictures: Pleasure and arousal in memory. *Journal of Experimental Psychology: Learning, Memory, Cognition*, 18, 379–390.

Cabeza, R., & Nyberg, L. (1997). Imaging cognition: An empirical review of PET studies with normal subjects. *Journal of Cognitive Neuroscience*, 9, 1–26.

Carstensen, L. L., Fung, H. F., & Charles, S. T. (2003). Socioemotional selectivity theory and the regulation of emotion in the second half of life. *Motivation and Emotion*, 27, 103–123.

Charles, S. T., Mather, M., & Carstensen, L. L. (2003). Ageing and emotional memory: The forgettable nature of negative images for older adults. *Journal of Experimental Psychology: General*, 132, 310–324.

Craik, F. I. M. (1986). A functional account of age differences in memory. In F. Klix & H. Hagendorf (Eds.), *Human memory and cognitive capabilities, mechanisms and performances* (pp. 409–422). Amsterdam: Elsevier.

Craik, F. I. M. (2002). Human memory and ageing. In L. Bäckman & C. von Hofsten (Eds.), *Psychology at the turn of the millennium* (Vol. 1 pp. 261–280). Hove, UK: Psychology Press.

Craik, F. I. M. (2005). On reducing age-related declines in memory and executive control. In J. Duncan, P. McLeod, & L. Phillips (Eds.), *Measuring the mind: Speed, control and age*. Oxford, UK: Oxford University Press.

Craik, F. I. M., Moroz, T. M., Moscovitch, M., Stuss, D. T., Winocur, G., Tulving, E., et al. (1999). In search of the self: A positron emission tomography study. *Psychological Science*, 10, 26–34.

Craik, F. I. M., & Tulving, E. (1975). Depth of processing and the retention of words in episodic memory. *Journal of Experimental Psychology: General*, 104, 268–294.

Czienskowski, U., & Giljohann, S. (2002). Intimacy, concreteness, and the "self-reference effect." *Experimental Psychology*, 49, 73–79.

Davidson, P. S. R., McFarland, C. P., & Glisky, E. L. (2006). Effects of emotion on item and source memory in young and older adults. *Cognitve, Affective, & Behavioral Neuroscience*, 6, 306–322.

Delis, D. C., Kramer, J., Kaplan, E., & Ober, B. A. (1987). *The California Verbal Learning Test*. San Antonio, TX: Psychological Corporation.

Denberg, N. L., Buchanan, T. W., Tranel, D., & Adolphs, R. (2003). Evidence for preserved emotional memory in normal older persons. *Emotion*, 3, 239–253.

Ferguson, T. J., Rule, G. R., & Carlson, D. (1983). Memory for personally relevant information. *Journal of Personality and Social Psychology*, 44, 251–261.

Fossati, P., Hevenor, S. J., Graham, S. J., Grady, C. L., Keightley, M. L., Craik, F., et al. (2003). In search of the emotional self: An fMRI study using positive and negative emotional words. *American Journal of Psychiatry*, 160, 1938–1945.

Gabrieli, J. D. E., Desmond, J. E., Demb, J. B., Wagner, A. D., Stone, M. V., Vaidya, C. J., et al. (1996). Functional magnetic resonance imaging of semantic memory processes in the frontal lobes. *Psychological Science*, 7(5), 278–283.

Gillihan, S. J., & Farah, M. J. (2005). Is self special? A critical review of evidence from experimental psychology and cognitive neuroscience. *Psychological Bulletin*, 131, 76–97.

Glisky, E. L. (2007). Changes in cognitive function in human ageing. In D. R. Riddle (Ed.), *Brain ageing: Models, methods, and mechanisms* (pp. 3–20). Boca Raton, FL: CRC Press.

Glisky, E. L., & Glisky, M. L. (2008). Memory rehabilitation in older adults. In D. Stuss, G. Winocur, & I. Robertson (Eds.), *Cognitive neurorehabilitation: Evidence and applications* (2nd ed., pp. 541–562). Cambridge, UK: Cambridge University Press.

Glisky, E. L., & Kong, L. L. (in press). Do young and older adults rely on different processes in source memory tasks? A neuropsychological study. *Journal of Experimental Psychology: Learning, Memory, and Cognition*.

Glisky, E. L., Polster, M. R., & Routhieaux, B. C. (1995). Double dissociation between item and source memory. *Neuropsychology*, 9(2), 229–235.

Glisky, E. L., Rubin, S. R., & Davidson, P. S. R. (2001). Source memory in older adults: An encoding or retrieval problem? *Journal of Experimental Psychology: Learning, Memory, and Cognition*, 27, 1131–1146.

Gutchess, A. H., Kensinger, E. A., Yoon, C., & Schacter, D. L. (2007). Ageing and the self-reference effect in memory. *Memory*, 15, 822–837.

Hart, R. P., Kwentus, J. A., Wade, J. B., & Taylor, J. R. (1988). Modified Wisconsin Card Sorting Test in elderly normal, depressed and demented patients. *Clinical Neuropsychologist*, 2, 49–56.

Kapur, S., Craik, F. I. M., Tulving, E., Wilson, A., Houle, S., & Brown, G. M. (1994). Neuroanatomical correlates of encoding in episodic memory: Levels of processing effect. *Proceedings of the National Academy of Sciences USA, 91,* 2008–2011.

Keenan, J. M., & Baillet, S. D. (1980). Memory for personally and socially significant events. In R. S. Nickerson (Ed.), *Attention and performance* (Vol. 8 pp. 651–659). Hillsdale, NJ: Lawrence Erlbaum Associates Inc.

Kelley, W. M. (2002). Finding the self? An event-related fMRI study. *Journal of Cognitive Neuroscience, 14,* 785–794.

Kensinger, E. A., & Corkin, S. (2003). Memory enhancement for emotional words: Are emotional words more vividly remembered than neutral words? *Memory & Cognition, 31,* 1169–1180.

Kensinger, E. A., Garoff-Eaton, R., & Schacter, D. L. (2007). Effects of emotion on memory specificity in young and older adults. *Journal of Gerontology: Psychological Sciences, 62B,* P208–P215.

Kester, J. D., Benjamin, A. S., Castel, A. D., & Craik, F. I. M. (2002). Memory in elderly people. In A. D. Baddeley, M. D. Kopelman, & B. A. Wilson (Eds.), *The handbook of memory disorders* (2nd ed., pp. 543–567). Chichester, UK: Wiley.

Klein, S. B., & Kihlstrom, J. F. (1986). Elaboration, organisation, and the self-reference effect in memory. *Journal of Experimental Psychology: General, 115,* 26–38.

Klein, S. B., & Loftus, J. (1988). The nature of self-referent encoding: The contributions of elaborative and organisational processes. *Journal of Personality and Social Psychology, 55,* 5–11.

Kuiper, N. A., & Rogers, T. B. (1979). Encoding of personal information: Self–other differences. *Journal of Personality and Social Psychology, 37,* 499–514.

Lou, H. C., Luber, B., Crupain, M., Keenan, J. P., Nowak, M., Kjaer, T. W., et al. (2004). Parietal cortex and representation of the mental self. *Proceedings of the National Academy of Sciences, 101,* 6827–2832.

MacPherson, S. E., Phillips, L. H., & Della Sala, S. (2002). Age, executive function and social decision making: A dorsolateral prefrontal theory of cognitive ageing. *Psychology & Ageing, 17,* 598–609.

Macrae, C. N., Moran, J. M., Heatherton, T. F., Banfield, J. F., & Kelley, W. M. (2004). Medial prefrontal activity predicts memory for self. *Cerebral Cortex, 14,* 647–654.

Marquine, M. J., & Glisky, E. L. (2005). *Self-knowledge and the self-reference effect in memory-impaired individuals.* Paper presented at the International Neuropsychological Society, St. Louis, MO.

Mather, M., & Carstensen, L. L. (2005). Ageing and motivated cognition: The positivity effect in attention and memory. *Trends in Cognitive Sciences, 9,* 496–502.

Mather, M., & Knight, M. (2005). Goal-directed memory: The role of cognitive control in older adults' emotional memory. *Psychology and Ageing, 20,* 554–570.

Miall, D. S. (1986). Emotion and the self: The context of remembering. *British Journal of Psychology, 77,* 389–397.

Mueller, J. H., Wonderlich, S., & Dugan, K. (1986). Self-referent processing of age-specific material. *Psychology and Ageing, 4,* 293–299.

Northoff, G., Heinzel, A., de Greck, M., Bermpohl, F., Dobrowolny, H., & Panksepp, J. (2006). Self-referential processing in our brain–A meta-analysis of imaging studies on the self. *NeuroImage, 31,* 440–457.

Ochsner, K. N., Knierim, K., Ludlow, D. H., Hanelin, J., Ramachandran, T., Glover, G., et al. (2004). Reflecting upon feelings: An fMRI study of neural systems supporting the attribution of emotion to self and other. *Journal of Cognitive Neuroscience, 16,* 1746–1772.

Park, D. C., & Gutchess, A. H. (2005). Long-term memory and ageing: A cognitive neuroscience perspective. In R. Cabeza, L. Nyberg, & D. Park (Eds.), *Cognitive neuroscience of ageing* (pp. 218–245). Oxford, UK: Oxford University Press.

Park, D. C., Lautenschlager, G., Hedden, T., Davidson, N. S., Smith, A. D., & Smith, P. (2002). Models of visuospatial and verbal memory across the adult life span. *Psychology and Ageing, 17,* 299–320.

Raz, N. (2000). Ageing of the brain and its impact on cognitive performance: Integration of structural and functional findings. In F. I. M. Craik & T. A. Salthouse (Eds.), *The handbook of ageing and cognition* (pp. 1–90, 2nd ed.). Mahwah, NJ: Lawrence Erlbaum Associates Inc.

Raz, N. (2005). The ageing brain observed in vivo: Differential changes and their modifiers. In R. Cabeza, L. Nyberg, & D. Park (Eds.), *Cognitive neuroscience of ageing* (pp. 19–57). Oxford, UK: Oxford University Press.

Reisberg, D., & Heuer, F. (2003). Memory for emotional events. In D. Reisberg & P. Hertel (Eds.), *Memory and emotion* (pp. 3–41). New York: Oxford University Press.

Reminger, S. L., Kaszniak, A. W., & Dalby, P. (2000). Age-invariance in the asymmetry of stimulus-evoked emotional facial muscle activity. *Ageing, Neuropsychology, and Cognition, 7,* 156–168.

Rogers, T. B., Kuiper, N. A., & Kirker, W. S. (1977). Self reference and the encoding of personal information. *Journal of Personality and Social Psychology, 35,* 677–688.

Rönnlund, M., Nyberg, L., Bäckman, L., & Nilsson, L-G. (2005). Stability, growth, and decline in adult life span development of declarative memory: Cross-sectional and longitudinal data from a population-based study. *Psychology and Ageing, 20,* 3–18.

Ryff, C. D. (1991). Possible selves in adulthood and old age: A tale of shifting horizons. *Psychology and Ageing, 6,* 286–295.

Salat, D. H., Buckner, R. L., Snyder, A. Z., Greve, D. N., Desikan, R. S. R., Busa, E., et al. (2004). Thinning of the cerebral cortex in ageing. *Cerebral Cortex, 14,* 721–730.

Schmitz, T. W., & Johnson, S. C. (2006). Self-appraisal decisions evoke dissociated dorsal-ventral aMPFC networks. *NeuroImage, 30,* 1050–1058.

Spreen, O., & Benton, A. L. (1977). *Neurosensory Center Comprehensive Examination for Aphasia* (revised ed.). Victoria, BC: University of Victoria Neuropsychology Laboratory.

Symons, C. S., & Johnson, B. T. (1997). The self-reference effect in memory: A meta-analysis. *Psychological Bulletin, 121*, 371–394.

Wagner, A. D. (2002). Cognitive control and episodic memory. In L. R. Squire & D. L. Schacter (Eds.), *Neuropsychology of memory* (3rd ed) (pp. 174–192). New York: Guilford Press.

Wechsler, D. (1981). *Wechsler Adult Intelligence Scale–Revised*. New York: Psychological Corporation.

Wechsler, D. (1997). *Wechsler Memory Scale–III*. San Antonio, TX: Psychological Corporation.

Wechsler, D. (1987). *Wechsler Memory Scale–Revised*. New York: Psychological Corporation.

Wechsler, D. (1999). *Wechsler Abbreviated Scale of Intelligence*. San Antonio, TX: Psychological Corporation, Harcourt Brace.

Williams, L. M., Brown, K. J., Palmer, D., Liddell, B. J., Kemp, A. H., Olivieri, G., et al. (2006). The mellow years?: Neural basis of improving emotional stability over age. *The Journal of Neuroscience, 26*, 6422–6430.

Zacks, R. T., Hasher, L., & Li, K. Z. H. (2000). Human memory. In F. I. M. Craik & T. A. Salthouse (Eds.), *The handbook of ageing and cognition* (2nd ed pp. 293–357). Mahwah, NJ: Lawrence Erlbaum Associates Inc.

MEMORY, 2009, 17 (2), 158–168

Ageing, remembering, and executive function

David Clarys, Aurelia Bugaiska, Géraldine Tapia, and Alexia Baudouin

Université François-Rabelais de Tours, France

This study was designed to investigate the relationship between executive functions and the age-related decline in episodic memory through the states-of-awareness approach. Following the presentation of a word list, a group of younger adults and a group of older adults undertook a recognition test in which they classified their responses according to the Remember-Know-Guess procedure (Gardiner & Richardson-Klavehn, 2000). In order to operationalise the executive function hypothesis, we investigated three specific executive functions (updating, shifting, and inhibition of a prepotent response) described in Miyake et al.'s (2000) theoretical model, and a complex executive task. The results revealed that fewer "R" responses were made during the recognition test by the older than the younger group, whereas there was no difference between the groups in the number of "K" responses. In addition, correlations indicated that remembering depended on executive function measures, whereas knowing did not. The hierarchical regression analyses showed that controlling for executive function, and particularly for the 2-back test, largely removed the age-related variance in remembering. These findings support the notion that executive dysfunction, and specifically updating decline, plays a central role in age-related memory loss.

Keywords: Ageing; Memory; States of Awareness; Executive Function.

Tulving (1983, 1985) suggested that a defining property of episodic and semantic memory systems is the phenomenological subjective experience that accompanies retrieval from them, and proposed a distinction between two kinds of consciousness: autonoetic and noetic. He showed that participants could readily understand the distinction between the two kinds of awareness, and could report them using Remember and Know responses. He used the term "remembering" to refer to the expression of autonoetic consciousness, which corresponds to episodic memory, and "knowing" to refer to the expression of noetic awareness, which corresponds to semantic memory. Remembering is characterised by recognition accompanied by the recollection of the mental representation constructed at encoding. Knowing is characterised by recognition

achieved without access to information about the learning context.

Tulving (1985) and Gardiner and his associates (Gardiner, 2001; Gardiner & Richardson-Klavehn, 2000) operationalised these two states of awareness with the R/K paradigm. This has been applied particularly in recognition tasks and consists of asking participants to state the nature of their recollective experience at the time of recognition. The participants have to classify each recognised item into one of two categories: "Remember" (R) or "Know" (K). An "R" response involves the participant's recollection of specific, previously encountered contextual details, while a "K" response indicates that the participant is sure that the item is a target but without any specific contextual recollection of the previously presented item. Gardiner and Conway

Address correspondence to: David Clarys, Université François Rabelais, Département de Psychologie, UMR-CNRS 6234 "Centre de recherches sur la cognition et l'apprentissage", 3 rue des Tanneurs, BP 4103, F-37041 Tours Cedex 1, France. E-mail: david.clarys@univ-tours.fr

This research was supported by the Collaborative Workshop Scheme 170-25-0008 of the AHRC, CNRS, ESRC, and MESR. The authors thank two anonymous reviewers for their helpful comments on an earlier version of this manuscript.

http://www.psypress.com/memory   DOI:10.1080/09658210802188301

(1999) suggested adding another category of response, "Guess" (G), when participants are not sure whether they saw the item during the learning task or not. This category avoids the possibility of participants choosing the "K" response when they are not sure that they have studied the item. Numerous experimental manipulations have strengthened this distinction, showing differential effects on "R" and "K" responses (for reviews, see Clarys, 2001; Gardiner, 2001).

Several studies have assessed the effects of ageing using the R/K paradigm, and a particularly compelling distinction between "R" and "K" responses has been observed. As a whole, two patterns of results emerge. Some studies have found that age is only associated with a decrease in Remember responses (Bugaiska et al., 2007; Bunce, 2003; Clarys, Isingrini, & Gana, 2002; Comblain, D'Argembeau, Van der Linden, & Aldenhoff, 2004; Fell, 1992; Lövden, Rönnlund, & Nilson, 2002; Perfect & Dasgupta, 1997), while others have also found an increase in the number of "K" responses (Bastin, Van der Linden, Michel, & Friedman, 2004; Bunce & Macready, 2005; Parkin & Walter, 1992; Perfect, Williams, & Anderton-Brown 1995; Piolino et al., 2006; Prull, Dawes, Martin, Rosenberg, & Light, 2006). Older adults are less likely to report recollective experience accompanying their recognition responses and more likely to report noetic consciousness. In a close approach, the studies that used the process-dissociation procedure (Jacoby, 1991, 1998) have shown a similar pattern of results. Indeed they observed no age-related differences in familiarity but an age-related decrease on recollection when process estimates were derived from the inclusion/exclusion method (for review, see Light, Prull, Lavoie, & Healy, 2000). It would thus be of interest to find an explanation for this decrease in autonoetic consciousness and highlight the factors involved.

One possible explanation for the differences in the proportion of R responses between younger and older people concerns executive functioning. Executive control is a multi-component construct that consists of a range of different processes that are involved in the planning, organisation, coordination, implementation, and evaluation of many of our non-routine activities (Glisky, 2007). The executive decline hypothesis for age-related decrease in cognitive performance (West, 1996), and particularly for memory, has received considerable empirical support (for reviews, see Moscovitch & Winocur, 1992; Parkin, 1997). This

hypothesis is based on neurobiological and neuropsychological evidence. It suggests that age-related declines in memory may be due to a selective decline in executive functions, traditionally thought to be associated with the functioning of the frontal lobes, which seem to be the area of the brain that is the earliest and most extensively affected by ageing (Raz, 2000; West, 1996). Further evidence for the role of executive functioning comes from studies showing that older participants perform less well than younger ones in tasks in which patients with frontal lobe damage also show impaired performance, such as control of interference (Dempster, 1992), memory for temporal order (Fabiani & Friedman, 1997; Parkin, Walter, & Hunkin, 1995), metamemory (Souchay, Isingrini, & Espagnet, 2000), and conscious awareness (Bunce, 2003; Parkin & Walter, 1992). Both groups are also impaired in source memory tasks (Craik, Morris, Morris, & Loewen, 1990; Glisky, Polster, & Routhieux, 1995), which can be considered as a deficit in the ability to encode the spatial and temporal context associated with an event (Parkin & Walter, 1992). All these observations have led to the hypothesis that age-related memory deficit may be due to a decline in executive functions.

The few studies that have investigated this possibility through the Remember/Know paradigm have produced conflicting results. One study showed correlations between measures of executive functioning and the amount of reported recollective experience in the oldest group of participants (Parkin & Walter, 1992), while other studies found weak (Bunce & Macready, 2005; Perfect & Dasgupta, 1997) or no evidence (Perfect et al., 1995). Parkin and Walter (1992) found that higher levels of "R" responding by the older adults were reliably correlated with better performance on the Wisconsin Card Sorting Test (WCST-Modified, Nelson, 1976). These data suggest that contextually based recognition ("R" responses) decreases as executive function declines. Bunce and Macready (2005) manipulated the time available for encoding operations and also recorded independent measures of executive functions and processing speed. They showed that processing speed, but not executive functioning, accounted for age-related variance in both remembering and knowing under the longer encoding condition. However, as the authors acknowledged, this result could be explained by the fact that the frontal tasks chosen (such as the FAS Word Fluency Test) did not assess the executive processes involved in elaborative re-hearsal and structuring with sufficient rigour. In a recent study, Bugaiska et al. (2007) investigated the relationships between the age-related decline in remembering, processing speed, and executive function. This function was assessed using a single complex executive task, the Wisconsin Card Sorting Test. The results showed that the effect of age in recollection experience is determined by executive function and not by diminution of processing speed.

As observed by the above authors, the associa-tion of the R/K paradigm and the executive decline hypothesis (West, 1996) provides some interesting avenues for future research. So the present study was conducted not to oppose again the executive-ageing hypothesis and the speed mediation hypothesis, but to better understand the role of executive function. More specifically we studied the precise nature and organisation of executive functions involved in the age-related decrease in remembering, using the recent theo-retical model of executive control proposed by Miyake et al. (2000). This model suggested that there are three specific executive functions: shift-ing between tasks or mental sets, updating, and inhibition of prepotent responses. Shifting ability involves the disengagement of an irrelevant task set and the active engagement of a relevant task set, as well as the capacity to perform a new operation when faced with proactive interference or negative priming. Updating is the capacity to control and code incoming information according to its relevance to the task. This ability enables old, non-relevant information in working memory to be replaced by new, more relevant information. Inhibition of prepotent responses refers to the ability to deliberately inhibit dominant or auto-matic irrelevant responses. Miyake et al. (2000) showed that these three specific functions are clearly distinguishable but not completely inde-pendent, seeming to possess some underlying commonalities.

The few previous studies that have examined executive functioning in the age-related deficit in remembering used only complex executive tasks and produced inconsistent results. Furthermore, none refers to an executive function model, and the tests used in these studies were not suffi-ciently specific. The main objective of the present study was to clarify these conflicting results and to better understand the role of executive function, highlighting the nature of the executive process involved. The originality of our research is to test

the executive hypothesis through the recent theoretical model of executive functioning pro-posed by Miyake et al. (2000). We combined the executive hypothesis and the two-states-of-aware-ness approach (Gardiner, 2001; Tulving, 1985) to investigate the role of the three specific and complex executive functions in age-related decre-ments in recollective experience. To date, no study has been conducted to examine Miyake et al.'s (2000) model in the context of state of awareness. The first objective of this study was to confirm the age-related difference in R responses. For K responses the predicted pattern of results is less clear because some authors have found an age-related difference while others have not. The second objective was to test the hypothesis that remembering is dependent on executive functions and that knowing is not. If this were true, "Remember" responses would be related to specific and complex executive functions but "Know" responses would not. The third and main objective was to examine the hypothesis that age-related declines in executive functions explain the observed decline in "Remember" responses during ageing. We hypothesised that specific executive functions, rather than a global decline in such functions, will account for the effect of age on "Remember" responses.

METHOD

Participants

A total of 88 adults living in a medium-sized metropolitan area participated in the study and were divided into two age groups. The first consisted of 44 younger adults (age range 18–33 years) and the second of 44 older adults (age range 61–85 years). All the participants came from the general community and lived in their own homes. They were screened for possible dementia with the Mini Mental States Examina-tion (MMSE, Folstein, Folstein, & McHugh, 1975) and for depression with the Geriatric Depression Scale (GDS; Yesavage et al., 1983). Only participants who obtained a score above the cut-off of 27 points on the MMSE and a score below the cut-off of 10 points on the GDS were included in the study.

The characteristics of the two groups are summarised in Table 1. The younger adults had more years of education than the older ones, but the older adults tended to perform better ($p = .07$)

TABLE 1
Means and standard deviations of participants' characteristics for the two age groups

| | Young (n =44) | | Old (n =44) | | |
	M	SD	M	SD	F(1, 86)
Age (years)	24.07	3.45	70.75	6.54	
Education (years)	12.14	2.20	10.55	3.72	5.97*
Mill Hill	30.14	6.19	32.57	6.30	3.34[§]

$^{§}p = .07$; $^{*}p < .05$.

on the Mill Hill Vocabulary Test (Deltour, 1993), a multiple-choice synonym vocabulary test.

Materials and procedure

Participants performed a recognition memory test using the Remember/Know/Guess method, and tests of executive function (Wisconsin Card Sorting Test, Number–letter task, 2-back test, and Stroop Colour-Word Test). All participants were tested individually and were informed that the experiment involved memory measures.

Remember Know/Guess measures

For the R/K/G paradigm, the material was the same as that used by Clarys et al. (2002) and consisted of two alternate study sets of 36 taxonomically unrelated concrete words. For each set, two different random orders were created. The sets were generated in such a way that the two lists were matched for word frequency and the number of letters per word. One set was presented at encoding and these words were used as target items in the following recognition test, while the other set provided the lures. Half the participants were presented with one set and half with the other, and they were not told how many items they had previously seen. The two sets of stimuli were counterbalanced across the two age groups. For the study phase, the words were presented on a computer screen at the rate of 5 s/word using Microsoft Power Point. The participants were told to read the words aloud and to remember them for a later test. The test phase was introduced following a retention interval of 5 minutes. The Stroop Colour-Word test (SCWT; Stroop, 1935) was administered during this interval and is described in the executive function section below.

For the recognition test, the complete set of 72 words (36 targets and 36 fillers) was presented in random order on the computer screen using Microsoft Power Point. For each word, the participants were asked if they recognised it from the earlier list. In addition, for each recognised word they had to indicate if their response was based on Remembering (R), Knowing (K), or Guessing (G). They were instructed to indicate an "R" response when the recognised word evoked some specific recollection from the learning sequence; for example, remembering a word because it brought to mind a particular association, image, or some other personal experience, or because something about its appearance or position could be recalled. "K" responses were to be given for the words that they felt confident about recognising but without any specific conscious recollection from the learning sequence. "G" responses were for words that they did not feel confident about recognising, and was used to avoid participants indicating a "K" response if they were not absolutely sure that they had seen the word in the study list. After the recognition phase, participants were asked to explain at least two of their Remember and two Know judgements to ensure that they had used the two types of response correctly: for R responses they had to give episodic details associated with the word encoding, and for K responses they had to show that they recognised the word but could not remember any specific detail about studying it. No participant was excluded on the basis of their explanations.

The dependent measures studied here were the proportion of overall correct recognitions (hits/targets) and false alarms (false alarms/lures), the proportion of correct recognitions and false alarms for "R", "K", and "G" responses, and the proportions of hits minus false alarms for overall recognition and for "R" and "K" responses. Data for correct and false Guess responses are presented in the tables but they were not analysed because they were only used to enhance the quality of K responses, and the number of responses was deemed to be too low.

Executive functioning tests

As in Miyake et al.'s study (2000), executive functioning was assessed using two kinds of executive test: complex executive tasks tapping various executive functions, and relatively simple executive tasks predominantly tapping each of the following specific executive functions: shifting, updating, and inhibition. The specific tasks were selected on the basis of proposals formulated by Miyake et al. (2000).

Wisconsin Card Sorting Test. The Wisconsin Card Sorting Test (WCST, modified by Nelson, 1976) is a standardised test designed to measure set formation and attentional shift, and as such is thought to assess complex executive functioning. It was administered and scored using standard procedures. This test requires participants to sort cards with geometric drawings varying in colour (yellow, green, red, or blue), shape (star, circle, cross, or square), and number (1, 2, 3, or 4), based on information provided by the examiner. The sorting rule changes throughout the test, thereby assessing the participant's ability to shift cognitive set. The WCST provides several scores and the specific measure given here is the number of perseverative errors, which are those most affected by age and the most representative of the executive function factor (Bryan, Luszcz, & Pointer, 1999).

Number–letter task. This task (Rogers & Monsell, 1995) was used to measure the shifting executive component. A number–letter pair (e.g., 5A) was presented in one of four boxes of a table. Participants were instructed to indicate whether the number was odd or even when the number–letter pair was presented in one of the top two boxes (number task), and whether the letter was a vowel or a consonant when the number–letter pair was presented in one of the bottom two boxes (letter task). The number–letter pair was presented only in the top two boxes for the first list of 32 target trials, only in the bottom two boxes for the second list of 32 target trials, and randomly in all four boxes for the third list of 32 target trials (switch trials). Thus, the trials with the first two lists required no task switching, whereas the third list required participants to shift between these two types of categorisation operations. In all trials, participants

responded by ticking one answer from a choice of four: "Odd", "Even", "Consonant", "Vowel". They were instructed to complete each list quickly and accurately, and completion times were measured. The cost of shifting between the two types of categorisation operations was calculated as the difference between the time to complete the third list, which required a mental shift, and the average of the times to complete the first two lists in which no shift was necessary. This shift cost served as the dependent variable.

2-back test. The 2-back letter task (Gevins & Cutillo, 1993) is hypothesised to tap the updating executive component. In this test the participant listens to a continuous sequence of letters and must decide and say whether each letter matches the one presented two back in the sequence. The letter list was composed of 30 items and the score was the number of correct responses.

Stroop Colour-Word test. The SCWT (Stroop, 1935) was used to measure the inhibition executive component. This task involves three subtests each displaying 100 stimuli. In the first (word reading), the participant is required to read words printed in black ink representing names of some basic colours. In the second subtest (colour naming), participants have to name the colour of crosses (XXX). In the last subtest (colour-word interference), they have to name the colour of the colour-word printed in incongruously coloured ink (e.g., the word "red" is written in green). In each subtest participants were required to name the colours aloud as quickly as possible for 45 seconds, and the number of correct responses was recorded. An interference score was computed as follows: colour-word interference score − [(word reading score × colour naming score)/(word reading score × colour naming score)].

RESULTS

Remembering, Knowing, and Executive measures

The means and standard deviations of hits, false alarms, and hits minus false alarms for overall recognition, "R", "K", and "G" responses, and the scores for executive measures are presented in Table 2. Separate analyses of variance (ANOVA) with age as a between-participants factor were performed on these measures. The analyses of hits revealed a significant age-related effect on

TABLE 2
Means and standard deviations for hits, false alarms, hits minus false alarms, and executive tasks as a function of age group

	Young (n = 44)		Old (n = 44)		
	M	SD	M	SD	F(1, 86)
Hits					
Overall recognition	.68	.13	.58	.18	8.11**
Remember	.30	.13	.23	.16	4.95*
Know	.30	.14	.28	.17	0.47 ns
Guess	.08	.05	.07	.07	–
False alarms					
Overall recognition	.15	.13	.22	.17	5.05*
Remember	.02	.04	.06	.11	4.64*
Know	.07	.07	.09	.07	1.35 ns
Guess	.06	.06	.07	.08	–
Hits minus False alarms					
Overall recognition	.53	.16	.36	.15	25.67***
Remember	.28	.13	.17	.11	17.62***
Know	.23	.14	.19	.15	1.67 ns
Executive function					
WCST	0.57	1.37	4.43	5.31	21.83***
2-back test	23.09	2.14	20.30	2.97	18.89***
Number–letter test	25.23	10.90	39.79	17.58	25.63***
SCWT	3.80	7.94	−7.93	13.62	24.36***

WCST: Wisconsin Card Sorting Test; SCWT: Stroop Colour-Word Test; *$p < .05$; **$p < .01$; ***$p < .001$; *ns*: non-significant.

overall recognition and on "R" responses, but no such effect on "K" responses. For the false alarms the separate analyses of variance showed a significant age-related increase in overall recognition and in "R" responses, but not in "K" responses. For hits minus false alarms an age-related decrease was observed for overall recognition and for "R" responses. For "K" responses there was no age-related effect. In this way, the older participants demonstrated a decrease in recognition, and more specifically in "R" responses. Thus, in line with our hypothesis, recognition associated with conscious recollection ("R" responses) declined with age, whereas recognition without conscious recollection ("K" responses) did not. However, we conducted a power analysis for the null findings of age and "K" responses. Our sample size (n = 88) provides a power of 0.22 at an alpha level of 0.05. Therefore our sample size does not have sufficient statistical power to detect a potential effect of age on "K" responses. From this sample size one cannot conclude that there is no age-related difference in "K" responses.

For executive tasks, as predicted, separate analyses of variance indicated a significant age effect on all of these measures. Thus, our study demonstrated an age-related decrease in executive functioning.

Correlations between executive functioning and Remember/Know measures (hits minus false alarms)

Correlations were performed to determine whether there was any relationship between executive measures and the two states of awareness. For "R" and "K" responses the measure used was hits minus false alarms. They were computed for each age group separately, and for the two age groups combined after age group had been partialled out. As recommended by Bryan and Luszcz (1996), the age group variable was used rather than individual age in the correlations and regression analyses. As participants were selected from two age groups, age was not normally distributed in this study, and correlations involving this type of distribution tend to be inflated due to overestimation of the range of scores. Therefore, age was coded as a qualitative variable (young = 1, old = 2). The correlation matrix within each age group separately (the younger below and the old above the diagonal) is presented in Table 3. Table 4 presents these correlations for all the participants

TABLE 3
Pearson correlations: Younger and older groups

Older Younger	1 WCST	2 2-back test	3 Number–letter test	4 SCWT	5 Remember	6 Know
1. WCST	–	−.25§	.29*	−.14	−.27¶	−.22
2. 2-back test	.31*	–	−.35*	−.35*	.71***s	−.16
3. Number–letter test	−.06	−.17	–	−.23	−.35*	−.04
4. SCWT	.00	−.05	−.25	–	.30*	.07
5. Remember	.03	.31*s	.00s	−.07	–	−.33*
6. Know	−.04	−.01	−.14	.14	−.52***	–

Pearson correlations between Remember, Know responses, and executive function measures for the younger (below the diagonal; $n = 44$) and for the older group (above the diagonal; $n = 44$).

WCST: Wisconsin Card Sorting Test; SCWT: Stroop Colour-Word Test; $§p = .10$; $¶p = .08$; $*p < .05$; $**p < .01$; $***p < .001$; s: significant difference between younger and older group correlations.

after age group was partialled out. For younger participants "R" responses only correlated significantly to the 2-back test whereas there was no significant correlation between "K" responses and executive function tasks. For older participants all executive measures correlated with "R" responses but not with "K" responses. The correlation between "R" responses and the 2-back test was very strong (.71) and was significantly greater in the older group than in the younger one (.31). When the two groups were combined and age group partialled out (Table 4), the analysis revealed that "R" responses correlated with the 2-back test and tended to correlate ($p = .08$) with the number–letter test. Conversely, there was no significant correlation with "K" responses. Thus, a correlational dissociation between "R" and "K" responses was observed, indicating that "R" responses correlated with executive tasks, whereas "K" responses did not correlate with any measure.

Hierarchical regression analyses

The role of the executive function tasks in the remembering variance was assessed using hier-

archical multiple regression analyses. As shown by the correlations matrix there was a strong correlation between "R" responses and the 2-back test. To exclude the possibility that this measure, which has the greatest first-order correlation with "R" responses, can alone account for the greatest proportion of variance in "R", three separate hierarchical regression analyses were conducted in order to test alternative models (order of entry). For "R" responses the measure used was hits minus false alarms. The results of these analyses are shown in Table 5. In the first analysis (Analysis 1) we entered first the three executive tasks least correlated with R responses: the number–letter test, the WCST, and the SCWT. Then we added the age group to examine whether prior entry of these three variables reduced the contribution of age group to a nonsignificant amount. Finally we entered the 2-back test to see whether this test accounted for a significant proportion of variance in R responses once age group was partialled out. The same procedure was repeated for Analysis 2, with the 2-back test entered before age group to examine whether prior entry of this test reduced the contribution of age group to a non-significant

TABLE 4
Pearson correlations: All participants

	WCST	2-back test	Number–letter test	SCWT	Remember
2-back test	−.15				
Number–letter test	.23*	−.30**			
SCWT	−.10	.23*	−.24*		
Remember	−.16	.52***	−.19§	.15	
Know	−.17	−.10	−.08	.09	−.42***

Pearson correlations between Remember, Know responses, and executive function measures for all the participants ($n = 88$) after age group was partialled out.

WCST: Wisconsin Card Sorting Test; SCWT: Stroop Colour-Word Test; $§p = .08$; $*p < .05$; $**p < .01$; $***p < .001$.

TABLE 5
Hierarchical regression analyses predicting "R" responses (hits minus false alarms) from age group and executive measures

Analyses	Variable	R^2	R^2 modified
Analysis 1	Number–letter task	.11	.11**
	WCST	.15	.04*
	SCWT	.18	.03
	Age group	.22	.04*
	2-back	.40	.18***
Analysis 2	Number–letter task	.11	.11**
	WCST	.15	.04*
	SCWT	.18	.03
	2-back	.39	.21***
	Age group	.40	.01
Analysis 3	2-back	.37	.37***
	Number–letter task	.38	.01
	WCST	.39	.01
	SCWT	.39	.00
	Age group	.40	.01

$n = 88$.
WCST: Wisconsin Card Sorting Test; SCWT: Stroop Colour-Word Test; *$p < .05$; **$p < .01$; ***$p < .001$.

amount. Finally, in the third analysis (Analysis 3), the 2-back test was entered first to see whether the other executive tasks and age group accounted for a significant proportion of variance in R responses after this measure was partialled out.

Analysis 1 shows that the number–letter task, the WCST, and the SCWT predicted 18% of the variance in remembering when entered first and that, after controlling for these measures, age group added a significant 4% to the variance. Analysis 1 indicates that the 2-back test, after controlling for the other executive tasks and age group, added a significant 18% to the variance in R responses. Analysis 2 shows that after controlling for the number–letter task, the WCST and the SCWT, the 2-back test added 21% to the variance in remembering. Age group no longer predicted "R" responses once executive functioning had been controlled. Finally, Analysis 3 indicates that the 2-back test predicted 37% of the variance in remembering when entered first. The other executive tasks and age group no longer predicted R responses after the 2-back test had been entered. These analyses indicate that the 2-back test is the main measure explaining variance in "R" responses, and more specifically, the age-related decline in remembering.

DISCUSSION

The aim of this study was to examine the precise nature and organisation of executive functions involved in the age-related decline in remembering, through a recent executive functions model (Miyake et al., 2000). First, we evaluated the effects of age in the two states of awareness. In line with our hypothesis, an age-related difference in the nature of awareness during recognition was observed. In accordance with previous studies (Bastin et al., 2004; Bugaiska et al., 2007; Bunce, 2003; Bunce & Macready, 2005; Clarys et al., 2002; Comblain et al., 2004; Fell, 1992; Lovden et al., 2002; Parkin & Walter, 1992; Perfect & Dasgupta, 1997; Perfect et al., 1995; Piolino et al., 2006; Prull et al., 2006), recognition with conscious recollection (R) was found to be impaired in ageing, whereas Know responses were not. Thus, the age-related decrease observed in overall recognition could be explained by the selective decline of responses associated with recollective experience, older adults failing to recollect specific contextual details that they had previously encountered. However, the power analysis indicated that this sample size is not sufficient to draw conclusions regarding the age-related difference in "K" responses.

The main objective of this study was to investigate the relationships between ageing, specific executive functions, and states of awareness. In line with the executive decline hypothesis (West, 1996) we found that older participants showed a marked decline in both complex and specific executive tasks. The results also indicated that the "R" responses were correlated with all the executive measures in the older group and only with the 2-back test in the younger group. When all the participants were included and the age group partialled out, "R" responses still correlated significantly with the 2-back test and there was a trend towards significance for the number–letter test. By contrast, there was no significant correlation between "K" responses and executive measures. It therefore appears that remembering is related to executive function, and particularly to the 2-back test, which is frequently used as a measure of the updating process. Our results, showing a correlational dissociation between "R" and "K" responses, are consistent with previous studies demonstrating that remembering and knowing can be dissociated by manipulating different variables (Clarys, 2001; Gardiner, 2001). These findings support the hypothesis of a functional dissociation between Remember and Know responses and provide data regarding their nature, indicating that "R", but not "K", responses depend on executive functions that correspond to strategic processes.

Three hierarchical regression analyses were also conducted to examine which executive task accounted for a significant proportion of R response variance, and whether the prior entry of these measures reduced the contribution of age group to a non-significant amount. The analyses indicated that the most important executive measure was the 2-back test, considered to evaluate the updating capacity. This measure appeared to be the best predictor of the variance in R responses and of the effects of age in remembering. The other executive tasks studied here seemed to be less involved in the Remember responses. The notion that executive deficit mediates the age-related decline in remembering has produced conflicting results in the literature. Our finding is consistent with two previous studies (Bugaiska et al., 2007; Parkin & Walter, 1992) but conflicts with others (Bunce & Macready, 2005; Perfect & Dasgupta, 1997; Perfect et al., 1995). These discrepant findings may be attributed to multiple confounds between participants, stimuli, timing, and various other important factors as the different tests used. For example, Bunce and Macready (2005) showed that processing speed but not executive functioning explained age-related variance in remembering. They used the digit-symbol substitution test (DSST) of the WAIS-R (Wechsler, 1981) as a speed test, but Parkin and Java (1999) showed that the DSST attenuated age-related differences in executive function in contrast to the digit cancellation task, which is a speed task requiring virtually no memory load, minimal attentional demands, and only a small motor component. Thus one can suggest that the DSST assessed executive functioning more than processing speed (Baudouin, Clarys, Vanneste, Isingrini, 2008). Therefore, while Bunce and Macready's (2005) study did not provide evidence that executive functioning is involved in the age-related difference in remembering, this could be because they used the DSST, which is based on high-level processing.

These executive functions may be involved at different stages of the initiation and control of memory processes. The updating process assumed to be evaluated by the 2-back test may be strongly involved in the elaboration and control of mental representation in memory during presentation of the material and during the recognition stage. This function could allow suitable strategies to be used at encoding and recognition to improve the memory trace, and may improve the learning and retrieval of information and the associated contextual details needed for recognition based on conscious recollection. This supports the notion that frontal lobe dysfunction does not produce a decrease in the storage capacity of memory but modifies the strategic processes accompanying mnemonic activities, such as initiation, execution, and the control of strategies occurring during information encoding and retrieval (Moscovitch, 1992). For example, during the encoding stage the updating process may help initiate encoding strategies, and during retrieval it may help initiate a strategic retrieval search and check that information has been correctly recalled. Older participants are thus less likely to initiate the elaborate rehearsal and structured encoding strategies that may aid conscious recollection and therefore produce fewer Remember responses.

The results of the present study support the hypothesis that updating is an important function involved in the age-related decrease in remembering. Executive functioning was assessed using two kinds of executive test: complex executive tasks tapping various executive functions, and relatively simple executive tasks predominantly tapping shifting, updating, and inhibition. However, the construct validities of complex executive tasks have not been completely established (Phillips, 1997; Rabbitt, 1997), despite their broad acceptance as measures of executive functioning. Many popular executive tasks seem to have been validated only on the criterion of being somewhat sensitive to frontal lobe damage, and the precise nature of the executive processes involved in the performance of these tasks is underspecified (Miyake et al., 2000). These tasks are not specific enough, and could involve both executive and non-executive processes. For these reasons, in contrast to specific executive measures, complex executive tasks do not appear to be able to explain the links between remembering responses and executive functioning. Our study therefore examined more specifically the precise nature and organisation of the executive functions involved in the age-related decline in remembering, including three specific tasks supposed to evaluate three relatively circumscribed lower level functions. However, each executive function was measured with only one indicator. Because of the potential for measurement error and for overlapping processes, it is not really possible to attribute any one task (2-back task) to a single process (updating). Another difficulty with the assessment of the updating function is that the 2-back test could involve processes of recognition memory similar to those involved in remembering. However the 2-back test is a short-term auditory memory task, whereas the episodic memory task involves long-term visual memory. To address these issues and confirm our results, further studies need to be conducted with at least three indicators for each of the specific executive functions.

In summary, the results of the present study support the hypothesis that specific executive deficits account for the age-related decline in memory performance. Miyake et al.'s theoretical model (2000) studied here seems to offer a useful approach for understanding executive functioning in ageing. The regression analysis strongly suggests that age-related differences in remembering can be accounted for by individual differences in executive measures and particularly in the 2-back test, which is supposed to tap the updating function. Conversely, "Knowing" was found not to depend on executive function and so was unaffected by ageing. The association of the two-states-of-awareness theory and the executive decline hypothesis, through the executive functioning model of Miyake et al. (2000), seems to provide some interesting results that need to be supported by further research investigating more specifically the close link between executive function and conscious awareness with more executive tasks for each specific executive component.

REFERENCES

Bastin, C., Van der Linden, M., Michel, A. P., & Friedman, W. J. (2004). The effects of ageing on location-based and distance-based processes in memory for time. *Acta Psychologica, 116*, 145–171.

Baudouin, A., Clarys, D., Vanneste, S., & Isingrini, M. (2008). *Executive functioning and processing speed in age-related effect in memory: Contribution of a coding task*. Manuscript submitted for publication.

Bryan, J., & Luszcz, M. A. (1996). Speed of information processing as a mediator between age and free-recall performance. *Psychology & Ageing, 11*, 3–9.

Bryan, J., Luszcz, M. A., & Pointer, S. (1999). The contribution of executive function and processing resources to age differences in the effects of strategy use on free recall. *Ageing; Neuropsychology and Cognition, 6*(4), 273–287.

Bugaiska, A., Clarys, D., Jarry, C., Taconnat, L., Tapia, G., Vanneste, S., et al. (2007). The effect of ageing in recollective experience: The processing speed and executive functioning hypothesis. *Consciousness & Cognition, 16*(4), 797–808.

Bunce, D. (2003). Cognitive support at encoding attenuates age differences in recollective experience among adults of lower frontal lobe function. *Neuropsychology, 17*, 353–361.

Bunce, D., & Macready, A. (2005). Processing speed, executive function, and age differences in remembering and knowing. *The Quarterly Journal of Experimental Psychology, 58A*(1), 155–168.

Clarys, D. (2001). Psychology of human memory: Theoretical and methodological progress. *L' Année Psychologique, 101*, 495–519.

Clarys, D., Isingrini, M., & Gana, K. (2002). Ageing and episodic memory: Mediators of age differences in remembering and knowing. *Acta Psychologica, 109*(3), 315–329.

Comblain, C., D'Argembeau, A., Van Der Linden, M., & Aldenhoff, L. (2004). The effect of ageing on the recollection of emotional and neutral picture. *Memory, 12*(6), 673–684.

Craik, F. I. M., Morris, L. W., Morris, R. G., & Loewen, E. R. (1990). Relations between source amnesia and frontal lobe functioning in older adults. *Psychology & Ageing, 5*, 148–151.

Deltour, J. J. (1993). *Echelle de vocabulaire de Mill Hill de J. C. Raven. Adaptation française et normes europeennes du Mill Hill et du Standard Progressive Matrices de Raven (PM38)*. Braine-le-Chateau: Editions l'application des techniques modernes.

Dempster, F. N. (1992). The rise and fall of the inhibitory mechanism: Toward a unified theory of cognitive development and aging. *Developmental Review, 12*, 45–75.

Fabiani, M., & Friedman, D. (1997). Dissociations between memory for temporal order and recognition memory in aging. *Neuropsychologia, 35*, 129–141.

Fell, M. (1992). Encoding retrieval and age effect on recollective experience. *The Irish Journal of Psychology, 13*, 62–78.

Folstein, M. F., Folstein, S. F., & Mc Hugh, P. R. (1975). Mini-Mental State: A practical method for grading the cognitive state of patient for the clinician. *Journal of Psychiatric Reseach, 12*, 189–198.

Gardiner, J. M. (2001). Episodic memory and autonoetic consciousness: A first person approach. *Philosophical Transactions of the Royal Society London B, 356*, 1351–1361.

Gardiner, J. M., & Conway, M. A. (1999). Levels of awareness and varieties of experience. In B. H. Challis & B. M. Velichkovsky (Eds.), *Stratification in cognition and consciousness* (pp. 237–254). Amsterdam/Philadelphia: John Benjamin Publishing Company.

Gardiner, J. M., & Richarson-Klavehn, A. (2000). Remembering and knowing. In E. Tulving & F. I. M. Craik (Eds.), *The Oxford handbook of memory*. Oxford, UK: Oxford University Press.

Gevins, A., & Cutillo, B. (1993). Spatiotemporal dynamics of component processes in human working memory. *Electroencephalography and Clinical Neurophysiology, 87*(3), 128–143.

Glisky, E. L. (2007). Changes in cognitive function in human aging. In D. Riddle (Ed.), *Brain aging: Methods, models, and mechanisms* (pp. 3–20). New York: CRC Press.

Glisky, E. L., Polster, M. R., & Routhieaux, B. C. (1995). Double dissociation between item and source memory. *Neuropsychology, 9*, 229–235.

Jacoby, L. L. (1991). A process dissociation framework: Separating automatic from intentional uses of memory. *Journal of Memory and Language, 30*, 513–541.

Jacoby, L. L. (1998). Invariance in automatic influences of memory: Toward a user's guide for the process-dissociation procedure. *Journal of Experimental Psychology: Learning, Memory and Cognition, 24*, 3–26.

Light, L. L., Prull, M. W., LaVoie, D. J., & Healy, M. R. (2000). Dual process theories of memory in old age. In T. J. Perfect & E. A. Maylor (Eds.), *Models of cognitive ageing* (pp. 238–300). Oxford, UK: Oxford University Press.

Lövdén, M., Rönnlund, M., & Nilson, G.-L. (2002). Remembering and knowing in adulthood: Effects of enacted encoding and relations to processing speed. *Aging, Neuropsychology, Cognition, 9*, 184–200.

Miyake, A., Friedman, N., Emerson, M., Witzki, A., Howerter, A., & Wager, T. (2000). The unity and diversity of executive functions and their contributions to complex frontal lobe tasks: A latent variable variable analysis. *Cognitive Psychology, 41*, 49–100.

Moscovitch, M. (1992). Memory and working-with-memory: A component process model based on modules and central systems. *Journal of Cognitive Neuroscience, 4*, 257–267.

Moscovitch, M., & Winocur, G. (1992). The neuropsychology of memory and ageing. In F. I. M. Craik & T. A. Salthouse (Eds.), *The handbook of ageing and cognition* (pp. 315–371). Hillsdale, NJ: Lawrence Erlbaum Associates Inc.

Nelson, H. E. (1976). A modified card sorting test sensitive to frontal lobe deficits. *Cortex, 12*, 313–324.

Parkin, A. J. (1997). Normal age-related memory loss and its relation to frontal lobe dysfunction. In P. Rabbitt (Ed.), *Methodology of frontal and executive function* (pp. 177–190). Hove, UK: Psychology Press.

Parkin, A. J., & Java, R. I. (1999). Deterioration of frontal lobe function in normal aging: Influences of fluid intelligence versus perceptual speed. *Neuropsychology, 13*, 539–545.

Parkin, A. J., & Walter, B. M. (1992). Recollective experience, normal aging, and frontal dysfunction. *Psychology & Aging, 7*, 290–298.

Parkin, A. J., Walter, B. R., & Hunkin, N. M. (1995). Relationships between normal aging, frontal lobe function and memory for temporal and spatial information. *Neuropsychology, 9*, 304–312.

Perfect, T. J., & Dasgupta, Z. R. R. (1997). What underlies the deficit in reported recollective experience in old age. *Memory & Cognition, 25*, 849–858.

Perfect, T. J., Williams, R. B., & Anderton-Brown, C. (1995). Age differences in reported recollective experiences are due to encoding effects, not response bias. *Memory, 3*, 169–184.

Phillips, L. H. (1997). Do "frontal tests" measure executive function? Issues of assessment and evidence from fluency tests. In P. Rabbitt (Ed.), *Methodology of frontal and executive functions* (pp. 191–213). Hove, UK: Psychology Press.

Piolino, P., Desgranges, B., Clarys, D., Guillery-Girard, B., Taconnat, L., Isingrini, M., et al. (2006). Autobiographical memory, autonoetic consciousness and self-perspective in aging. *Psychology and Aging, 21*(3), 110–125.

Prull, M. W., Dawes, L. L. C., Martin, A. M., Rosenberg, H. F., & Light, L. L. (2006). Recollection and familiarity in recognition memory: Adult age differences and neuropsychological test correlates. *Psychology & Aging, 21*(7), 107–118.

Rabbitt, P. N. (1997). Introduction: Methodologies and models in the study of executive function. In P. Rabbitt (Ed.), *Methodology of frontal and executive function*. Hove, UK: Psychology Press.

Raz, N. (2000). Ageing of the brain and its impact on cognitive performance: Integration of structural and functional findings. In F. I. M. Craik & T. A. Salthouse (Eds.), *The handbook of ageing and cognition. Second edition*. Hillsdale, NJ: Lawrence Erlbaum Associates.

Rogers, R. D., & Monsells, (1995). Costs of a predictable switch between simple cognitive tasks. *Journal of experimental psychology: General, 124*, 207–231.

Souchay, C., Isingrini, M., & Espagnet, L. (2000). Ageing, episodic memory, feeling-of-knowing, and frontal functioning. *Neuropsychology, 2*, 299–309.

Stroop, J. R. (1935). Studies of interference in serial verbal reactions. *Journal of Experimental Psychology, 89*, 669–679.

Tulving, E. (1983). *Elements of episodic memory*. Oxford, UK: Oxford University Press.

Tulving, E. (1985). Memory and consciousness. *Canadian Psychologist, 26*, 1–12.

Wechsler, D. (1981). *Manual for Wechsler Adult Intelligence Scale–Revised*. San Antonio, TX: Psychological Corporation.

West, R. L. (1996). An application of prefrontal cortex function theory to cognitive aging. *Psychological Bulletin, 120*, 272–292.

Yesavage, J. A., Brink, T. L., Rose, T. L., Lum, O., Huang, V., Adey, M., et al. (1983). Development and validation of a geriatric depression screening scale – a preliminary report. *Journal of Psychiatric Research, 17*(1), 37–49.

MEMORY, 2009, 17 (2), 169–179

Psychology Press
Taylor & Francis Group

Committing memory errors with high confidence: Older adults do but children don't

Yee Lee Shing, Markus Werkle-Bergner, Shu-Chen Li, and Ulman Lindenberger

Max Planck Institute for Human Development, Berlin, Germany

We investigated lifespan differences of confidence calibration in episodic memory, particularly the susceptibility to high-confidence errors within samples of children, teenagers, younger adults, and older adults. Using an associative recognition memory paradigm, we drew a direct link between older adults' associative deficit and high-confidence errors. We predicted that only older adults would show high-confidence error even though their memory performance was at a similar level to that of children. Participants of all ages showed higher confidence following correct responses compared to incorrect responses, demonstrating the ability to calibrate subjective confidence in relation to memory accuracy. However, older adults were disproportionately more likely to indicate high confidence following erroneously remembered word pairs than participants of the other three age groups. Results are discussed in relation to the misrecollection account of high-confidence errors and ageing-related decline in hippocampus-dependent episodic memory functions.

Keywords: Memory development; Metamemory; Confidence judgement; False memory.

In everyday life we often find ourselves introspecting about how sure we are of our memories about certain issues or events. The ability to match (or "calibrate") subjective confidence with memory accuracy reflects the efficacy of one aspect of metacognitive memory monitoring (e.g., Brewer & Wells, 2006; Johnson, 2006; Loftus, 2003). Young adults typically provide higher confidence judgements after correct than after incorrect answers, indicating well-attuned calibration in matching accuracy and confidence (e.g., Roebers, 2002). In situations when young adults are "miscalibrated", overconfidence with respect to incorrect responses (henceforth termed *high-confidence error*) is a

common phenomenon (e.g., Maki & Swett, 1987; Schneider & Laurion, 1993).

MEMORY ACCURACY AND CONFIDENCE CALIBRATION: TRENDS IN DEVELOPMENT AND AGEING

Researchers in the fields of child development (e.g., Pressley, Levin, Ghatala, & Ahmad, 1987; Roebers, 2002) and cognitive ageing (e.g., Jacoby & Rhodes, 2006) have noted that the ability to be well "calibrated" in judging the "goodness" of one's memory changes with age. An early study

Address correspondence to: Yee Lee Shing, (yshing@mpib-berlin.mpg.de), Markus Werkle-Bergner (werkle@mpib-berlin.mpg.de), Shu-Chen Li (shuchen@mpib-berlin.mpg.de), or Ulman Lindenberger (lindenberger@mpib-berlin.mpg.de), all at the Center for Lifespan Psychology, Max Planck Institute for Human Development, Lentzeallee 94, D-14195 Berlin, Germany.

This study was carried out in the context of the Research Group "Binding: Functional Architecture, Neuronal Correlates, and Ontogeny", funded by the German Research Foundation (DFG FOR 448), and conducted in partial fulfilment of the doctoral dissertation of the first author. The first and second authors would like to express gratitude for the support of the International Max Planck Research School, LIFE, especially LIFE faculty members Chad Dodson and Lael Schooler for their helpful feedback. We express gratitude to the research assistants and participants of the study.

http://www.psypress.com/memory   DOI:10.1080/09658210802190596

(Pressley et al., 1987) showed that early-grade schoolchildren provided high-confidence ratings after both correct and incorrect responses, demonstrating a lack of differentiation according to accuracy. Children in later elementary school years can already differentially rate correct responses with higher confidence than incorrect ones (see also Roebers, von der Linden, Schneider, & Howie, 2007, with an event-recall paradigm). However, if prompted with misleading information, as is often done in false memory and eyewitness paradigms, even older children's confidence judgements are then less well calibrated than the judgements of younger adults, showing overconfidence with respect to incorrect responses (Roebers, 2002; Roebers & Howie, 2003). At the other end of the lifespan, older adults have been shown to experience greater difficulties in monitoring newly learned information than younger adults (e.g., Dodson & Krueger, 2006; Souchay, Isingrini, & Espagnet, 2000). Using an eyewitness misinformation paradigm, Dodson and Krueger (2006) found that older adults give high-confidence ratings to a greater proportion of falsely recognised items than younger adults.

Various potentially overlapping mechanisms have been suggested to account for the increase of false memory in ageing. Prominent accounts include compromised recollection (Jacoby, 1999), deficient inhibitory control (Jacoby & Rhodes, 2006), and impaired source monitoring (Henkel, Johnson, & DeLeonardis, 1998). Recently Dodson, Bawa, and Krueger (2007) found that high-confidence errors are particularly likely under conditions that require recollections of specific details of a memory episode. Specifically, this "misrecollection account" suggests that older adults' high-confidence errors may arise from their susceptibility to miscombine features from separate events, such that associations based on miscombined features become subjectively indistinguishable from associations based on correctly combined features (e.g., Chalfonte & Johnson, 1996; Naveh-Benjamin, Hussain, Guez, & Bar-On, 2003). This account is consistent with findings pointing towards pronounced age-associated declines in the hippocampus (e.g., Persson et al., 2006; Raz et al., 2005), which is important for episodic memory functioning. Age-associated impairments in this region have been linked to older adults' difficulties in forming new associations, and in separating new associations from memories stored in long-term memory (Dase-

laar, Fleck, Dobbins, Madden, & Cabeza, 2006; Wilson, Gallagher, Eichenbaum, & Tanila, 2006).

AIMS AND OVERVIEW OF THE PRESENT STUDY

Thus far, child developmental and ageing research on memory accuracy and confidence calibration have been pursued separately and relied primarily on the paradigms of eyewitness misinformation (e.g., Ghetti, Qin, & Goodman, 2002; Roebers, 2002; Jacoby, Bishara, Hessels, & Toth, 2005) or source monitoring (e.g., Dodson et al., 2007). In these paradigms basic associative mechanisms of episodic memory (i.e., binding processes) are usually couched within various contextual details whose features could be manipulated to yield misinformation or shifts in memory sources. Under these conditions, younger children and older adults tend to overestimate their memory performance, particularly with respect to false memories. However, no study to date has directly compared children and older adults on memory-accuracy calibration and their susceptibility to high-confidence memory errors. To minimise age differences in the ability to process contextual details and to more directly relate memory-monitoring functions to basic associative mechanisms of memory, an associative recognition paradigm without addition of misinformation or source information was used.

According to the two-process account (Yonelinas, 2002), memory for past events can be based on retrieval accompanied by specific contextual details (recollection) or on the feeling that an event is old or new without recovering specific details (familiarity). Existing evidence suggests that recollection depends more on the hippocampus, whereas familiarity depends more on the rhinal cortex, and that healthy ageing has greater effects on recollection than on familiarity (e.g., Jacoby, 1999). Recent findings by Daselaar et al. (2006) suggest that older adults compensate for hippocampal (recollection) deficits by relying more on the rhinal cortex (familiarity), possibly guided by top-down frontal modulation. Based on these findings we predicted that older adults, due to their deficits in forming associations during encoding and their greater reliance on familiarity during retrieval, would be more likely to miscombine features originating from different familiar events into illusory memory with high confidence than younger adults. In contrast to our prediction regarding older adults, we did not expect that 10- to 12-year-old children and adolescents would be particularly prone to commit memory errors with high confidence because the medial temporal brain regions (including the hippocampus and the rhinal cortex) operate relatively well by middle childhood (e.g., Giedd et al., 1999; Menon, Boyett-Anderson, & Reiss, 2005; Ofen et al., 2007; Sowell et al., 2003).

In addition to individual differences in the efficacy of associative mechanisms, strategic processes also affect episodic memory (see also Shing, Werkle-Bergner, Li, & Lindenberger, in press; Werkle-Bergner, Müller, Li, & Lindenberger, 2006). These processes may include the organisation and manipulation of the elements of a memory episode during encoding, storage, or retrieval (Craik & Lockhart, 1972; Levin, 1988; Paivio, 1971). For example, memory encoding can be aided by the use of mediators generated from verbal and imagery elaboration (Richardson, 1998). The child developmental literature suggests that it is not until the end of the elementary-school years that children make use of the full range of memory strategies (for a review, see Schneider & Pressley, 1997). On the other hand, the cognitive ageing literature suggests that older adults do not utilise memory strategies as efficiently as younger adults (for a review, see Kausler, 1994). Therefore in this study we also examined the extent to which high-confidence errors can be reduced by instructing an elaborative imagery strategy to the participants. Given recent evidence suggesting that older adults show more limited memory plasticity than children as a function of mnemonic training (Brehmer, Li, Müller, v. Oertzen, & Lindenberger, 2007), we expected that older adults would continue to show more high-confidence errors than individuals in other age groups even after strategy instruction.

METHOD

Participants

Our lifespan sample consisted of four age groups: 43 children (aged 10–12, $M = 11.2$, $SD = 0.6$), 43 teenagers (aged 13–15, $M = 14.4$, $SD = 0.4$), 42 younger adults (aged 20–25, $M = 23.3$, $SD = 1.6$), and 42 older adults (aged 70–75, $M = 73.2$, $SD = 1.7$). The age differences between the children and teenagers were chosen to reflect assumed

developmental differences in maturity of the prefrontal cortex (Giedd et al., 1999). All participants were residents of Berlin, Germany and travelled to our laboratory for testing on their own, or were accompanied by a parent in the case of younger children. The children and teenagers were attending the highest school track in Germany (the *Gymnasium*) that allows for university admission. The younger adults were mostly university students but none of them was a psychology student (to minimise pre-existing difference in knowledge of memory strategy). The older adults lived independently in the community. All participants reported having normal or corrected-to-normal visual and auditory acuity. Participants also filled out demographic questionnaires assessing subjective well-being and subject health condition, in which participants showed no significant age difference in these dimensions. Descriptive information of the participants is summarised in Table 1.

Design and procedure

We systematically varied demands on an associative recognition memory task (cf. Naveh-Benjamin, 2000) along the dimensions of associative demand and strategic elaboration in a fully crossed within-person repeated measures design. The task entailed presenting lists of word pairs for study and then testing either for the single words (item recognition) or for the associations between the words (pair recognition). Given the emphasis on binding as a candidate mechanism for high-confidence error, here we focused only on pair recognition.[1]

Associative-demand manipulation. Word pairs of either two unrelated German–German (GG) words or of one German word and a Malay word[2] (GM) were used. The Malay word was the direct translation of the German word. For our German participants the GM pairs demanded more associative processing than the GM pairs, as there is a lack of pre-existing knowledge of the unfamiliar Malay language.

---

[1] Other details of the study can be obtained by contacting the authors.

[2] Malay is written in the Latin alphabet and the phonemes are pronounceable for German speakers. None of the participants in our sample knew this language, thus it was equally unfamiliar for all age groups.

TABLE 1
Descriptive characteristics of sample

Measures	Children M (SD)	Teenager M (SD)	Younger adults M (SD)	Older adults M (SD)
Age	11.2 (0.6)	14.4 (0.4)	23.3 (1.6)	73.2 (1.7)
Male: Female percentage (%)	47: 53	51: 49	48: 52	50:50
Well-being	4.9 (2.3)	4.6 (2.4)	4.9 (2.7)	5.4 (2.9)
Subjective health	3.4 (0.7)	3.1 (0.6)	3.1 (0.8)	3.1 (0.7)
Digit symbol (cognitive mechanics)	45.7 (7.3)	57.3 (9.3)	62.8 (10.9)	43.4 (9.5)
Vocabulary (cognitive pragmatics)	9.4 (4.1)	13.5 (4.4)	20.6 (4.5)	27.9 (4.1)

Standard deviation in brackets. See reference for calculation of well-being score (total score 12; the lower the better) in Radloff (1977). Questionnaire of subjective health was constructed by the authors (scale from 1 to 5; the higher the better).

Strategic elaboration manipulation. The levels of strategic elaboration were manipulated using the encoding instruction. At pre-strategy memory assessment, participants were simply instructed to study the word pairs for an upcoming pair recognition test. This was followed by a strategy training session, in which participants were instructed and practised on an elaborative imagery strategy (Richardson, 1998). The essence of the strategy was to elaborate on the word pairs with visual imagery that dynamically integrated the two words (Paivio, 1969). For the German–Malay condition, a variant of the imagery strategy known as the keyword strategy was instructed. Participants were told to first find a meaningful connection (i.e., the keyword) for the Malay word through either its phonological or orthographic characteristics. Then participants integrated the keyword with the German word through imagery. In the strategy instruction session participants were introduced to the main principles of the strategy and intensively practised applying it. Detailed feedback was provided to improve the quality of the imageries. After the strategy-training session, participants' memory performance was assessed in two sessions of post-strategy memory assessment. On average, the time interval between testing sessions was between 2 and 4 days.

Pre- and post-strategy memory assessments. In a counterbalanced block design, 45 GG or GM word pairs were presented sequentially on the computer screen during the encoding phase. Presentation time was 3 seconds for younger adults and 6 seconds for the other age groups to avoid ceiling or floor performance in the different age groups. At the recognition phase, 60 memory probes were presented consecutively on the computer screen. Half of the pair probes were exact replication pairs from the encoding phase

(target pairs); 15 probes were rearranged pairs, composed of recombinations of words taken from different study pairs at encoding; 15 probes were new–new pairs, composed of words that never appeared at encoding. Participants were instructed to press the "old" response button for intact pairs and the "new" response button for both the rearranged and new–new pairs. The distinction between the two types of lure probes was based on the rationale that the rearranged pairs elicited a higher familiarity signal than the new–new pairs, which also required higher fidelity of the recollection process to avoid committing false alarm (FA) responses (Yonelinas, 2002). In the analysis we focused on confidence judgements following FAs on rearranged pairs.

Confidence rating. Following each old/new judgement during the recognition phase, participants made a confidence judgement of their decision on a 3-point scale ranging from 1 (unsure) to 3 (sure), without time restriction. To aid the children in understanding the scale, each of the response buttons corresponding to the three increasing levels of confidence was labelled by stickers with one, two, or three stars.

RESULTS

Overview of analyses

Confidence judgements of trials in which an old/new judgement was given in less than 400 ms were likely to be invalid or anticipatory responses and were discarded from analyses (less than 1% of overall data). Rates of hits ("old" responses to target) and FAs ("old" responses to rearranged lures) were computed respectively for each block types. On average, teenagers and younger adults produced much fewer FAs than children and older adults. Whereas children showed comparable levels of FAs to older adults at pre-strategy assessment, they reduced the FA rate more than older adults after strategy instruction (see Table 2). For the two response types (hit or FA), percentages of "sure" judgements were calculated. For analyses of confidence rating with respect to these two response types, individuals who did not produce FAs logically yielded missing data and were excluded from the statistical analyses. Overall, this resulted in 7% and 9% of missing data in children and older adults for the GG condition, respectively, before strategy instruction, and 12% missing data in both age groups after strategy instruction. In teenagers and younger adults, the amount of missing data is larger (i.e., 10–43%). There were no missing data in the GM condition. Given that we did not have specific predictions regarding the two post-strategy sessions, we collapsed across the participants' performance on the two post-strategy sessions to reduce data complexity.

The percentages of "sure" judgements following hits and FAs (see Figure 1) were analysed with a $2 \times 2 \times 4$ (response type: hits vs FAs x assessment: pre- vs post-strategy $\times$ 4 age groups) mixed MANOVA, separately for the GG and GM conditions. We examined three main hypotheses: (1) all participants would show more "sure" judgements on hit than FA responses; (2) older adults would show more "sure" responses on FAs (i.e., high-confidence error) than other age groups, including children; (3) high-confidence

errors in older adults would remain even after strategy instruction. For all effects we also calculated p_{rep} using the approximation of Killeen (2005) and partial eta squared (η^2). Significant age effects were followed up by post hoc all possible pairwise comparisons with Bonferroni adjustment.

GG condition

The results are shown in the upper panels of Figure 1. The $2 \times 2 \times 4$ omnibus test yielded a significant main effect of response type, $F(1, 109) = 275.35$, $p_{rep} > .99$, $\eta^2 = .72$, and significant interactions between response type and assessment, $F(1, 109) = 14.81$, $p_{rep} > .99$, $\eta^2 = .12$, as well as between response type and age, $F(3, 109) = 10.56$, $p_{rep} > .99$, $\eta^2 = .23$. The three-way interaction was not significant, $F < 1$. The main effect of response type was driven by a higher percentage of "sure" judgements following hit responses than FA responses ($M_{hit} = 80.40$ vs $M_{FA} = 35.40$). Therefore, as expected, participants in all age groups differentiated between correct and incorrect responses, demonstrating appropriate memory accuracy and confidence calibration in general. In addition, the interaction between response type and assessment showed that the difference in confidence following hit and FA responses was enlarged after strategy instruction ($\triangle$ pre-strategy $= 37.40$ vs $\triangle$ post-strategy $= 52.60$).

TABLE 2
Mean and standard error (in parentheses) of hit rates for target pairs and FA rates for rearranged lure pairs at pre- and post-strategy assessments

Age group	Hit rate		False alarm rate	
	Pre-strategy	Post-strategy	Pre-strategy	Post-strategy
German–German				
Children	.69 (.02)	.81 (.02)	.31 (.03)	.12 (.01)
Teenager	.80 (.02)	.86 (.02)	.22 (.02)	.08 (.01)
Younger adults	.82 (.02)	.88 (.01)	.16 (.03)	.06 (.01)
Older adults	.81 (.02)	.84 (.02)	.34 (.04)	.21 (.03)
German–Malay				
Children	.60 (.02)	.68 (.02)	.40 (.02)	.32 (.02)
Teenager	.68 (.03)	.73 (.02)	.38 (.02)	.29 (.02)
Younger adults	.77 (.02)	.79 (.01)	.45 (.03)	.27 (.02)
Older adults	.76 (.02)	.80 (.02)	.55 (.03)	.48 (.03)

In the GG condition children showed comparable FA rates to older adults at pre-strategy assessment, $t(76) = -.76$, $p = .45$, and lower FA rates compared to older adults after strategy instruction, $t(61) = -3.27$, $p = .002$. In the GM condition children and older adults differed in the FA rate both before, $t(74) = -3.48$, $p = .001$, and after strategy instruction, $t(77) = -4.66$, $p = .00$.

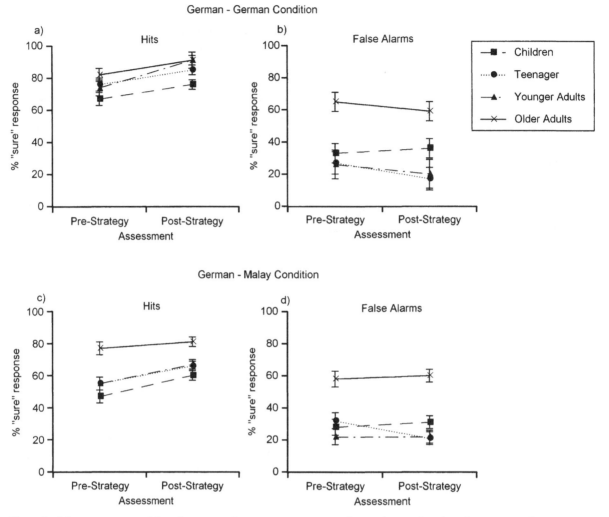

Figure 1. Mean percentages of "sure" responses from pre- to post-strategy instruction as a function of age group and response type (i.e., hit or FA) in the GG and GM conditions.

To interpret the interaction between response type and age, we examined mean percentages of "sure" judgements (separately for hits or FAs) derived from the pre- and post-strategy assessments with one-way ANOVAs (age as factor). For both response types, there was a significant age effect—hit: $F(3, 166) = 6.99$, $p_{rep} > .99$, $\eta^2 = .11$; FA: $F(3, 154) = 8.19$, $p_{rep} > .99$, $\eta^2 = .14$. For confidence judgements following hits, post hoc comparisons showed that children were significantly lower in the percentage of "sure" judgements ($M_{children} = 73.77$) compared to the other age groups ($.93 < p_{rep} < .99$; $82.22 < M < 87.26$). There was no difference among the remaining three age groups. For confidence judgements associated with FAs, post hoc comparisons showed that older adults were significantly higher in the percentage of "sure" judgements ($M_{olderadults} = 56.83$) compared to the other age groups ($p_{rep} > .92$, $22.00 <$

$M < 35.17$), including children ($M_{children} = 35.17$, $p_{rep} = .97$). There was no difference among the remaining three age groups. Therefore our prediction that older adults should show more high-confidence errors, including the comparison to children, was supported. Furthermore, this effect was observable both at pre- and post-strategy instruction sessions as indicated by the nonsignificant three-way interaction.

GM condition

The results are shown in the bottom panel of Figure 1. The $2 \times 2 \times 4$ omnibus test yielded significant main effect of assessment, $F(1, 164) = 6.80$, $p_{rep} = .95$, $\eta^2 = .04$, and response type, $F(1, 164) = 418.17$, $p_{rep} > .99$, $\eta^2 = .72$; significant interactions between response type and age, $F(3, 164) = 9.54$, $p_{rep} > .99$, $\eta^2 = .15$, as well as between assessment and response type, $F(1, 164) = 27.42$, $p_{rep} > .99$, $\eta^2 = .14$; and a significant three-way interaction, $F(3, 164) = 3.61$, $p_{rep} > .94$, $\eta^2 = .06$. To interpret the highest-order interaction, we examined the confidence judgements following hits or FAs separately using two-way ANOVAs (assessment by age group).

For confidence judgements following hit responses there were significant main effects of assessment, $F(1, 166) = 31.13$, $p_{rep} > .99$, $\eta^2 = .16$, and age group, $F(3, 166) = 12.47$, $p_{rep} > .99$, $\eta^2 = .18$. Specifically, participants showed higher percentages of "sure" responses following hit responses after strategy instruction ($M_{pre\text{-}strategy} = 58.65$, $M_{post\text{-}strategy} = 68.09$). Older adults, on average, showed significantly more "sure" responses ($M_{older\ adults} = 78.70$) compared to the other age groups ($p_{rep} > .99$, $53.10 < M < 61.10$). The remaining three age groups did not differ from each other. The interaction between assessment and age group was not significant, $F(3, 166) = 1.31$, $p_{rep} = .66$, indicating that the change from pre- to post-strategy assessment was equal across age group.

For confidence judgements following FA responses, the only significant effect was age, $F(3, 164) = 18.91$, $p_{rep} > .99$, $\eta^2 = .26$. Post hoc comparisons revealed that older adults, similar to the GG condition, showed significantly more high-confidence errors ($M_{older\ adults} = 59.00$) compared to the other age groups ($p_{rep} > .99$, $22.10 < M < 29.10$), including children ($M_{children} = 29.10$). The three remaining age groups did not differ from each other. Therefore our prediction that older adults should show more high-confidence error, including the comparison to children, was supported. Furthermore, this pattern did not diminish even after strategy instruction. We also examined whether older adults showed even more "sure" responses on FAs than other age groups in the GM condition. In a 2×4 (associative demand; GG vs GM × four age groups) ANOVA, we did not find main or interaction effect involving the associative condition factor. Therefore our prediction was not supported.

DISCUSSION AND CONCLUSION

Results from this study can be summarised in three main points. First, participants of all age groups showed more "sure" judgements following hit than FA responses, demonstrating their general ability to calibrate confidence level according to memory accuracy. In both the GG and GM conditions the differences between the confidence ratings of hit and FA responses were enlarged after strategy instruction, indicating the effects of strategy use on the calibration of confidence judgement. Inspecting Figure 1 indicates that this effect was driven primarily by an increase of "sure" response following hit responses. In other words, changes in strategy use as induced by instruction increased participants' performance as well as the confidence in their performance.

Second, as predicted by the misrecollection account, older adults showed more "sure" responses following FA errors than all other age groups. Children, while performing the memory task at a similar level as older adults (before strategy instruction), did not show such a pattern of high-confidence errors when they produced FAs. This finding is consistent with evidence gathered from developmental and lifespan studies showing that children's ability in associative binding is mature relatively early (Cowan, Naveh-Benjamin, Kilb, & Saults, 2006; Shing et al., in press; Sluzenski, Newcombe, & Kovacs, 2006; Werkle-Bergner et al., 2006). Our results also lend support to the view that the efficacy of associative binding mechanisms is compromised in old age and, furthermore, contributes to lifespan differences in high-confidence errors for rearranged lure pairs.

Third, our study extended the literature by showing that instructing an elaborative imagery strategy does not eliminate or reduce negative adult age differences in high-confidence errors. It is important to point out that, overall, the participants' performance was significantly improved after strategy instruction, as reflected in increased hit and reduced FA rates. However, as long as FAs were committed, older adults persistently experienced the phenomenological feeling of high confidence and more so than the other age groups. Similar observations can be made on the pattern of high-confidence errors in the GG and GM conditions. The two conditions were designed to vary the demands on associative binding. As can be seen in Table 2, participants' performance in the GM condition was very much lowered (i.e., lower hit and higher FA rates), demonstrating the difficulty of the high associative-demand condition. However, given the occurrence of FAs, participants (including older adults) were equally likely to associate the

FAs with high confidence (as reflected in the percentage of "sure" responses) in the GM and GG conditions. This seems to suggest that, while older adults are vulnerable in making high-confidence errors when memory retrieval require specific details, the extent of the difficulty in integrating the memory feature at encoding does not affect the relative occurrence of high-confidence errors. At the same time, the greater associative difficulty in the GM condition resulted in poorer performance and may have led children, teenagers, and younger adults to be less likely to give "sure" judgements following hit responses in the GM condition. However, this was not the case for older adults, as reflected in the significant difference between older adults and the other age groups in percentages of "sure" judgements following hit responses. Apparently, older adults lacked sensitivity to the difference in difficulty between the two conditions. These findings need to be corroborated by further investigations to determine whether they are substantially related to more general ageing-induced deficits in meta-cognitive monitoring (cf. Hertzog & Dunlosky, 2005; Souchay & Isingrini, 2004).

The findings above also suggest that the locus of the mechanism causing the high-confidence errors in older adults is not yet clearly identified. Developmentally, differences in children and older adults' memory functioning may manifest themselves at encoding and/or retrieval processes. The misrecollection account suggests that older adults have a propensity to miscombine features of different events, which in turn causes convincing high-confidence errors in false memories (Dodson et al., 2007). Assuming the manipulations on strategy instruction and associative demand mainly influenced the encoding operation, the similar levels of high-confidence errors in older adults across the conditions indicate that the errors were driven not by encoding but by retrieval difficulty. That is, older adults may have difficulty in specifying the sources of the familiarity signals at retrieval (e.g., Henkel et al., 1998; Jacoby, 1999). An alternative memory strategy that is worth investigating is the distinctiveness heuristic, which is a mode of responding emphasising participants' metacognitive awareness at retrieval, such that accurate recognition of studied items should require recollection of distinctive details (e.g., Schacter, Israel, & Raccine, 1999). The heuristic has been shown to reduce false memory and improve confidence-accuracy calibration in children (Ghetti et al., 2002) and

older adults (Dodson & Schacter, 2002; Schacter et al., 1999). In as much as the pattern of high-confidence errors is reduced in older adults after the distinctiveness heuristic is instructed, the results would point towards retrieval problems as the cause of high-confidence errors.

It is important to point out that, while our study directly tested the link between the misrecollection account and associative mechanisms, our data do not disprove other alternative explanatory frameworks of false memories in ageing (e.g., inhibitory deficit, decline in recollection process). On the contrary, it is most likely that the various mechanisms at memory encoding, representation, and retrieval interact and underlie different aspects of false memory and high-confidence error phenomena. One line of research that may be informative is the neurocomputational framework proposed by Li and colleagues (e.g., Li, Lindenberger, & Sikström, 2001), in which senescent changes in aspects of cognition are simulated in relation to age-related reductions in the efficacy of dopaminergic neuromodulation (see Bäckman & Farde, 2005, for a review). Using the model it was shown that neuromodulational deficiency results in less distinct internal representation, especially in task conditions that require associative binding (Li, Naveh-Benjamin, & Lindenberger, 2005). In accordance with the misrecollection account, although at a different level, the neurocomputational model suggests that older adults' high-confidence errors may have been the behavioural manifestation of the highly activated but less distinctive internal hidden-layer representations of memory items in the simulated old networks. From the perspective of the ageing hippocampal model (Wilson et al., 2006), this would correspond to the lack of distinction between newly learned information and existing memory traces, possibly due to deteriorating functional connectivity between the entorhinal cortex and hippocampus. Extending the neurocomputational theory on deficient neuromodulation leading to less distinctive representations (e.g., Li et al., 2001, 2005), a conjecture can also be derived to interpret why the ageing-related deficit in memory calibration is specific to false-alarm responses but not to hits. This is because, by default, hit responses are derived from having "afferent sensory copies" of the associations formed in memory. There is no evidence indicating that older adults are less able to calibrate when they detect a match between stimuli and memory representation. On the other hand, for the FAs for rearranged pairs, although there were separate afferent sensory copies of each of the items encoded in memory, there were no actual "afferent sensory copies" of these associations. Any associations of these come from illusory conjunctions. Thus, one would expect the negative consequences of less distinctive representations to be more prominent when needing to verify memory representations that lack the actual sensory encoding aspects; that is, the rearranged lure pairs (cf. Craik, 1983).

At the same time, ageing affects the functioning of strategic processes possibly via senescent changes in structure and connectivity of the prefrontal cortex (Buckner, 2004; Raz et al., 2005; West, 1996). Prefrontally mediated strategic processes during memory encoding, storage, and retrieval are mainly understood to increase the signal-to-noise ratio in the face of competing representations and to bias memory search operations in task-appropriate ways (Miller & Cohen, 2001; Rugg & Wilding, 2000; Simons & Spears, 2003). Given that rejecting the rearranged pairs puts particularly high demands on controlled processing during retrieval to overcome response tendencies triggered by familiarity signals, our findings suggest that older adults' high-confidence errors may have resulted from a reduced distinctiveness of memory traces in combination with less efficient strategic support at retrieval. This chain of effects may provide a viable explanation for the high-confidence error phenomenon in old age and calls for future studies in this direction for corroboration. Furthermore, it is important to recognise that older adults differ considerably in their mean levels and rates of decline of the cognitive and neural functioning. The multiple factor framework (Buckner, 2004) postulates that distinct age-related cascades targeting different brain systems may vary in their levels of progression across individuals (see also Hedden & Gabrieli, 2004). Specifically, a dissociation between nondemented ageing and Alzheimer's disease has been documented, such that individuals with dementia show substantial reduction in hippocampal volume while only mild effects are present in nondemented ageing (e.g., Head, Snyder, Girton, Morris, & Buckner, 2005). In this context it is worth noting that older adults varied considerably in the proportion of high confidence. Some older adults always expressed high confidence following FA responses, whereas others usually expressed lower confidence following FA responses (similar to younger adults and children). Given our conjecture that high-confidence error

may be related to hippocampal decline, future research should combine behavioural experiments with neuroimaging measures and longitudinal assessments to find out the extent to which high proportions of high-confidence false alarms form part of normal ageing or signal later risk for dementia (cf. Bäckman & Small, 2007).

REFERENCES

Bäckman, L., & Farde, L. (2005). The role of dopamine systems in cognitive aging. In R. Cabeza, L. Nyberg, & D. Park (Eds.), *Cognitive neuroscience of aging: Linking cognitive and cerebral aging* (pp. 58–84). New York: Oxford University Press.

Bäckman, L., & Small, B. J. (2007). Cognitive deficits in preclinical Alzheimer's disease and vascular dementia: Patterns of findings from the Kungsholmen project. *Physiology & Behavior, 92,* 80–86.

Brehmer, Y., Li, S-C., Müller, V., v. Oertzen, T., & Lindenberger, U. (2007). Memory plasticity across the lifespan: Uncovering children's latent potential. *Developmental Psychology, 43*(2), 465–478.

Brewer, N., & Wells, G. L. (2006). The confidence–accuracy relationship in eyewitness identification: Effects of lineup instructions, foil similarity, and target-absent base rates. *Journal of Experimental Psychology: Applied, 12,* 11–30.

Buckner, R. L. (2004). Memory and executive function in aging and AD: Multiple factors that cause decline and reserve factors that compensate. *Neuron, 44,* 195–208.

Chalfonte, B. L., & Johnson, M. K. (1996). Feature memory and binding in young and older adults. *Memory & Cognition, 24*(4), 403–416.

Cowan, N., Naveh-Benjamin, M., Kilb, A., & Saults, J. S. (2006). Life-span development of visual working memory: When is feature binding difficult. *Developmental Psychology, 42*(6), 1089–1102.

Craik, F. I. M. (1983). On the transfer of information from temporary to permanent memory. *Philosophical Transactions of the Royal Society of London, B302,* 341–359.

Craik, F. I. M., & Lockhart, R. S. (1972). Levels of processing: A framework for memory research. *Journal of Verbal Learning and Verbal Behavior, 11,* 671–684.

Daselaar, S. M., Fleck, M. S., Dobbins, I. G., Madden, D. J., & Cabeza, R. (2006). Effects of healthy ageing on hippocampal and rhinal memory functions: An event-related fMRI study. *Cerebral Cortex, 16,* 1771–1782.

Dodson, C. S., Bawa, S., & Krueger, L. E. (2007). Ageing, metamemory, and high-confidence errors: A misrecollection account. *Psychology and Ageing, 22*(1), 122–133.

Dodson, C. S., & Krueger, L. E. (2006). I misremember it well: Why older adults are unreliable eyewitnesses. *Psychonomic Bulletin & Review, 13,* 770–775.

Dodson, C. S., & Schacter, D. L. (2002). Ageing and strategic retrieval processes: Reducing false memories with a distinctiveness heuristic. *Psychology and Aging, 17*(3), 405–415.

Ghetti, S., Qin, J., & Goodman, G. S. (2002). False memories in children and adults: Age, distinctiveness, and subjective experience. *Developmental Psychology, 38*(5), 705–718.

Giedd, J. N., Blumenthal, J., Jeffries, N. O., Castellanos, F. X., Liu, H., Zijdenbos, A., et al. (1999). Brain development during childhood and adolescence: A longitudinal MRI study. *Nature Neuroscience, 2*(10), 861–863.

Head, D., Snyder, A. Z., Girton, L. E., Morris, J. C., & Buckner, R. L. (2005). Frontal–hippocampal double dissociation between normal ageing and Alzheimer's disease. *Cerebral Cortex, 15*, 732–739.

Hedden, T., & Gabrieli, J. D. E. (2004). Insights into the aging mind: A view from cognitive neuroscience. *Nature Reviews Neuroscience, 5*, 87–97.

Henkel, L. A., Johnson, M. K., & DeLeonardis, D. M. (1998). Ageing and source monitoring: Cognitive processes and neuropsychological correlates. *Journal of Experimental Psychology: General, 127*, 251–268.

Hertzog, C., & Dunlosky, J. (2005). Ageing, metacognition, and cognitive control. In B. H. Ross (Ed.), *The psychology of learning and motivation* (pp. 215–251). San Diego, CA: Academic Press.

Jacoby, L. L. (1999). Ironic effects of repetition: Measuring age-related differences in memory. *Journal of Experimental Psychology: Learning, Memory and Cognition, 25*, 3–22.

Jacoby, L. L., Bishara, A. J., Hessels, S., & Toth, J. P. (2005). Aging, subjective experience, and cognitive control: Dramatic false remembering by older adults. *Journal of Experimental Psychology: General, 134*(2), 131–148.

Jacoby, L. L., & Rhodes, M. G. (2006). False remembering in the aged. *Current Directions in Psychological Science, 15*(2), 49–53.

Johnson, M. K. (2006). Memory and reality. *American Psychologist, 61*, 760–771.

Kausler, D. H. 1994. *Learning and memory in normal aging.* New York: Academic Press.

Killeen, P. R. (2005). An alternative to null-hypothesis significance tests. *Psychological Science, 16*(5), 345–353.

Levin, J. R. (1988). Elaboration-based learning strategies: Powerful theory = powerful application. *Contemporary Educational Psychology, 13*, 191–295.

Li, S-C., Lindenberger, U., & Sikström, S. (2001). Aging cognition: From neuromodulation to representation. *Trends in Cognitive Sciences, 5*(11), 479–486.

Li, S-C., Naveh-Benjamin, M., & Lindenberger, U. (2005). Aging neuromodulation impairs associative binding: A neurocomputational account. *Psychological Science, 16*(6), 445–450.

Loftus, E. F. (2003). Make-believe memories. *American Psychologist, 58*(11), 867–873.

Maki, R. H., & Swett, S. (1987). Metamemory for narrative text. *Memory & Cognition, 15*(1), 72–83.

Menon, V., Boyett-Anderson, J. M., & Reiss, A. L. (2005). Maturation of medial temporal lobe response and connectivity during memory encoding. *Cognitive Brain Research, 25*, 379–385.

Miller, E. K., & Cohen, J. D. (2001). An integrative theory of prefrontal cortex function. *Annual Review of Neuroscience, 24*, 167–202.

Naveh-Benjamin, M. (2000). Adult age differences in memory performance: Tests of an associative deficit hypothesis. *Journal of Experimental Psychology: Learning, Memory and Cognition, 26*, 1170–1187.

Naveh-Benjamin, M., Hussain, Z., Guez, J., & Bar-On, M. (2003). Adult age differences in episodic memory: Further support for an associative-deficit hypothesis. *Journal of Experimental Psychology: Learning, Memory and Cognition, 29*, 826–837.

Ofen, N., Kao, Y-C., Sokol-Hessner, P., Kim, H., Whitfield-Gabrieli, S., & Gabrieli, J. D. E. (2007). Development of the declarative memory system in the human brain. *Nature Neuroscience, 10*(9), 1198–1205.

Paivio, A. (1969). Mental imagery in associative learning and memory. *Psychological Review, 76*, 241–263.

Paivio, A. (1971). *Imagery and verbal processes.* New York: Holt, Rinehart & Winston.

Persson, J., Nyberg, L., Lind, J., Larsson, A., Nilsson, L-G., Ingvar, M., et al. (2006). Structure–function correlates of cognitive decline in aging. *Cerebral Cortex, 16*, 907–915.

Pressley, M., Levin, J. R., Ghatala, E. S., & Ahmad, M. (1987). Test monitoring in young grade school children. *Journal of Experimental Child Psychology, 43*, 96–111.

Radloff, L. S. (1977). The CES-D scale: A self-report depression scale for research in the general population. *Journal of Applied Psychology Measurement, 1*, 385–401.

Raz, N., Lindenberger, U., Rodrigue, K. M., Kennedy, K. M., Head, D., Williamson, A., et al. (2005). Regional brain changes in ageing healthy adults: General trends, individual differences, and modifiers. *Cerebral Cortex, 15*(11), 1676–1689.

Richardson, J. T. E. (1998). The availability and effectiveness of reported mediators in associative learning: A historical review and an experimental investigation. *Psychonomic Bulletin & Review, 5*(4), 597–614.

Roebers, C. M. (2002). Confidence judgements in children's and adults' event recall and suggestibility. *Developmental Psychology, 38*(6), 1052–1067.

Roebers, C. M., & Howie, P. (2003). Confidence judgements in event recall: Developmental progression in the impact of question format. *Journal of Experimental Child Psychology, 85*, 352–371.

Roebers, C. M., von der Linden, N., Schneider, W., & Howie, P. (2007). Children's metamemorial judgements in an event recall task. *Journal of Experimental Child Psychology, 97*, 117–137.

Rugg, M. D., & Wilding, E. L. (2000). Retrieval processing and episodic memory. *Trends in Cognitive Sciences, 4*(3), 108–115.

Schacter, D. L., Israel, L., & Raccine, C. (1999). Suppressing false recognition in younger and older adults: The distinctiveness heuristics. *Journal of Memory and Language, 40*, 1–24.

Schneider, S. L., & Laurion, S. K. (1993). Do we know what we've learned from listening to the news? *Memory and Cognition, 21*(2), 198–209.

Schneider, W., & Pressley, M. (1997). *Memory development between two and twenty* (2nd ed.). Mahwah, NJ: Lawrence Erlbaum Associates Inc

Shing, Y. L., Werkle-Bergner, M., Li, S-C., & Lindenberger, U. (in press). Associative and strategic components of episodic memory: A lifespan dissociation. *Journal of Experimental Psychology: General.*

Simons, J. S., & Spiers, H. J. (2003). Prefrontal and medial temporal lobe interactions in long-term memory. *Nature Reviews Neuroscience, 4*, 637–648.

Sluzenski, J., Newcombe, N., & Kovacs, S. L. (2006). Binding, relational memory, and recall of naturalistic events: A developmental perspective. *Journal of Experimental Psychology: Learning, Memoryand Cognition, 32*(1), 89–100.

Souchay, C., & Isingrini, M. (2004). Age related differences in metacognitive control: Role of executive functioning. *Brain And Cognition, 56*(1), 89–99.

Souchay, C., Isingrini, M., & Espagnet, L. (2000). Aging, episodic memory feeling-of-knowing, and frontal functioning. *Neuropsychology, 14*, 299–309.

Sowell, E. R., Peterson, B. S., Thompson, P. M., Welcome, S. E., Henkenius, A. L., & Toga, A. W. (2003). Mapping cortical change across the human lifespan. *Nature Neuroscience, 6*(3), 309–314.

Werkle-Bergner, M., Müller, V., Li, S-C., & Lindenberger, U. (2006). Cortical EEG correlates of successful memory encoding: Implications for lifespan comparisons. *Neuroscience and Biobehavioral Reviews, 30*, 839–854.

West, R. L. (1996). An application of prefrontal cortex function theory to cognitive aging. *Psychological Bulletin, 120*(2), 272–292.

Wilson, I. A., Gallagher, M., Eichenbaum, H., & Tanila, H. (2006). Neurocognitive aging: Prior memories hinder new hippocampal encoding. *Trends in Neurosciences, 29*(12), 662–670.

Yonelinas, A. P. (2002). The nature of recollection and familiarity: A review of 30 years of research. *Journal of Memory and Language, 46*(3), 441–517.

MEMORY, 2009, 17 (2), 180–196

Differential effects of age on prospective and retrospective memory tasks in young, young-old, and old-old adults

Lia Kvavilashvili, Diana E. Kornbrot, and Veronica Mash
University of Hertfordshire, Hatfield, UK

Janet Cockburn
University of Reading, UK

Alan Milne
University of Aberdeen, UK

Remembering to do something in the future (termed prospective memory) is distinguished from remembering information from the past (retrospective memory). Because prospective memory requires strong self-initiation, Craik (1986) predicted that age decrements should be larger in prospective than retrospective memory tasks. The aim of the present study was to assess Craik's prediction by examining the onset of age decline in two retrospective and three prospective memory tasks in the samples of young (18–30 years), young-old (61–70 years), and old-old (71–80 years) participants recruited from the local community. Results showed that although the magnitude of age effects varied across the laboratory prospective memory tasks, they were smaller than age effects in a simple three-item free recall task. Moreover, while reliable age decrements in both retrospective memory tasks of recognition and free recall were already present in the young-old group, in laboratory tasks of prospective memory they were mostly present in the old-old group only. In addition, older participants were more likely to report a retrospective than prospective memory failure as their most recent memory lapse, while the opposite pattern was present in young participants. Taken together, these findings highlight the theoretical importance of distinguishing effects of ageing on prospective and retrospective memory, and support and extend the results of a recent meta-analysis by Henry, MacLeod, Phillips, and Crawford (2004).

Keywords: Prospective memory; Retrospective memory; Ageing and memory; Young-old; Old-old.

Remembering to post a letter, make a phone call, or take a medication are important everyday tasks that rely on prospective memory—one's ability to remember and carry out intended actions at some point in the future. Prospective memory tasks have been classed into two broad

Address for correspondence: Lia Kvavilashvili, School of Psychology, University of Hertfordshire, College Lane, Hatfield, Herts, AL10 9AB, UK. E-mail: L.Kvavilashvili@herts.ac.uk

It is with great regret that we have to inform readers of the recent death of Alan Milne. He will be sadly missed.

Research presented in this paper was supported by a grant from the Economic and Social Research Council to Lia Kvavilashvili, Diana Kornbrot, Janet Cockburn and Alan Milne. Portions of research described in this paper were presented at the 1st International Conference on Prospective Memory in July 2000 (University of Hertfordshire), the Experimental Psychology Society Meeting in January 2001 (University College London), and the Psychonomic Meeting in November 2002 (Kansas City). We are grateful to Fiona Kyle for helping us to collect data and to young and old volunteers who took part in the study. The assistance of the University Medical Centre in recruiting volunteers is also gratefully acknowledged.

DOI:10.1080/09658210802194366

categories. In event-based tasks one has to remember to do something in response to a certain event (e.g., posting a letter when you pass the post box in the street). In time-based tasks the action has to be carried out at a particular time (e.g., making a phone call at 2:00 pm). Because there is no external event in time-based tasks, signifying the opportunity for recall, they require more self-initiated processing and are considered to be more difficult to remember than event-based tasks (e.g., Einstein, McDaniel, Richardson, Guynn, & Cunfer, 1995; Kvavilashvili & Fisher, 2007; Sellen, Louie, Harris, & Willkins, 1997).[1] However, an important feature that is common to all prospective memory tasks is the absence of an explicit prompt for recall at the time of retrieval. Hence, prospective memory has often been referred to as one's ability to "remember to remember", and distinguished from retrospective memory that is almost always instigated by an explicit prompt to recall the past information (e.g., "How was your holiday last week?", "Please recall all the words that you saw earlier in the experiment").

Despite this self-cued aspect of prospective memory, each prospective memory task also consists of a retrospective component. After having remembered that something needs to be done, one also has to remember "what" it is that needs to be done. This retrospective component is usually minimal and it is the prospective, "remembering to remember" aspect of the task that is problematic to both adults and children (Meacham, 1977; Zimmerman & Meier, 2006).

According to Craik (1986), this self-cued aspect of prospective memory should be even more problematic for older adults, who are generally known to experience difficulties with self-initiated, strategic retrieval. He predicted that age effects should be particularly pronounced in prospective memory and even exceed those observed in free recall retrospective memory tests, which are known to require high levels of internal strategic processes and produce large

age decrements. However, in stark contrast to Craik's prediction, initial naturalistic studies of prospective memory (where participants had to remember to send postcards or make phone calls at certain dates/times) failed to obtain significant age effects (Devolder, Brigham, & Pressley, 1990; Martin, 1986; Moscovitch, 1982; Patton & Meit, 1993; Rendell & Thomson, 1993; West, 1988, Study 1). Furthermore, no age effects were obtained in the first laboratory study of event-based prospective memory in which participants were busily engaged in an ongoing short-term memory test and additionally had to remember to press a key every time they encountered a particular target word in the ongoing task (Einstein & McDaniel, 1990). These findings prompted Einstein and McDaniel to conclude that "prospective memory seems to be an exciting exception to typical age-related decrements in memory" (p. 724). However, research that has accumulated since 1990 has produced contradictory patterns of findings that are much more difficult to interpret.

Age effects were initially identified in laboratory studies that investigated time-based prospective memory, e.g., Einstein et al. (1995), in which there was no age effect in the event-based condition but older participants were significantly worse in the time-based condition. Einstein et al. (1995) explained this pattern of results (i.e., age by type of task interaction) as being in line with Craik's (1986) theoretical model, which assumes large age-related memory decrements for tasks with high degree of self-initiation. However, subsequent studies reported age effects even in event-based prospective memory tasks. Currently, the results with event-based tasks are mixed, with some studies consistently failing to obtain age effects (e.g., Cherry & LeCompte, 1999; Cherry et al., 2001; Cherry & Plauche, 2004; Einstein & McDaniel, 1990; Einstein et al., 1995; Marsh, Hicks, Cook, & Mayhorn, 2007; Reese & Cherry; 2002), and others resulting in significant age effects (Mäntylä, 1993, 1994; Maylor, 1993, 1996, 1998; Maylor, Smith, Della Sala, & Logie, 2002; Park, Hertzog, Kidder, Morrel, & Mayhorn, 1997; Smith & Bayen, 2006; West & Craik, 1999, 2001; Zimmerman & Meier, 2006).

It has been pointed out that the majority of laboratory studies that failed to obtain age effects have adjusted (i.e., reduced) the difficulty of ongoing task (into which prospective memory target events are embedded) for older participants. For example, if the ongoing activity

---

[1] Kvavilashvili and Ellis (1996) have also distinguished activity-based tasks that involve remembering to do something before or after finishing a certain activity, for example, taking a pill after the breakfast (see also Harris, 1984). Because these tasks do not involve the interruption of ongoing activity, as something is to be done during the "gap" between the two consecutive activities, Kvavilashvili and Ellis (1996) have suggested that activity-based tasks may be easier to remember than event- and time-based tasks both of which usually require the interruption of ongoing activity.

involved answering general knowledge questions, the presentation rate would be slower for older participants (Einstein et al., 1995; Experiment 3) to compensate for their reduced speed of processing, or in the case of a short-term memory test, they would be presented with fewer items to remember (Einstein & McDaniel, 1990; Cherry & Plauche, 2004). Another important variable that can potentially account for discrepant findings is the nature of an event-based task, where performance may vary considerably as a function of cue event and its relation to the ongoing activity (focal vs non-focal cues) (Einstein & McDaniel, 2005; McDaniel & Einstein, 2007). With focal cues, a prospective memory event (e.g., the word "president") is processed as part of an ongoing activity (e.g., answering general knowledge questions). With non-focal cues, a target event (e.g., a face with glasses) requires additional processing since it is irrelevant to the processing of material in the ongoing task (e.g., naming the photos of celebrities). Age effects should therefore be more pronounced in event-based tasks with non-focal than focal cues (see also the task-appropriate account of Maylor, 1998). Recently several studies have started to address this issue explicitly by manipulating the nature of cues and/or the ongoing activity as a function of age (e.g., Rendell, McDaniel, Forbes, & Einstein, 2007; Zimmerman & Meier, 2006).

Although considerable progress has been made in trying to solve the basis for discrepant findings in laboratory studies of event-based prospective memory, most studies have failed to explicitly address the prediction made by Craik (1986) about the differential effects of age on prospective and retrospective memory. Given that age effects have been obtained in many laboratory studies of prospective memory, Craik's prediction needs to be addressed by comparing age effects in prospective and retrospective memory tasks within the same participant population to see if larger effects are obtained for the former than the latter (e.g., see Kvavilashvili, Messer, & Ebdon, 2001; Uttl, Graf, Miller, & Tuokko, 2001). However, the majority of published studies used only one or two prospective and retrospective memory tasks and did not report or compare the effect sizes (but see Zeintl, Kliegel, & Hofer, 2007).

In this respect, a major advance was made by a seminal meta-analysis of 26 studies on prospective memory and ageing which covered a total of 152 study-level effects with a large number of young ($N = 1426$) and old ($N = 1462$) participants (see Henry et al., 2004). This meta-analysis resulted in several key findings. First, negative correlations with age in laboratory time-based tasks ($r = -.39$) were not reliably larger than in event-based tasks ($r = -.34$). This finding contradicts the view that time-based tasks impose greater demands on self-initiated processes than event-based tasks. Second, the magnitude of age effects in laboratory event-based tasks was minimal, with focal cues and/or undemanding ongoing tasks ($r = -.14$) explaining only a very small percentage of variance (1.9%) in performance, and fairly large for tasks that imposed high attentional demands ($r = -.40$) explaining 16.4% of variance. Third, contrary to Craik's prediction, the magnitude of age effects on prospective memory was reliably smaller than in retrospective free recall tasks, and did not differ from those in recognition tasks. This finding has important implications for the understanding of mechanisms involved in prospective memory retrieval and indicates that self-initiation in prospective memory tasks may be mediated by predominantly automatic than by attentionally demanding controlled processes (cf. Kvavilashvili & Fisher, 2007).

Despite these interesting findings several important questions still need to be addressed. First, it remains unclear whether the patterns of findings obtained in meta-analysis of 26 studies with several thousand participants are robust enough to emerge within a single study. Second, if age effects are more pronounced in retrospective than in prospective memory tasks, then older adults should report experiencing more problems in everyday retrospective than prospective memory tasks. Finally, in order to gain better insight into differential effects of age on prospective and retrospective memory it is necessary to compare the onset of age decline in different prospective and retrospective memory tasks within one participant population by having at least two groups of old participants who are in their 60s and 70s (young-old and old-old).

The important information about the onset of decline in prospective memory and how it differs from that of retrospective memory is largely missing due to an existing practice in ageing research of using only one group of old participants whose age varies considerably (from as young as 55 to 80 or above in some studies). The results of few existing studies that have used age cohorts have shown that old participants in their

60s are reliably better on prospective memory tasks than those in their 70s (e.g., Bisiacchi, 1996; Dobbs & Rule, 1987, the red pen task; Huppert, Johnson, & Nickson, 2000; Maylor, 1996; Uttl et al., 2001; Zimmerman & Meier, 2006) with an accelerated decline starting only after 75 years of age (Mäntylä & Nilsson, 1997, analysis on conditionalised scores). Moreover, the studies that also included a sample of young adults showed that age effects were obtained only when young adults' prospective memory performance was compared to an old-old group in their 70s, but not when it was compared to young-old group in their 60s (Dobbs & Rule, 1987; Zimmerman & Meier, 2006; but see Maylor, 1998, who obtained age effect between young and old groups in their 50s to early 60s). It thus appears that by collapsing old participants of various ages into one single group important age effects on prospective memory may be masked.

The aim of the present study was to extend the findings of Henry et al.'s (2004) meta-analysis by addressing the set of important issues outlined above. Thus, in order to test Craik's (1986) prediction in more fine-grained manner, we compared the onset of decline in prospective and retrospective memory in three groups of participants (young, young-old, and old-old). Retrospective memory was assessed by tests of free recall and recognition. Prospective memory was assessed by three different laboratory-based tasks.

The main experimental task was modelled after Einstein et al. (1995, Experiment 3). Thus, participants had to answer a long set of general knowledge questions presented on the computer screen (ongoing task). In the event-based condition, participants had to type in six numbers (1, 2, 3, 4, 5, and 6) when they received a question about "telephone". In the time-based condition, they had to do this once in every 3 minutes. Unlike Einstein et al. (1995) we also had an activity-based condition in which participants had to type in the numbers after they finished each block of trials during a short 15-second rest interval between the blocks (see Footnote 1). Prospective memory performance was scored as a proportion of correct, on time, responses out of six opportunities, which in each condition occurred once in every 3 minutes during a 19-minute task of answering general knowledge questions.

In addition to this main experimental task, participants were also assigned to two additional event-based tasks during a 90-minute experimental session. Thus, participants had to remember to write down a name of a colour if they noticed that the task they were working on was on a coloured sheet of paper (there were three response opportunities). In another task, modelled after Dobbs and Rule (1987), participants had to remember to request a red pen when later in the session they were asked to copy a geometric figure (one response opportunity). These tasks can be considered as more "naturalistic" than our main experimental task because retrieval opportunities are separated by longer delay intervals filled with various activities (mimicking the complexities of everyday prospective memory task situations). In addition, the difficulty of ongoing tasks is not adjusted according to the age group. The few studies that used such "naturalistic" laboratory tasks have all reported significant age effects (Cockburn & Smith, 1991; Dobbs & Rule, 1987; Huppert et al., 2000; Kliegel, McDaniel, & Einstein, 2000; Mäntylä & Nilsson, 1997; Uttl et al., 2001; West, 1988, Study 2; Zeintl et al., 2007).

Several important predictions were made in the present study. First, it was predicted that the magnitude of age effects in the laboratory tasks of prospective memory would vary depending on the nature of tasks. For example, largest age effects would be obtained for the time-based condition in the main experimental task and for the event-based colour task as the latter involved a non-focal cue (the colour of the paper was irrelevant to the task the participant was working on at the time).

Furthermore, it was expected that age effects would be significantly larger in a simple three-item retrospective free recall task (see Method section) than in any of the laboratory prospective memory tasks. Most importantly, it was hypothesised that different patterns of decline would be observed in retrospective and prospective memory tasks. In particular, it was expected that while age effects in free recall and recognition tasks would be present in the young-old participants (those in their 60s), age effects in prospective memory tasks would be present only in the old-old (those in their 70s) but not in the young-old participants. Taken together, this pattern of findings would mean that for young-old, and especially old-old participants, everyday retrospective memory tasks should be more problematic than prospective memory tasks. This idea was assessed informally by asking all participants to recall their most recent everyday memory failure.

METHOD

Participants

The sample consisted of 223 participants, recruited from the local community in order to minimise differences due to background and education levels: 72 young (21 males, 51 females, mean age 23.50 years, $SD = 3.60$; range 18–30), 79 young-old (36 males, 43 females, mean age 66.05, $SD = 3.07$, range 61–70), and 72 old-old (30 males, 42 females, mean age 75.06, $SD = 2.77$, range 71–80). The majority ($N = 157$) were recruited by letters to residents on the local doctor's (general practitioner's) register and the remaining 66 (51 young and 15 old) by advertising in the local newspaper, job centre, youth centre etc.

In the young group 61% were employed, 8% were unemployed, 28% were students from various universities/colleges, and 3% were housewives. In the old group 75% were retired, 11% were semi-retired, 7% were working full time, and 7% were housewives.

No participant reported any of the following conditions: serious head injury; stroke, mental health, and/or memory problems (diagnosed by a doctor). None of the young women were pregnant at time of testing. All older participants were healthy and residing in the community. In an initial telephone interview with the experimenter none of them reported experiencing problems with vision, hearing, or physical mobility. English was the first language for all the participants.

Table 1 lists scores on background variables by age group. There was no reliable difference on self-rated general health between young and old participants on a 5-point rating scale with 1 =

poor and 5 = excellent ($F = 1.08$). However, in comparison to young adults, both groups of older adults rated their health as being better than that of their peers on a 5-point rating scale where 1 = worse, 3 = same, and 5 = significantly better ($p = .03$ and $p = .0004$ for young-old and old-old groups, respectively).

Vocabulary, estimated from scores on the Spot-the-Word Test of the Speed and Capacity of Language Processing Test (SCOLP; Baddeley, Emslie, & Nimmo-Smith, 1993), was reliably better in both young-old and old-old participants than in the young group (both $ps < .0001$). Young-old were also significantly better than young participants in the General Knowledge Task ($p = .017$), while the difference between the young and old-old was not significant ($p = .70$). These results indicate that any superiority in performance of the younger group in memory tests was not likely to be due to different crystallised cognitive ability. A test of general cognitive functioning revealed an opposite trend. Although all the old participants scored at least 24/30 on Mini Mental State Examination (MMSE; Folstein, Folstein, & McHugh, 1975), their scores were reliably lower than in the young group ($ps < .001$ for both groups of old participants). Similarly, young-old and old-old participants were reliably worse on the Speed of Comprehension Test of the SCOLP than the young group ($p = .04$ and $p = .001$, respectively). Finally, in common with other studies (cf. Freeman & Ellis, 2003; Huppert et al., 2000), young participants had spent significantly more years in full time education than either young-old ($p = .0001$) or old-old ($p < .0001$). The difference between the two old

TABLE 1
Participants' mean scores on several background variables as a function of age group

	Age group				
	Young ($N = 72$)	Young-old ($N = 79$)	Old-old ($N = 72$)	F value (2, 220)	Effect size (η^2)
Health rating	3.93 (0.70)	4.09 (0.80)	3.94 (0.69)	1.08	–
Health (self vs peers)	3.26 (0.61)	3.57 (0.61)	3.74 (0.73)	7.76	.07
Vocabulary (SCOLP– Spot-The-Word Test)	48.58 (4.25)	53.19 (4.16)	52.92 (4.62)	25.99	.19
General knowledge questions	0.50 (0.09)	0.55 (0.10)	0.52 (0.13)	4.08	.04
MMSE	29.06 (0.96)	28.23 (1.28)	27.64 (1.31)	25.99	.19
Speed of Processing (SCOLP–Speed of Comprehension)	74.26 (13.15)	69.32 (13.60)	64.06 (10.80)	11.82	.10
Years of education	14.01 (2.23)	12.43 (2.53)	11.35 (2.21)	23.83	.18

Standard deviations in brackets. See text for details of these measures.

groups was also significant in the expected direction ($p = .01$).

Materials

Speed and capacity of language comprehension test (SCOLP). This consists of Speed of Comprehension and Spot-the-Word Tests (Baddeley et al., 1993). Version B of both tests was used. In the Speed of Comprehension Test participants have 2 minutes in which to work through a maximum of 100 sentences and rate them as true or false as quickly and accurately as possible. The performance is scored as a total number of sentences rated in 2 minutes. In the Spot-the-Word Test participants have to identify a real word in 60 pairs of words consisting of a word and a nonword. There is no time limit on this test and performance is scored as a total number of correct responses out of 60.

Retrospective memory tests. (a) In the recognition memory test participants were presented with 18 sets of four words on a coloured sheet of A4 paper and asked to identify the one word in each set that they had just seen in the Spot-the-Word Test (see Baddeley et al., 1993). The performance was scored as the proportion of correct responses out of possible 18. (b) The three-item free recall test was part of the MMSE. Participants were told that their memory would be tested and were asked to repeat the three words "apple", "penny" and "table". This was followed by counting backwards in sevens from 100, and after five responses participants were asked to recall the three words. Performance was scored as the proportion of correctly recalled words.

General knowledge task (GKT). This was a 19-minute ongoing task for the main experimental prospective memory task of typing in six numbers. The GKT consisted of a computer analogue of stacks of cards (12 cm × 18 cm) presented on the screen with one general knowledge question per card. A total of 117 general knowledge questions were used, adapted from the pool of 160 questions used by Einstein et al. (1995) by selecting those questions most appropriate for a British sample. Six target questions about the American presidents used by Einstein et al. (1995) were changed into political and historical questions relevant to a British population. In the event-based condition, six of these questions were replaced by the six target questions about the

"telephone". The "telephone" questions were not used in activity- and time-based conditions lest they acted as incidental reminders to the participants (the main experimental prospective memory task involved typing in six numbers as if "making a phone call to a friend").

Presentation rate of the cards varied across the age groups. Following Einstein et al. (1995), presentation rate for each card was 12 seconds in the young group and 15 seconds in the old groups. With the presentation rate of 12 and 15 seconds per question, 88 and 70 questions respectively were randomly chosen from a pool 117 and presented in a random order. In the event-based condition, the target telephone questions occurred in fixed positions (once in every 3 minutes).

Design

For the main prospective memory task of typing in six numbers while answering general knowledge questions the design was a 3 age (young vs young-old vs old-old) × 3 type of task (event- vs time- vs activity-based) between-participants factorial. There were at least 24 participants in each of the resultant nine cells. For all the other tasks as dependent variables, the design was one-factor between-participants ANOVA with age as the independent variable. Unless otherwise specified, the number of participants in each of the three age groups was 72, 79, and 72 for young, young-old and old-old, respectively.

Procedure

Participants were tested individually by one of the three female experimenters (two of them being the first and the third author) in offices in the same building and with a similar layout. On average, testing sessions lasted 1½ to 2 hours including a short break of 10–15 minutes. All participants received a payment of £10 for their time and travel expenses.

At the beginning of the session the experimenter read a short description of the aims of the project and some of the tasks that had to be performed during the session. After signing a consent form participants made two ratings about their health, provided basic demographic information, and described their most recent memory failure. Participants were then informed that some of the paper and pencil tasks throughout the session would be printed on coloured sheets of paper. When presented with one of these coloured sheets, they had to remember to write the name of that colour anywhere on the page as soon as they noticed that the paper was coloured (this was the prospective event-based colour task). It was made clear that they would not be reminded of this task by the experimenter. Three opportunities throughout the session to make this response occurred in the recognition memory test (green paper), a brief 14-item questionnaire (yellow) and the MMSE interlocked pentagons subtask (peach).

Next, participants were informed that they would be tested on a general knowledge task (GKT). It was explained that each question would appear in the centre of a computer screen as though it was written on a card within a stack of several cards, and that there would be several such stacks. As each question was answered the stack would (visibly) diminish by one so that when all the questions from the stack had been answered there would be a blank screen for several seconds. This was described as a rest interval, which would be followed by a tone indicating that the next stack of cards was about to appear on the screen.

Participants were reassured that there would be a variety of questions and that nobody was expected to get them all right. They were also encouraged to guess if necessary. They were given the opportunity to question the instructions and then given a practice session of eight questions, consisting of a stack of three cards, a 15-second rest interval, then a stack of five cards.

The practice session was followed by the instructions for the main prospective memory task. The experimenter informed the participants that a secondary aim of the study was to explore how people remember to do things in the future, such as remembering to pass on a message to a friend or making a phone call at a certain time. In order to study their memory for future actions the experimenter wanted them to remember to do something additional while they were engaged in answering the questions. Thus, in the activity-based condition participants were asked to give an imaginary phone call to a friend every time they finished answering a stack of cards by typing in six numbers 1, 2, 3, 4, 5, 6 on the number pad of the computer keyboard. In the event-based condition they had to do this every time they saw a question containing the word "telephone". In the time-based condition they had to type in numbers every 3 minutes, i.e., at 3, 6, 9, 12, 15, and 18 minutes. They could check the elapsed time by pressing a space bar, which showed a small digital clock on the screen for a few seconds. Participants could not check the time on their own wristwatches as all participants had been asked to remove them at the beginning of the session (cf. Einstein et al., 1995).

Participants were encouraged to ask questions and the experimenter moved on only after she had made sure they had understood the instructions. There was then a filled delay of approximately 10–12 minutes before participants were asked to carry out the GKT (see Einstein & McDaniel, 1990). During this period participants completed both components of the SCOLP and the recognition memory test. This test was presented on the green sheet of paper and thus represented the first target occasion for the event-based colour task.

The participants then carried out the GKT. The prospective memory task of typing in six numbers was not mentioned at this point. The GKT lasted for 19 minutes and contained a total of six opportunities to respond prospectively, which occurred at 3-minute intervals in all conditions (activity-, event-, and time-based). The first question together with four possible answers (denoted as A, B, C, and D) was presented on the first (top) card of a stack. After a few seconds a prompt "Please enter your selection (A–D)" appeared on the bottom of the card and the participant had to type in the correct answer by pressing one of four designated keys marked (as A, B, C, D) on the keyboard. This was followed by feedback on the same card, indicating whether the participant had run out of time or whether the response option chosen was correct or not. The correct answer together with a cumulative percentage score at that point in the task was also presented. Then the card disappeared and revealed the second question written on the next card in the stack and so on. In line with Einstein et al. (1995), the feedback period always lasted for 3 seconds, but the amount of time the questions were displayed and the time participants were given to enter their response after the prompt varied according to participants' age (in the young group 6 and 3 seconds, and in the old group 8 and 4 seconds, respectively). Each stack of cards represented a block of trials. In all experimental conditions there were seven blocks of trials (one short and six long). In the event- and time-based conditions the first short block lasted for 1 minute and the remaining long blocks for 2 minutes 45 seconds. In the activity-based condition the first long block lasted for 3 minutes, blocks 2–6 for 2 minutes 45 seconds, and the final short block for 45 seconds. The rest intervals between the blocks were always 15 seconds. This sequence of long and short blocks ensured that retrieval occasions occurred in every 3 minutes in the middle of the blocks in event- and time-based conditions (requiring an interruption of ongoing activity), but at the end of the blocks in the activity-based condition.

On completion of the GKT participants who forgot to type in six numbers on all six occasions were given successive questions or prompts (increasing in specificity) to find out whether failure was due to complete forgetting of the instructions (i.e., a retrospective memory failure) or a failure to carry out the task at an appropriate moment. Thus participants were asked if, in addition to answering general knowledge questions, they were also supposed to do something else (first prompt), whether they had to do something on a particular occasion (3 minutes, rest interval, telephone question) (second prompt), or what was it that they were supposed to do every 3 minutes/rest interval/telephone question (third prompt). If participants could not recall the prospective memory task even after this most specific prompt they were given a recognition test consisting of three possible tasks (tap with a finger, type in six numbers, type in six letters) from which they had to choose the correct one (i.e., type in six numbers).

After probing, participants were asked to fill a short 14-item questionnaire, which was presented on the yellow sheet of paper and thus represented the second target occasion for the event-based colour task introduced in the beginning of the session. This was followed by a short (coffee/tea) break.

At the beginning of the second half of the session participants were given the instructions for the event-based red pen task. They were told that if at some stage in the session they were asked to copy a geometric figure, they had to request a red pen with which to draw it. After this, participants were engaged in a self-paced cognitive task presented on the computer, lasting 10–15 minutes and unrelated to the present study. This was followed by the MMSE, which included the retrospective memory free recall task (recalling the words "apple", "penny", and "table") (see

Materials section above). In addition, the last item contained two cue events for remembering the event-based red pen and colour prospective memory tasks. The experimenter gave the participant a sheet of peach-coloured paper with two interlocked pentagons and asked them to copy the figure in the space underneath. As soon as the participants heard this request they had to remember to ask for the red pen. Subsequently they also had to remember to write the colour of the paper on the sheet. As soon as participants finished copying the pentagons post-experimental probing questions were asked about the red pen task and then the colour task in the same way as for the main prospective memory task of typing in six numbers (see above).

RESULTS

This section is broken down into subsections corresponding to the different prospective and retrospective memory tasks described above. Participants' descriptions of their most recent memory failure as a function of age were also analysed. For all analyses the alpha level was set at .05, the Tukey HSD test was used for post hoc comparisons and effect sizes were measured by partial eta-squared (η^2) with small, medium, and large effects defined as .01, .06, and .16, respectively (Cohen, 1977).

Self-reported memory failure

Out of 223 participants, 17 could not remember their most recent memory failure (4 young, 7 young-old, and 6 old-old). The data of a further four participants were missing due to experimenter error. The remaining 202 participants provided either a specific example of their most recent failure or their most frequently occurring failure (when they were unable to retrieve the most recent one). Participants' descriptions of their memory lapses were categorised either as *prospective* (i.e., forgetting to turn up for an appointment, pass on a message, return a phone call, send a letter etc.), *retrospective* (forgetting a name, a word, where one put something, etc.), or *other* which mostly were absent-minded errors (going upstairs and forgetting why, opening a fridge to fetch a cup, repeating a simple action twice, etc.).

Percentage of participants as a function of age group and type of reported memory failure are presented in Table 2. As one can see from this table, young participants were more likely to report prospective memory lapses (53%) than young-old (18%) and old-old participants (19%). In contrast, both young-old and old-old participants were more likely to report retrospective memory lapses (54% and 55%, respectively) than young participants (35%). They were also more likely to report absent-minded errors (28% and 26%) than young participants (12%). These age differences in percentages of reported errors were highly significant $\chi^2 = 26.13$, $df = 4$, $N = 202$, $p < .0005$.

Retrospective memory tasks

Recognition was measured as the proportion of correctly recognised words (out of a possible 18) in the recognition component of the Spot-the-Word Test. Free recall was measured as the proportion of correctly recalled words (out of possible three) in the recall component of Mini Mental State examination. The mean proportions of correctly recognised and recalled words are presented in Table 3. One-way ANOVAs on these means with age as an independent variable revealed significant effects of age both for recognition, $F(2, 220) = 18.91$, $MSE = .01$, $p < .0001$, $\eta^2 = .15$, and for free recall, $F(2, 220) = 34.20$, $MSE = .01$, $p < .0001$, $\eta^2 = .24$. Post hoc comparisons revealed identical patterns for recognition and recall: young participants recognised and recalled significantly more words than either young-old ($ps < .0005$) or old-old ($ps < .0005$) participants, while differences between the two old group were not significant ($p = .54$ and $p = .19$, respectively). These large age effects were not

due to large participant numbers per age group (at least 72). Identical results were obtained when the analysis was repeated on participants in the activity, event-, and time-based conditions of the main experimental task with only 24 participants per age group.

Prospective memory tasks

Main experimental task – typing in six numbers. This task was embedded within the general knowledge question answering task and varied in terms of type of prospective memory cue (event vs time vs activity). As pointed out in the Method section, old participants were better or equally as good as young participants at answering questions in the general knowledge task (see Table 1 for means).

Out of 223 participants, 121 remembered to type in numbers on all six occasions (50 young, 46 young-old, and 25 old-old), 75 remembered on some but not on all occasions (20 young, 24 young-old and 31 old-old), and 27 participants forgot on all six occasions (2 young, 9 young-old, and 16 old-old). Post-experimental probing of these participants revealed that there was only one 79-year-old participant (in the activity-based condition) who could not identify the prospective memory task even at the fourth most specific prompt involving recognition of the correct action. All other participants remembered about the task either at the first (2 young, 6 young-old, and 5 old-old), second (2 young-old and 2 old-old), third (1 young-old and 1 old-old), or the final fourth prompt (7 old-old).

Participants in the activity- and event-based conditions tended to respond to the target occasions immediately or not at all. Prospective memory performance in these conditions was measured as a proportion of these on-time

TABLE 2

Percentage of participants as a function of type of reported memory failure (prospective vs retrospective vs other) and age group (young vs young-old vs old-old)

| Age group | *Type of reported memory failure* | | | |
	Prospective	*Retrospective*	*Other*	*Total*
Young	53% (35)	35% (23)	12% (8)	100% (66)
Young-old	18% (13)	54% (38)	28% (20)	100% (71)
Old-old	19% (12)	55% (36)	26% (17)	100% (65)
Total	30% (60)	48% (97)	22% (45)	100% (202)

Raw numbers in brackets.

TABLE 3
Mean scores on prospective and retrospective memory tasks as a function of age (young vs young-old vs old-old)

Memory tasks	Young	Young-old	Old-Old	Effect size (η^2)
RM – Recognition	.85 [a] [b] (.12)	.75 (.14)	.73 (.12)	.15
RM – Free Recall	.90 [a] [b] (.19)	.62 (.31)	.54 (.31)	.24
PM – Main experimental task				
Activity-based	.96 [b] (.20)	.85 [b] (.35)	.66 (.48)	.04
Event-based	.73 (.29)	.69 (.32)	.54 (.34)	.019
Time-based (strict scoring – 15 s)	.88 [a] [b] (.24)	.47 (.40)	.36 (.31)	.13
Time-based (lenient scoring – 60 s)	.92 [b] (.21)	.76 (.35)	.68 (.33)	.03
PM – Event-based colour	.68 [b] (.29)	.59 [b] (.37)	.37 (.40)	.12
PM – Event-based red pen	.92 [b] (.28)	.79 (.41)	.66 (.48)	.07

Results of post hoc comparisons between means of three age groups are denoted by subscripts a and b. Standard deviations in brackets.
[a]Reliably better than young-old. [b]Reliably better than old-old.

responses (cf. Einstein & McDaniel, 1990; Einstein et al., 1995). In contrast, participants in the time-based condition were predominantly responding late rather than not at all (i.e., few responses were made at exactly 3-minute intervals). Performance in this task was therefore measured as a proportion of responses that occurred within 15 seconds of the target time.

The mean proportions of correct prospective memory responses (out of possible 6) are presented in Table 3 as a function of age group (young vs young-old vs old-old) and the type of prospective memory task (event- vs time- vs activity-based). These means were entered into a 3 (age) × 3 (task) between-participants ANOVA. This analysis revealed a significant main effect of task, $F(2, 214) = 10.60$, $MSE = .112$, $p < .0001$, $\eta^2 = .09$. Post hoc tests showed that performance in the activity-based condition ($M = .82$, $SD = .38$) was significantly better than in the event- ($M = .66$, $SD = .33$) and time-based ($M = .57$; $SD = .39$) conditions ($p = .007$ and $p < .0001$, respectively). Although performance in the event-based condition was numerically higher than in the time-based condition, this difference was not statistically significant ($p = .27$). There was also a reliable main effect of age, $F(2, 214) = 18.17$, $MSE = .112$, $p < .0001$, $\eta^2 = .145$. Post hoc tests showed that young participants were reliably better ($M = .86$, $SD = .26$) than young-old participants ($M = .67$, $SD = .38$) who were reliably better than old-old participants ($M = .52$, $SD = .40$) ($p = .003$ and $p = .016$). However, this main effect was qualified by a significant age by condition interaction $F(4, 214) = 2.49$, $MSE = .112$, $p = .04$, $\eta^2 = .04$.

Tests of simple main effects showed that age effects were significant in the activity-based,

$F(2, 214) = 4.87$, $MSE = .112$, $p = .009$, $\eta^2 = .04$, and the time-based conditions, $F(2, 214) = 16.14$, $MSE = .112$, $p < .0001$, $\eta^2 = .13$, but not in the event-based condition, $F(2, 214) = 2.12$, $MSE = .112$, $p = .12$, $\eta^2 = .019$. Follow-up post hoc tests indicated that in the activity-based condition performance of young and young-old participants did not reliably differ from each other ($p = .24$) but young were reliably better than old-old participants ($p = .002$). Although young-old participants were numerically better ($M = .85$) than old-old participants ($M = .66$), this difference was marginally significant ($p = .05$). In contrast, in the time-based condition young participants were reliably better than both young-old and old-old participants (both $ps < .0001$) who did not differ from each other ($p = .24$).

However, it is important to note that the results of the above analysis were different when we adopted a more lenient scoring criteria for the time-based task, used by Einstein et al. (1995), by expanding the time window for correct responses up to 60 seconds from the target time. This substantially enhanced the time-based scores in all three age groups ($M = .92$, $M = .76$, and $M = .68$ in young, young-old. and old-old groups, respectively), and the age effect in time-based condition was substantially reduced, $F(2, 214) = 3.38$, $MSE = .109$, $p = .036$, $\eta^2 = .03$. Moreover, post hoc tests showed that performance of young and young-old participants was not reliably different ($p = .12$), but both groups were reliably better than old-old group ($p < .0001$ and $p = .026$, respectively).

Event-based colour task. In this task participants had to remember to write down the colour of the paper as soon as they noticed that a task they were carrying out was presented on a coloured sheet of paper. The performance score was the proportion of correct responses out of a possible three. Out of 223 participants, 62 remembered to perform this task on all three occasions (23 young, 25 young-old, 14 old-old), 107 participants remembered on one or two occasions (44 young, 39 young-old, 24 old-old), and 54 forgot on all three occasions (5 young, 15 young-old, and 34 old-old). Post-experimental probing of these participants revealed that only 12 participants recalled the task at the very first prompt (4 young-old and 8 old-old). The majority (78%) recalled the task on the successively specific prompts. While 32 participants (4 young, 9 young-old, and 19 old-old) recalled the task on the second and the third prompt, 10 participants (1 young, 2 young-old, and 7 old-old) needed the fourth most specific prompt to be able to recognise the correct action.

The mean proportions of correct prospective memory responses were .68 ($SD = .29$) in the young group, .59 ($SD = .37$) in the young-old group, and .37 ($SD = .40$) in the old-old group. These means were entered into a one-way between-participants ANOVA with age group as an independent variable. This analyses resulted in a significant main effect of age, $F(2, 220) = 14.58$, $MSE = .126$, $p < .0001$, $\eta^2 = .12$. Post hoc analysis showed that while young and young-old participants' scores did not reliably differ from each other ($p = .27$), they were both reliably higher than the scores of old-old participants ($p < .0001$ and $p = .001$, respectively).

Event-based red pen task. During the Mini-Mental-State-Examination (towards the end of the session) participants had to request a red pen to carry out the task of copying a geometric figure. Out of 223 participants, 173 remembered to request the red pen and were given a score of 1 (66 young, 61 young-old, and 46 old-old). The remaining 50 participants who forgot to do so were given a score of 0 (6 young, 18 young-old, and 26 old-old). Post-experimental probing of these 50 participants revealed that only 13 participants recalled the task at the very first prompt (3 young, 3 young-old, and 7 old-old). The majority (i.e., 31) recalled the task on the last most specific prompt, which involved the recognition of the to-be-performed action (3 young, 12 young-old, and 16 old-old). Four old participants (2 young-old and 2 old-old) were unable to even recognise the correct action. The data of these

four participants were excluded from the analysis. Mean scores of young, young-old, and old-old participants were entered into a one-way ANOVA with age as an independent variable. This resulted in a significant main effect of age, $F(2, 216) = 7.61$, $MSE = .16$, $p = .001$, $\eta^2 = .07$. Post hoc comparisons showed that performance of young participants ($M = .92$, $SD = .28$) did not differ from that of young-old participants ($M = .79$, $SD = .41$) ($p = .14$) but was reliably better than old-old participants ($M = .66$, $SD = .48$) ($p < .0001$). The difference between young-old and old-old was not significant ($p = .10$).[2]

GENERAL DISCUSSION

Research in prospective memory has grown enormously over the past decade and addresses a variety of important questions (see Einstein & McDaniel, 2005; Kliegel, McDaniel, & Einstein, 2008; McDaniel & Einstein, 2007). Investigating age effects on prospective remembering has been, and continues to be, a major focus of this research (Ellis & Kvavilashvili, 2000; Henry et al., 2004). Increased interest in this topic is understandable given that the ability of an ageing population to lead an independent life in the community depends crucially on their preserved prospective memory functioning. This research is also important theoretically as it can shed light on processes involved in prospective remembering (e.g., absence of age effects would be indicative of the involvement of predominantly automatic processes), and inform us about the relationship between prospective and retrospective memory (e.g., similar or different patterns of decline).

The major aim of the present study was to evaluate Craik's (1986) prediction about differential age effects on prospective and retrospective memory tasks, and to replicate some of the results of Henry et al.'s (2004) meta-analysis in a single study. This was achieved by comparing the onset of age decline in several retrospective and prospective memory tasks in three groups of partici-

---

[2] Since the variable for remembering the red pen was binary, a more sensitive logistic regression analysis was also conducted. As with ANOVA, there was a significant main effect of age group $\chi^2(2) = 15.1$, $p = .002$, with a modest effect size (Nagelkerke $r^2 = .10$). However, post hoc comparisons resulted in a significant difference between young and young-old, $\chi^2(1) = 12.5$, $p = .0004$, and marginally significant difference between young-old and old-old, $\chi^2(1) = 3.3$, $p = .068$.

pants: young, young-old, and old-old. On the whole, results replicated the main findings of the meta-analysis (outlined in the introduction) and in addition established different patterns of age decline in prospective and retrospective memory tasks. The latter finding underscores the importance of dividing older participants into at least two groups of younger and older adults (who are in their 60s and 70s) in prospective memory research.

Differential effects of age on prospective and retrospective memory

The first and most important finding was that, contrary to Craik's prediction (1986), effects of age on prospective memory were smaller than on retrospective memory. Thus, age effects in recognition and especially free recall tasks were fairly large, and explained 15% and 24% of variance in performance, respectively. These percentages are almost identical to those found in the Henry et al. (2004) meta-analysis (14% for recognition and 27% for free recall). By contrast, although reliable age effects occurred in all three laboratory tasks of prospective memory (the main experimental task of typing in six numbers, as well as event-based colour and red pen tasks), these were noticeably smaller than in the free recall task. The largest age effects were obtained in those prospective memory tasks that imposed relatively high demands on participants' processing resources, such as in the time-based condition of the main experimental task (but only when using a strict scoring criterion of a short, 15-second time window) and in the non-focal event-based colour tasks. However, even in these tasks age effects did not explain more than 13% and 12% variance in performance, respectively. In the Henry et al. (2004) meta-analysis the laboratory time-based and non-focal event-based tasks explained similar 15% and 16% of variance (see Table 2 of Henry et al., 2004).

Taken together, these findings extend the results of Henry et al.'s (2004) meta-analysis in several important ways. For example, according to Henry et al. (2004), one potential problem with interpreting the presence of larger age effects in free recall than in prospective memory tasks is that "the former are typically associated with list lengths that are substantially longer than those used in the latter" (p. 34). To counter this problem, in the present study we used the simplest possible free recall task with three items only, but still observed a large age effect, comparable to those obtained with multi-item lists. Importantly, this large age effect in free recall was not due to impaired cognitive functioning in older samples. Older adults scored significantly higher than young on the vocabulary test (Spot-the-Word Test), and the vast majority (i.e., 96%) scored 26 and above on the MMSE. In addition, the exclusion of six old participants who scored close to the cut off point of the MMSE (one participant scored 24 and five scored 25) did not change the pattern of results or the magnitude of age effects reported in Table 3.

Another novel finding concerns recognition memory. At first sight, the similar effect sizes obtained for recognition and prospective memory tasks (both in meta-analysis and in our study) might be interpreted as indicative of some similarities between these two forms of memory, given that event-based tasks may depend to some extent on noticing or recognising the event as an appropriate cue for action (e.g., Cherry et al., 2001; Einstein & McDaniel, 1996; McDaniel & Einstein, 2007; Reese & Cherry, 2002). However, our results concerning the onset of age decline in young-old and old-old participants show that this may not be the case. Post hoc comparisons revealed that a reliable age decline in recognition memory (and in free recall) was already present in the young-old group (61–70). In prospective memory tasks, however, the decline started mainly in the old-old group (71–80) (see Table 3).

In order to pinpoint the onset of decline more precisely, we further subdivided the groups of young-old and old-old into 5-year age bands of 61–65, 66–70, 71–75, and 76–80, with at least 36 participants in each subgroup. Post hoc tests with these five age groups showed that age decline for both recognition and free recall was present in the youngest age group of 61–65. By contrast, decline in prospective memory tasks was present only in the groups older than 61–65. Specifically, in the main experimental and event-based colour tasks it was present in the 71–75 group, and in the red pen task in the 66–70 group.

These findings are important for current research on ageing and prospective memory for the following reasons. First, they can explain the large variability in prospective memory scores that often exists within a group of older adults with a wide age range (typically 60 to 80 years and above) (e.g., Kidder, Park, Hertzog, & Morell, 1997; Park et al., 1997; Salthouse, Berish, &

Siedlecki, 2004; West & Craik, 1999). Second, they can potentially explain some of the contradictory findings in the literature concerning the presence or absence of age effects in prospective memory. It appears that age effects can disappear, or be substantially reduced, in studies in which the older sample consists primarily of individuals in their 60s, and be more likely to emerge when the older sample is predominantly in their 70s and above.

The pattern of findings concerning the differential effects of age on prospective and retrospective memory tasks was further supported by the analysis of participants' most recent self-reported memory failure. While old participants were more likely to report retrospective memory failure (54.5%) than young adults (35%), the latter were more likely to report prospective memory failure (53%) than older adults (18.5%) (see Table 2).[3] One possible explanation is that older adults have fewer prospective memory tasks to complete in everyday life and therefore they have less opportunity to experience prospective memory failures. However, the results of a study on participants' real-life intentions by Freeman and Ellis (2003) have shown that there were no age effects in the number of completed prospective memory tasks within a 1-week period. In fact, older people had a reliably higher proportion of intended and successfully completed tasks than young adults.

In conclusion, the results of the present study indicate that, in laboratory tasks, age effects are stronger and the decline starts earlier for retrospective than prospective memory. In addition, older adults reported experiencing more retrospective than prospective memory failures in their everyday life. These conclusions appear to contradict the results of a recent study by Zeintl et al. (2007) who compared performance of older

adults (aged 65 to 80) in three prospective and three retrospective memory tasks. They found larger age effects for prospective than retrospective memory tasks. The discrepancy between our results and those of Zeintle et al. (2007) may stem from the fact that they did not have a group of younger adults in their study. Indeed, when we calculated correlations between the chronological age and prospective and retrospective memory scores in our older participants only (N = 151), the obtained pattern was almost identical to that of Zeintl et al. (2007). Correlations between age and retrospective memory tasks were small and non-significant ($r = -.14$, $p = .08$; and $r = -.14$, $p = .079$ for recall and recognition, respectively), while correlations between age and prospective memory tasks ranged between $-.20$ and $-.34$ and were statistically significant. Taken together, results from Zeintl et al. (2007) and our study suggest that the decline in retrospective memory tasks starts in early 60s (possibly even earlier) with relatively little further decline in the 70s and early 80s, whereas decline in prospective memory tasks starts later but then continues at a more steady rate. Clearly, this is an interesting avenue for future research.

Performance on prospective memory tasks

An additional set of findings concerns the variable performance levels on different laboratory prospective memory tasks, as well as differential age effects on these tasks. Results from the main experimental task showed that performance in the activity-based condition was better than in both event- and time-based conditions (given strict scoring criterion for the time-based task). This might be due to the less demanding nature of this task as participants did not need to interrupt an ongoing activity to type in the numbers (see Kvavilashvili & Ellis, 1996). It should be noted that Kvavilashvili et al. (2001) observed negative effects of interruption in young children even in an event-based task. Thus, the findings indicate that a more systematic examination of the effects of task interruption on prospective memory may help us to have a better insight into similarities and differences between the event-, time-, and activity-based tasks.

Another interesting finding was that performance in the time-based condition varied greatly depending on the scoring criterion adopted.

---

[3] A similar pattern has also been obtained with the Everyday Memory Questionnaire by Martin (1986) as older adults scored better on prospective memory items (keeping appointments, paying bills, and taking medications), and younger adults on retrospective items (remembering names, telephone numbers, and sports results). However, other questionnaire studies (see e.g., Dobbs & Rule, 1987; Smith, Della Sala, Logie & Maylor, 2000) did not obtain any differences between prospective and retrospective items as a function of age. This could be due to problems that older adults may have when trying to retrospectively evaluate the frequency of different types of memory failures experienced in everyday life. In this respect, asking participants to recall their most recent failure can substantially reduce demands on retrospective memory and produce more valid results.

When we used a relatively strict criterion of counting a response as correct if it occurred within 15 seconds of the critical time, performance was worst in the time-based condition for both groups of older adults, and the effect of age explained 13% of the variance in performance (see Table 3). However, when we adopted a more lenient 60-second time window for scoring correct responses, the performance in the older groups substantially improved and the size of the age effect was markedly diminished, and comparable to that found for event- and activity-based conditions. Given that different studies have used a very wide range of time windows from few seconds (e.g., Maylor et al., 2002; Park et al., 1997) to 90 seconds (Martin & Schumann-Hengsteler, 2001), it is obvious that performance levels will vary across the studies, which may partly contribute to contradictory findings in the literature about the differential effects for age on time-based prospective memory.

It is important to point out that performance levels in three event-based tasks also varied substantially, with performance being highest in the red pen task ($M = .77$), lowest in the colour task ($M = .55$) and intermediate in the main (event-based) telephone task ($M = .65$). This pattern seems to be in line with the multi-process theory of McDaniel and Einstein (2007), which would predict that performance in the non-focal colour task should be worse than in the red pen and telephone tasks, since both are focal event-based tasks. However, in the telephone task, the target word "telephone" was a familiar and less distinctive word in the context of answering general knowledge questions,[4] whereas the target event in the red pen task (the words "please copy this geometric figure") was relatively unfamiliar and distinctive in the context of other predominantly verbal sub-items of Mini Mental State Examination. Previous findings on the positive effects of unfamiliar distinctive targets on prospective memory (Brandimonte & Passolunghi, 1994; McDaniel & Einstein, 1993) would suggest that performance in the red pen task should be superior to the telephone task. These predictions were indeed supported by the results of an additional analysis of variance on those participants who were in the event-based condition of

the main prospective memory task (24 young, 28 young-old, and 24 old-old).

This large variability in event-based scores as a function of target event characteristics can at least partly account for the contradictory findings in the literature concerning variable effects of age on event-based prospective memory (cf. Cherry et al., 2001; McDaniel & Einstein, 2007). It is interesting, however, that a reliable age effect was obtained in the red pen task, even though it was a focal task with a distinctive cue. As noted in the introduction, this could be due to the fact that the red pen task (as well as the colour task) is different from the typical laboratory tasks in two respects: they both have longer and/or irregular delay intervals and the target event(s) does not occur within one single ongoing activity. It is also noteworthy that the majority of older adults (32 out of 44) who forgot the red pen task also had difficulties remembering prospective memory instructions. Thus, 64% remembered the task at the fourth most specific prompt involving the recognition of the correct action and a further 9% (two young-old and two old-old) could not event recognise the correct action. Similar difficulties (albeit to a lesser degree) were encountered with remembering the task instructions for the colour task (see Results section). There is now a growing number of studies indicating that age decrements in prospective memory can be at least partly explained by the increased difficulty older adults have in remembering the retrospective component of prospective memory instructions (e.g., Cherry et al., 2001; Mäntylä & Nilsson, 1997; Salthouse et al., 2004).

Methodological considerations

A couple of methodological points need to be considered in the light of the present findings. First, it can be argued that by equating the difficulty of the ongoing question-answering task we artificially reduced the size of age effects in the main experimental prospective memory task. However, in order to properly assess age effects on prospective memory it is necessary to ensure that both age groups have equal amounts of attentional resources available for the execution of prospective memory tasks. Due to cognitive slowing, older adults needed more time to read the questions/type in their responses. If they had not been given the extra 3 seconds they would have had fewer processing resources avail-

---

[4] For example, "What is the telephone number for Directory Enquiries?" Answers: 999, 192, 129, 555, or "What is the lowest value coin used in public telephones?": 1p, 2p, 5p, 10p.

able for the prospective memory tasks than young adults. This would give an unfair advantage to the younger group.[5] Moreover, age effects in those prospective memory tasks (colour and red pen tasks) in which no equating of ongoing task difficulty took place were still smaller than in the simple (retrospective) free recall task.

The second methodological issue concerns ceiling effects in the young sample for some of the memory tasks (e.g., both the retrospective memory tasks, as well as the activity-based, time-based, and red pen prospective memory tasks). Ceiling effects are known to reduce the size of age effects (e.g., Uttl, 2005). While this criticism may apply to the activity-based, time-based, and red pen tasks, it does not apply to the two event-based tasks—the telephone and the colour tasks. Performance on these tasks was not near ceiling, but there was still no age effect in the former, and in the latter the age effect explained 13% of variance. Although this is a medium to large effect, it is still smaller than the age effect in the free recall task (24%). Moreover, since the ceiling effect was present in the free recall task as well, the age effect on free recall task would probably have been even larger if we had used a longer word list to avoid ceiling effects.

Conclusions and future directions

Results of the present study have both practical and theoretical implications, and raise key questions for future research. The results strongly suggest that the collapsing of old participants of various ages into one single group can mask interesting and important age effects on prospective memory. It is of little help to a layperson, who is 60 and concerned about his or her current or near-future prospective memory, to be informed of the results of the study in which older sample comprises individuals aged 60 to 80 and above. What is urgently needed from both practical and theoretical perspectives is to be able to determine the onset of age decline in different types of prospective memory tasks. Most importantly,

future research will need to compare the onset of decline in prospective and retrospective memory tasks in a more systematic fashion by including a wider range of retrospective memory tasks such as cued recall, story recall, and implicit memory (perhaps even autobiographical memories), to get a better understanding of differential effects of age on prospective and retrospective memory.

Findings from our study, comparing age effects in several prospective memory tasks with a restricted number of retrospective memory tasks, suggest the involvement of different retrieval mechanisms in these two types of memory tasks (see also Zeintl et al., 2007). One possibility is that prospective and retrospective memory draw on different memory structures. Our results concerning the differential onset of age decline in these tasks seem to support this idea. Converging evidence has also been obtained in several other studies that identified separate factors for prospective and retrospective memory tasks using exploratory factor analysis (Maylor et al., 2002; Uttl et al., 2001), or examined the construct validity of event-based prospective memory tasks (Salthouse et al., 2004).

Another possibility is that prospective and retrospective memory tasks differ mainly in terms of the amount of automaticity involved in retrieval. The relatively small age effects on prospective memory obtained in the present study provide some support for the idea that the retrieval of prospective memory tasks is, to some degree, an automatic process. Thus, in terms of automaticity one can regard memory tasks as lying on a continuum, with the implicit memory tasks at the one end of the continuum representing mostly automatic processes (with small or no age effects), and the free recall tasks at the other end representing mostly strategic/controlled processes (with large age effects). Prospective memory tasks appear to occupy an intermediate position, in that they seem to be largely automatic, but at the same time also contain some controlled strategic processes (hence the small to medium size age effects in some tasks). This conflicts with Craik's (1986) functional model of ageing and memory, which places prospective memory at the strategic/controlled end of the continuum, but is in line with the multi-process theory of prospective memory which stipulates that, depending on circumstances, prospective memory can be subserved by both automatic and controlled processes (see

---

[5] A question about available processing resources is not properly solved even when young and old participants have similar performance levels on the ongoing activity. This is because older adults may need to put more effort (available attentional resources) into ongoing tasks than young to maintain similar levels of performance (cf. Kvavilashvili & Fisher, 2007).

McDaniel & Einstein, 2007). Hence, when examining the effects of age, future research will need to carefully specify the resource demands and other components of both prospective and retrospective memory tasks as well as the age composition of older populations.

REFERENCES

Baddeley, A., Emslie, H., & Nimmo-Smith, I. (1993). The spot-the-word test: A robust estimate of verbal intelligence based on lexical decision. *British Journal of Psychology, 32*, 55–65.

Bisiacchi, P. (1996). The neuropsychological approach in the study of prospective memory. In M. Brandimonte, G. O. Einstein, & M. A. McDaniel (Eds.), *Prospective memory: Theory and applications* (pp. 297–317). Mahwah, NJ: Lawrence Erlbaum Associates Inc.

Brandimonte, M. A., & Passolunghi, M. C. (1994). The effect of cue familiarity, cue-distinctiveness, and retention interval on prospective remembering. *The Quarterly Journal of Experimental Psychology, 47A*, 565–588.

Cherry, K. E., & LeCompte, D. C. (1999). Age and individual differences influence prospective memory. *Psychology and Aging, 14*, 60–76.

Cherry, K. E., Martin, R. C., Simmons-D'Gerolamo, S. S., Pinkston, J. B., Griffing, A., & Gouvier, W. D. (2001). Prospective remembering in younger and older adults: Role of the prospective cue. *Memory, 9*, 1–17.

Cherry, K. E., & Plauche, M. F. (2004). Age differences in prospective memory: Role of task complexity and prospective support. In S. Sohov (Ed.), *Advances in psychology research* (Vol. 28, pp. 28–41). Hauppauge, NY: Nova Science Publishers, Inc.

Cockburn, J., & Smith, P. T. (1991). The relative influence of intelligence and age on everyday memory. *Journal of Gerontology: Psychological Sciences, 46*, 31–36.

Cohen, J. (1977). *Statistical power analysis for the behavioral sciences.* New York: Academic Press.

Craik, F. I. M. (1986). A functional account of age differences in memory. In F. Clix & H. Hagendorf (Eds.), *Human memory and cognitive capabilities: Mechanisms and performances* (pp. 409–422). Amsterdam: Elsevier.

Devolder, P. A., Brigham, M. C., & Pressley, M. (1990). Memory performance awareness in younger and older adults. *Psychology and Aging, 5*, 291–303.

Dobbs, A. R., & Rule, B. G. (1987). Prospective memory and self-reports of memory abilities in older adults. *Canadian Journal of Psychology, 41*, 209–222.

Einstein, G. O., & McDaniel, M. A. (1990). Normal ageing and prospective memory. *Journal of Experimental Psychology: Learning Memory and Cognition, 16*, 717–726.

Einstein, G. O., & McDaniel, M. A. (1996). Retrieval processes in prospective memory: Theoretical approaches and some new empirical findings. In M. Brandimonte, G. O. Einstein, & M. A. McDaniel (Eds.), *Prospective memory: Theory and applications* (pp. 115–142). Hillsdale, NJ: Lawrence Erlbaum Associates Inc.

Einstein, G. O., & McDaniel, M. A. (2005). Prospective memory: Multiple retrieval processes. *Current Directions in Psychological Science, 14*, 286–290.

Einstein, G. O., McDaniel, M. A., Richardson, S. L., Guynn, M. J., & Cunfer, A. R. (1995). Ageing and prospective memory: Examining the influence of self-initiated retrieval processes. *Journal of Experimental Psychology: Learning, Memory and Cognition, 21*, 996–1007.

Ellis, J. A., & Kvavilashvili, L. (2000). Prospective memory in 2000: Past, present and future directions. *Applied Cognitive Psychology, 14*, S1–S9.

Folstein, M. F., Folstein, S. E., & McHugh, P. R. (1975). "Mini-Mental State": A practical method for grading the cognitive state of patients for the clinician. *Journal of Psychiatric Research, 12*, 189–198.

Freeman, J. E., & Ellis, J. A. (2003). The intention superiority effect for naturally occurring activities: The role of intention accessibility in everyday prospective remembering in young and older adults. *International Journal of Psychology, 38*, 215–228.

Harris, J. E. (1984). Remembering to do things: A forgotten topic. In J. E. Harris & P. E. Morris (Eds.), *Everyday memory, actions and absent-mindedness* (pp. 71–92). London: Academic Press.

Henry, D. H., MacLeod, M. S., Phillips, L. H., & Crawford, J. R. (2004). A meta-analytic review of prospective memory and aging. *Psychology and Aging, 19*, 27–39.

Huppert, F. A., Johnson, T., & Nickson, J. (2000). High prevalence of prospective memory impairment in the elderly and in early-stage dementia: Findings from a population-based study. *Applied Cognitive Psychology, 14*, S63–S81.

Kidder, D. P., Park, D. C., Hertzog, C., & Morrell, R. (1997). Prospective memory and aging: The effects of working memory and prospective memory task load. *Aging, Neuropsychology, and Cognition, 4*, 93–112.

Kliegel, M., McDaniel, M. A., & Einstein, G. O. (2000). Plan formation, retention, and execution in prospective memory: A new approach and age-related effects. *Memory & Cognition, 28*, 1041–1049.

Kliegel, M., McDaniel, M. A., & Einstein, G. O. (Eds.). (2008). *Prospective memory: Cognitive, neuroscience, developmental, and applied perspectives.* Mahwah, NJ: Lawrence Erlbaum Associates Inc.

Kvavilashvili, L., & Ellis, J. (1996). Varieties of intention: Some distinctions and classifications. In M. Brandimonte, G. Einstein, & M. McDaniel (Eds.), *Prospective memory: Theory and Applications* (pp. 23–51). Hillsdale, NJ: Lawrence Erlbaum Associates Inc.

Kvavilashvili, L., & Fisher, L. (2007). Is time-based prospective remembering mediated by self-initiated rehearsals?: Role of cues, ongoing activity, age and motivation. *Journal of Experimental Psychology: General, 136*, 112–132.

Kvavilashvili, L., Messer, D., & Ebdon, P. (2001). Prospective memory in children: The effects of age and task interruption. *Developmental Psychology, 37*, 418–430.

Mäntylä, T. (1993). Priming effects in prospective memory. *Memory, 1*, 203–218.

Mäntylä, T. (1994). Remembering to remember: Adult age differences in prospective memory. *Journal of Gerontology: Psychological Sciences, 49*, 276–282.

Mäntylä, T., & Nilsson, L-G. (1997). Remembering to remember in adulthood: A population-based study on aging and prospective memory. *Aging, Neuropsychology, and Cognition, 4*, 81–92.

Marsh, R. L., Hicks, J. L., Cook, G. I., & Mayhorn, C. B. (2007). Comparing older and younger adults in an event-based prospective memory paradigm containing an output monitoring component. *Aging, Neuropsychology, and Cognition, 14*, 168–188.

Martin, M. (1986). Ageing and patterns of change in everyday memory and cognition. *Human Learning, 5*, 63–74.

Martin, M., & Schumann-Hengsteler, R. (2001). How task demands influence time-based prospective memory performance in young and old adults. *International Journal of Behavioral Development, 25*, 386–391.

Maylor, E. (1993). Aging and forgetting in prospective and retrospective memory tasks. *Psychology and Aging, 3*, 420–428.

Maylor, E. A. (1996). Age-related impairment in an event-based prospective memory task. *Psychology and Aging, 11*, 74–78.

Maylor, E. A. (1998). Changes in event-based prospective memory across the adulthood. *Aging, Neuropsychology, and Cognition, 5*, 107–128.

Maylor, E. A., Smith, G., Della Sala, S., & Logie, R. H. (2002). Prospective and retrospective memory in normal aging and dementia: An experimental study. *Memory and Cognition, 30*, 871–884.

Meacham, J. A. (1977). Soviet investigations of memory development. In R. V. Kail & J. W. Hagen (Eds.), *Perspectives on the development of memory and cognition*. Hillsdale, NJ: Lawrence Erlbaum Associates Inc.

McDaniel, M. A., & Einstein, G. O. (1993). The importance of cue familiarity and cue distinctiveness in prospective memory. *Memory, 1*, 23–41.

McDaniel, M. A., & Einstein, G. O. (2007). *Prospective memory: An overview and synthesis of an emerging field*. Los Angeles: Sage Publications.

Moscovitch, M. (1982). A neuropsychological approach to memory and perception in normal and pathological aging. In F. I. M. Craik & S. Trehub (Eds.), *Aging and cognitive processes* (pp. 55–78). New York: Plenum Press.

Park, D. C., Hertzog, C., Kidder, D. P., Morrell, R. W., & Mayhorn, C. B. (1997). Effect of age on event-based and time-based prospective memory. *Psychology and Aging, 12*, 314–327.

Patton, G. W. R., & Meit, M. (1993). Effect of ageing on prospective and incidental memory. *Experimental Aging Research, 19*, 165–176.

Reese, C. M., & Cherry, K. E. (2002). The effects of age, ability, and memory monitoring on prospective memory task performance. *Aging, Neuropsychology, and Cognition, 9*, 98–113.

Rendell, P. G., McDaniel, M. A., Forbes, R. D., & Einstein, G. O. (2007). Age-related effects in prospective memory are modulated by ongoing task complexity and relation to target cue. *Aging, Neuropsychology, and Cognition, 14*, 236–256.

Rendell, P. G., & Thompson, D. M. (1993). The effect of ageing on remembering to remember: An investigation of simulated medication regiments. *Australian Journal of Ageing, 12*, 11–18.

Salthouse, T. A, Berish, D. E., & Siedlecki, K. L. (2004). Construct validity and age sensitivity of prospective memory. *Memory and Cognition, 32*, 1133–1148.

Sellen, A. J., Louie, G., Harris, J. E., & Wilkins, A. J. (1997). What brings intentions to mind? An in situ study of prospective memory. *Memory, 5*, 483–507.

Smith, G., Della Sala, S., Logie, R. H., & Maylor, E. A. (2000). Prospective and retrospective memory in normal ageing and dementia: A questionnaire study. *Memory, 8*, 311–321.

Smith, R. E., & Bayen, U. J. (2006). The source of adult age differences in event-based prospective memory: A multinomial modelling approach. *Journal of Experimental Psychology: Learning, Memory, and Cognition, 32*, 623–635.

Uttl, B. (2005). Age-related changes in event cued prospective memory proper. In N. Ohta, C. M. MacLeod, & B. Uttl (Eds.), *Dynamic cognitive processes* (pp. 273–303). Tokyo: Springer-Verlag.

Uttl, B., Graf, P., Miller, J., & Tuokko, H. (2001). Pro- and retrospective memory in late adulthood. *Consciousness and Cognition, 10*, 451–472.

West, R., & Craik, F. I. M. (1999). Age-related decline in prospective memory: The roles of cue accessibility and cue sensitivity. *Psychology and Aging, 14*, 264–272.

West, R., & Craik, F. I. M. (2001). Influences on the efficiency of prospective memory in younger and older adults. *Psychology and Aging, 16*, 682–696.

West, R. L. (1988). Prospective memory and aging. In M. M. Gruneberg, P. E. Morris, & R. N. Sykes (Eds.), *Practical aspects of memory: Current research and issues (vol. 2)* (pp. 119–125). Chichester, UK: Wiley.

Zeintl, M., Kliegel, M., & Hofer, S. (2007). The role of processing resources in age-related prospective and retrospective memory within old age. *Psychology and Aging, 22*, 826–834.

Zimmerman, T. D., & Meier, B. (2006). The rise and decline of prospective memory performance across the lifespan. *The Quarterly Journal of Experimental Psychology, 59*, 2040–2046.

MEMORY, 2009, 17 (2), 197–207

Episodic memory deficits slow down the dynamics of cognitive procedural learning in normal ageing

Hélène Beaunieux, Valérie Hubert, Anne Lise Pitel, Béatrice Desgranges, and Francis Eustache

Inserm-EPHE-Université de Caen/Basse-Normandie, France

Cognitive procedural learning is characterised by three phases, each involving distinct processes. Considering the implication of episodic memory in the first cognitive stage, the impairment of this memory system might be responsible for a slowing down of the cognitive procedural learning dynamics in the course of ageing. Performances of massed cognitive procedural learning were evaluated in older and younger participants using the Tower of Toronto task. Nonverbal intelligence and psychomotor abilities were used to analyse procedural dynamics, while episodic memory and working memory were assessed to measure their respective contributions to learning strategies. This experiment showed that older participants did not spontaneously invoke episodic memory and presented a slowdown in the cognitive procedural learning associated with a late involvement of working memory. These findings suggest that the slowdown in the cognitive procedural learning may be linked with the implementation of different learning strategies less involving episodic memory in older participants.

Keywords: Ageing; Episodic memory; Cognitive procedural learning; Procedural memory; Tower of Hanoi; Tower of Toronto task; Working memory.

Procedural memory is defined as the memory system in charge of the encoding, storage, and retrieval of procedures that underlie motor, verbal, and cognitive skills. Procedural learning is the process whereby a procedure is encoded in procedural memory. Previous investigations of cognitive procedural learning have suggested that skills undergo three characteristic phases (cognitive, associative, and autonomous) involving different cognitive processes in the course of the learning of complex procedures (ACT model, Adaptive Control of Thoughts; Anderson, 2000). According to the ACT model, learning a new cognitive procedure requires highly controlled processes in the initial cognitive phase and more automatic ones in the final autonomous phase. The boundaries of these procedural learning

stages can notably be delimited using an experimental method (Ackerman & Cianciolo, 2000) consisting in analysing the correlations' changes with practice between the procedural learning level and the cognitive determinants specific to each learning phase. We have previously used the Tower of Toronto (TT) task to further categorise these three learning phases in younger adults, analysing the cognitive determinants of procedural performance levels for each trial in the learning process (Beaunieux et al., 2006). Our findings confirmed the existence of two such determinants for the cognitive phase (nonverbal intellectual abilities) and autonomous phase (psychomotor abilities), which proved to be the best markers of their boundaries. They also helped us to improve our understanding of the

---

Address correspondence to: Francis Eustache, Inserm-EPHE-Université de Caen/Basse-Normandie, Unité U 923, Laboratoire de neuropsychologie, CHU Côte de Nacre, 14033 Caen Cedex, France. E-mail: neuropsycho@chu-caen.fr

The authors would like to thank the reviewers and the associate editor (Chris Moulin) for their valuable comments.

---

http://www.psypress.com/memory   DOI:10.1080/09658210802212010

roles played by the two memory systems, episodic memory and working memory, in the implementation of the learning strategies. Episodic memory is currently described as the memory system notably in charge of the encoding, storage, and retrieval of personally experienced events, associated with a precise spatial and temporal context of encoding and a specific state of consciousness (Tulving, 2001). According to Baddeley (2000, 2003), working memory is a memory system composed of both slave systems and a central executive considered as similar to the executive functions (Baddeley, 1996).

This cognitive theoretical framework of procedural learning, fitting with neuroimaging data (Hubert et al., 2007), could be useful in explaining the different conclusions reached by studies on the effects of ageing on cognitive procedural learning. Because of differences in performance levels, some studies have concluded that the learning of cognitive procedures is impaired in older participants (Davis & Bernstein, 1992). Others, because of the absence of any effect of age on performance improvement, have concluded that cognitive procedural learning is preserved in normal ageing. These latter studies have reported normal ability in elderly participants to automate cognitive procedure such as solving the TH (Tower of Hanoi; Vakil & Agmon-Ashkenazi, 1997) or the TT task (Peretti, Danion, Gierski, & Grange, 2002). Nevertheless these studies do not analyse cognitive procedural learning dynamics with direct reference to Ackerman's conceptions (1988, 1990). Only the study of Head, Raz, Gunning-Dixon, Williamson, and Acker (2002) supports the idea, in accordance with Ackerman's (1988) conception, that in the course of ageing, cognitive variables such as executive functions and working memory involved in the first stage of procedural learning, and particularly vulnerable to age (West, 1996), might be responsible for the effect of age on cognitive procedural learning. However, this study only proposed a few learning trials. Only the first stages of the acquisition were examined, not the autonomous one, i.e., the encoding into procedural memory. Further investigations including a large number of trials seem to be required to study the effect of age on cognitive procedural dynamics; i.e., the linking of the three learning phases. In the same way, the contribution of episodic memory to cognitive procedural learning difficulties in older participants has to be defined. Baddeley and Wilson (1994) have stressed the major contribution of

episodic memory in procedural learning. Recently we showed the involvement of episodic memory in automation of the TT task in young participants (Beaunieux et al., 2006). Owing to the well-established effect of age on episodic memory, it might be hypothesised that the dynamics of cognitive procedural learning would be disturbed.

Above and beyond the issue of the preservation or deterioration of procedural memory in healthy ageing (based on indicators of improvements or performance levels respectively), we set out to use these two indicators to find out how and why ageing may affect procedural learning abilities. We therefore decided to study cognitive procedural learning using a combined methodology issue from our two previous studies (Beaunieux et al., 2006; Hubert et al., 2007), in order to specify the effect of age on the dynamics of cognitive procedural learning and the implication of episodic memory in the phenomenon. The aims were (1) to study, in older participants, the dynamics of cognitive procedural learning using the TT task, and (2) to characterise the contributions of episodic memory and working memory during the acquisition of this cognitive procedure.

METHOD

Participants

A total of 100 unpaid volunteers from two different age groups (50 younger and 50 older participants) were tested. The 50 young participants were selected from the 100 of our previous study (Beaunieux et al., 2006), according to their vocabulary level (measured by the Mill Hill Scale; Deltour, 1998) in order to be matched to the 50 elderly participants. A health questionnaire was used to screen all the participants for any history of neurological or psychiatric conditions, head injury, and alcohol or drug abuse. Two participants were excluded for traumatic head injury and three for drug abuse. Because the procedural task involved the processing of colours, participants were also screened for colour blindness using the Ishihara Test (Ishihara, 1997). Three participants were excluded for colour blindness. We made sure that none of the participants was familiar with the TT problem. We ensured that no participants in the older sample showed signs of neurodegenerative pathologies by checking that they performed within normal limits on the Mattis Dementia Rating Scale (MDRS). Five older participants were excluded for a score outside normal limits on the MDRS. The study was conducted in line with the Declaration of Helsinki. The overall characteristics of the participants are reported in Table 1.

Materials

The experimental protocol featured two sessions separated by an interval of 1 week. The first session was taken up by the procedural learning of the TT task while participants underwent a set of supplementary cognitive tasks in the second session.

Session 1: Procedural task (TT task). The TT task consisted of a rectangular base and three pegs. Four different-coloured disks were used: one black, one red, one yellow, and one white. The TT disks were initially stacked on the leftmost peg, with the darkest one at the bottom and the lightest one on top. The task consisted in rebuilding this configuration on the rightmost peg, obeying the following two rules: only one disk may be moved at a time, and a darker disk may never be placed on top of a lighter one. These rules were read out to the participants and explained through examples of authorised and unauthorised moves. All the instructions were printed on a sheet of paper placed near the participant. Participants were just asked to solve the problem; no reference was made to completing it in the fewest possible moves or shortest possible time.

TABLE 1
Characteristics and cognitive scores of the younger and older participants

	Younger (N = 50)	Older (N = 50)	p value
Sex ratio (males/ females)	26/24	22/28	–
Age			
Mean (SD)	22.2 (4.5)	67.5 (8.3)	.0001
Range	18–34	55–95	
Vocabulary level (Mill Hill)			
Mean (SD)	26.0 (2.7)	26.3 (4.8)	.72
Dementia rating (MDRS)			
Mean (SD)	/	142.2 (1.8)	–

SD = Standard deviation; max. score of the Mill Hill = 34; MDRS = Mattis Dementia Rating Scale, cut-off score = 138, max. score = 144.

We also added a rule that provided a cue for the participants: begin by putting the white disk on the middle peg. This instruction was given in order to avoid a probably random choice by the participants. The TT device was connected to a computer, which recorded the completion time (in seconds) and the number of moves per trial for each participant. The minimum number of moves for the four-disk TT task is 15. As we gave a clue for the first move, this move (and the time it took) was not taken into account. The optimum solution was thus 14 moves.

To enable them to reach the autonomous phase, the participants performed 40 trials of the TT task (eight blocks of 5 consecutive trials, with a 5-minute break between each block). This number of trials is largely sufficient for younger participants to reach the autonomous phase (Beaunieux et al., 2006) and, according to Peretti et al. (2002), may also be sufficient for older ones.

Session 2: Cognitive tasks. As in the study by Beaunieux et al. (2006), we assessed nonverbal intelligence and psychomotor functions. *Nonverbal intellectual functions* were assessed using the Block Design subtest of the Wechsler Adult Intelligence Scale (WAIS-III; Wechsler, 2001, French version). In order to assess *psychomotor abilities*, we asked the participants to carry out two disk transfer tasks. The aim was to transfer four disks (one by one) from the leftmost peg to the middle peg, then to the rightmost peg, and finally back to the leftmost one. The only instruction we gave was to use only one hand. This transfer task was performed twice (before and after the procedural learning of the TT task).

We also measured the efficiency of episodic memory and working memory. *Episodic memory* was assessed using an abridged form of the California Verbal Learning Test (CVLT) and pairing and free recall of the digit symbol coding. During the CVLT, 16 words were presented only once and participants immediately had to recall them. Free recall of the digit symbol coding consists in delayed recall of as many of the previously seen symbols as possible. Lastly, *working memory* was assessed by means of span tests: the WAIS-III digit forward span (Wechsler, 2001) allowed us to evaluate the slave systems of working memory. The ability to handle information in working memory was also measured, using the Letter Number Sequencing test taken from the WAIS-III.

Statistical analyses

Assessment of cognitive procedural learning. Performances of the 50 younger and 50 older participants on the TT task were assessed by means of two variables: the number of moves and the total problem-solving time (in seconds) per trial. Aggregating the data by block would yield a more stable estimate of performance for each group and limit the number of subsequently calculated correlations. A multivariate analysis of variance (MANOVA) was carried out, with performances on the four blocks (of 10 trials) as the repeated measure and groups as a between-participants factor. Complementary analyses on each session were conducted by mean of *t*-tests.

Effect of ageing on supplementary cognitive tasks. For episodic memory and working memory we calculated a composite score corresponding to the sum of the scores collected with the tests evaluating each cognitive function (episodic memory composite score maximum = 43, working memory composite score maximum = 30). In order to test the effect of age on the nonprocedural components, *t*-tests were therefore used to compare the younger and older groups for each composite score. Intellectual and psychomotor raw scores were also compared by means of *t*-tests.

Delimitation of the three learning phases of the TT task for each group. The three learning phases were determined in a three-stage analysis carried out separately for each group. As in the first stage of the statistical analyses of Hubert et al. (2007), the delimitation of the three learning phases was done for each individual participant, using the number of moves per trial. The length of the cognitive phase therefore corresponded to the number of trials during which the participant failed to find the optimum solution. The length of the associative phase corresponded to the number of trials during which the participant solved the procedure in 14 moves or near this optimum solution. Lastly, the length of the autonomous phase corresponded to the number of trials during which the participant solved the procedure in 14 moves.

In the same way as Beaunieux et al. (2006), the second stage consisted of correlations between the intelligence and psychomotor scores on the one hand and performances in terms of total time per block of the TT task on the other hand. We

chose not to consider the number of moves here, as it was not sufficiently sensitive—this variable loses its variability once the participants have found the solution to the problem and thus does not fully reflect the automation of the cognitive procedure.

In the third and last stage we compared the correlations with intelligence with those with psychomotor abilities (calculated for each block) by means of Steiger's Z* statistic (Steiger, 1980) which tests for the differences in each of the two correlation matrix. Our aim was thus to delimit the three phases for the older group in order to compare them with those of the younger group.

For the two groups, we expected a greater contribution of nonverbal intellectual abilities than psychomotor abilities during the cognitive phase, and the opposite results during the autonomous phase, the associative phase being characterised by no significant difference between the two cognitive determinants.

Effect of age on the dynamics of cognitive procedural learning. In order to study the effect of age on the dynamics of cognitive procedural learning we first compared the average length of the each three phases in the two groups by means of *t*-tests.

We then compared the involvement of the intelligence and psychomotor abilities in cognitive procedural learning in the two groups by applying Fisher's test (Fisher, 1921). First we assessed the age-related differences in correlations between nonverbal intellectual abilities and procedural learning performances (total time per block). The differences for each block were expressed as *z* scores. The same analysis was carried out for the correlations between psychomotor abilities and performances (total time per block). A contribution of nonverbal intellectual abilities or psychomotor abilities statistically more significant in the younger group than in the older one will result in *z* score > 1.65, whereas *z* score < −1.65 will translate as the opposite result.

In consideration of the effect of age on cognitive procedural levels in ageing, we expected that the cognitive and associative phases would be longer for the older group.

Characterising the procedural learning phases for each group. Lastly, in order to study the contributions of episodic memory and working memory during cognitive procedural learning, we examined the correlations between the episodic and working memory composite scores and procedural learning performance (total time per block) for each group. We also compared the involvement of these components in the two groups by applying Fisher's test (Fisher, 1921). We expected a differential involvement of episodic and working memory in the two groups.

RESULTS

Assessment of cognitive procedural learning

Regarding the time taken to solve the TT task, the MANOVA showed a significant group effect, $F(1, 98) = 33.5$; $p < .0001$, a significant block repetition effect, $F(3, 294) = 223.7$; $p < .0001$, and a significant interaction between block and group, $F(3, 294) = 12.6$; $p < .0001$ (Figure 1A). T-tests conducted for each block showed that there was a significant difference between the two groups on the four blocks—block 1: $t(98) = 4.8$, $p < .0001$; block 2: $t(98) = 4.9$, $p < .0001$; block 3: $t(98) = 5.3$, $p < .0001$; block 4: $t(98) = 4.1$, $p < .0001$.

In terms of the number of moves, to the MANOVA revealed a significant effect of group, $F(1, 98) = 18.9$; $p < .0001$, a significant block repetition effect, $F(3, 294) = 94.6$; $p < .0001$, and a significant interaction between the two effects, $F(3, 294) = 2.9$; $p < .03$ (Figure 1B). T-tests conducted for each block showed that there was a significant difference between the two groups on the four blocks—block 1: $t(98) = 3.1$, $p = .003$; block 2: $t(98) = 3.3$, $p = .0015$; block 3: $t(98) = 4.9$, $p < .0001$; block 4: $t(98) = 4.6$, $p < .0001$.

Effect of ageing on supplementary cognitive tasks

The comparison of the mean cognitive scores of the younger and the older groups is show in Table 2. Results did not reveal a significant effect of age on nonverbal intelligence abilities, but showed a significant deleterious effect of age on psychomotor abilities, episodic memory, and working memory.

Delimitation of the three learning phases for each group

Length of the learning phases (Hubert et al., 2007). Table 3 reports the length of the three

learning phases in the two groups. Broadly speaking, the cognitive phase of the younger group covered trials 1–4, the associative phase trials 5–18, and the autonomous phase trials 19–40. The cognitive phase of the older group covered trials 1–13, the associative phase trials 14–33, and the autonomous phase trials 34–40.

Correlational analyses (Beaunieux et al., 2006). In the younger group, nonverbal intelligence was significantly correlated with procedural performance levels in the first half of the learning process, during the blocks 1 and 2. Psychomotor abilities were significantly correlated with procedural performance levels from the second block onwards (Figure 2A). The comparison of the two sets of correlations (nonverbal intellectual abilities and psychomotor abilities) revealed that there was no significant difference in favour of the involvement of intellectual capacities. During the blocks 3 and 4 there was a significant difference in favour of psychomotor abilities: $t(37) = -3.5$, $p = .0013$ and $t(37) = -5.2$, $p < .0001$ respectively.

In the older group, nonverbal intelligence abilities were significantly correlated with procedural performance levels during the blocks 1, 2, and 4, while psychomotor abilities were significantly correlated with procedural performance levels during blocks 3 and 4; i.e., one block later than for the younger group (Figure 2B). The comparison of the two sets of correlations showed that there were no significant overall differences but a tendency for block 1 to reveal a greater contribution of intellectual abilities, $t(37) = 1.5$, $p = .13$. Contrary to the younger participants there were no significant differences in favour of the psychomotor abilities.

Effect of age on the dynamics of cognitive procedural learning

Comparison of the mean length of the learning phases in the two groups showed that the cognitive and the associative phases of the older participants were significantly longer than in the younger group, whereas the autonomous phase was significantly shorter (Table 3).

Using Fisher's test, the analyses revealed that the involvement of intellectual abilities in performances did not differ significantly between the two groups, but tended to be significant ($p < .06$) in favour of the older group in block 4

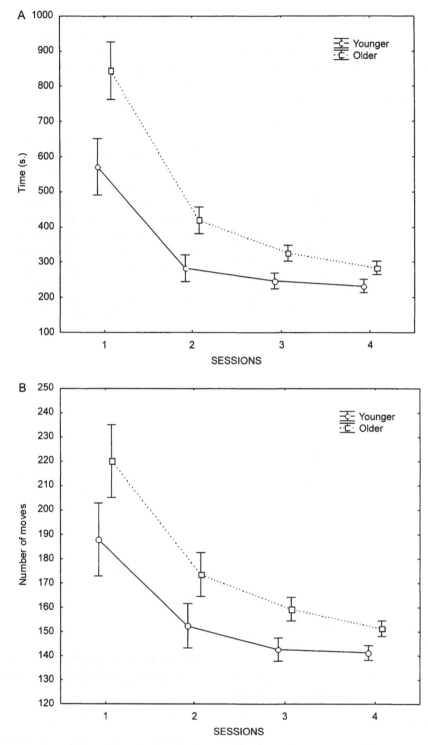

Figure 1. Performance trends in terms of completion time (A) and moves (B) per block during the four learning blocks in the Tower of Toronto task. The results show a significant learning effect across the four blocks, a significant group effect, and a significant interaction between learning and group.

TABLE 2
Cognitive scores of the younger and older participants

Cognitive function	Task	Dependent variable	Max. score	Younger (N=50) Mean (SD)	Older (N=50) Mean (SD)	t	p value
Intelligence abilities	Block Design	Number of marks	20	10.7 (2.0)	10.9 (1.9)	0.5	.62
Psychomotor abilities	Disk transfer task	Average of the two transfer times	–	2.8 (0.5)	3.1 (0.5)	2.8	.007
Episodic memory	California Verbal Learning Test	Number of correctly recalled words	16	7.7 (2)	8.1 (2.4)	0.9	.36
	Digit symbol coding		27	23.7 (3.8)	14.8 (6)	−8.8	.0001
	Composite score*		**43**	**31.3 (4.8)**	**22.8 (7.3)**	**−6.9**	**.0001**
Working memory	Digit forward span	Maximum number of correctly recalled items	9	6.0 (0.1)	5.3 (0.1)	−4.3	.0001
	Letter Number sequencing test		21	12.6 (0.3)	10.1 (0.3)	−4.2	.0001
	Composite score*		**30**	**16.0 (1.9)**	**13.8 (1.6)**	**−6.1**	**.0001**

SD = Standard deviation; *the composite scores (in bold) were used in all statistical analyses; degree of freedom = 98 for all the analyses.

TABLE 3
Length of the three learning phases (number of trials) in the younger and older participants

	Younger (N=50) Mean (SD)	Older (N=50) Mean (SD)	t	p value
Cognitive phase	4.1 (4.3)	13.1 (10.4)	5.2	< .001
Associative phase	13.9 (8.8)	19.7 (10.4)	2.8	.006
Autonomous phase	21.9 (11.1)	7 (9.5)	−7.2	< .001

SD = Standard deviation; degree of freedom = 98 for all analyses.

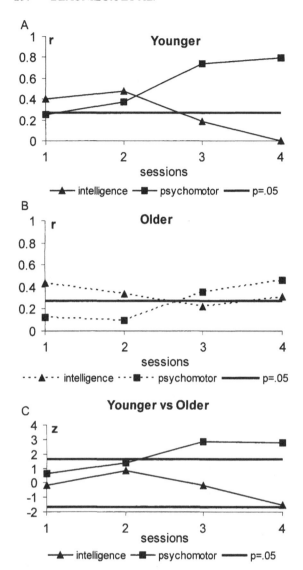

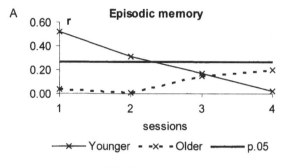

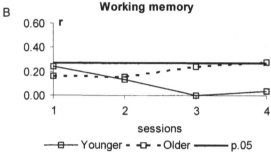

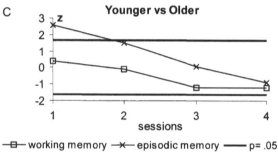

Figure 2. Effect of age on the dynamics of cognitive procedural learning. (A) Correlations between procedural performance levels (time in seconds) and the intelligence and psychomotor scores for the younger participants. The boldface horizontal line corresponds to the statistical threshold $p = .05$. The correlations located above this line are significant. (B) Correlations between procedural performance levels (time in seconds) and the intelligence and psychomotor scores for the older participants. The boldface horizontal line corresponds to the statistical threshold $p = .05$. The correlations located above this line are significant. (C) Comparison of the inter-group determinants (correlations). Calculated z-value, assessing the existence or otherwise of a significant difference between the two groups for the two determinants (intelligence and psychomotor abilities), calculated for each trial. The boldface horizontal lines correspond to the tabulated z-value $p = .05$. The calculated z-values located above or below these lines are significant. The difference is in favour of the younger subjects for $z > 1.65$ and in favour of the older participants for $z < -1.65$.

Figure 3. Correlations between procedural performance levels (time in seconds) and (A) episodic memory and (B) working memory scores in younger participants and older participants. (C) Calculated z-value, assessing the existence or otherwise of a significant difference between the two groups for these two components (episodic memory and working memory). The boldface horizontal lines correspond to the statistical threshold $p = .05$. The correlations or the tabulated z-value located above these lines are significant.

(Figure 2C). By contrast, the correlations with the psychomotor abilities were significantly stronger for the younger group than for the older during blocks 3 and 4.

Characterising the procedural learning phases for each group

The correlations between episodic and working memory and procedural performances indicated that episodic memory was significantly correlated with performance levels only in the first half of the learning process and only in the younger group (Figure 3A). We did not observe any significant correlations between episodic memory and procedural performance levels for the older group.

In the younger group, working memory was not significantly correlated with learning performance, but seemed to be more involved at the beginning of the learning process and gradually decreased thereafter (Figure 3B). In the older group, working memory was significantly correlated to the performance levels only in block 4.

Fisher's test showed only that the correlations with episodic memory were significantly superior in the younger group than in the older one in block 1 (Figure 3C). Regarding working memory, there were statistical tendencies for the two last blocks in favour of a greater involvement in the older group than in the younger one.

DISCUSSION

The results of the present investigation confirm first of all the beneficial effect of trial repetition on performance both in terms of time and number of moves required to solve the TT task in younger and older participants. However, the significant interaction indicated that because of the additional time and moves necessary to solve the TT task in the older participants, they had to improve their performance with practice more than the younger ones. Post hoc comparisons showed that older participants did not catch up with the younger performance levels at the end of the learning process. These results are consistent with those of Peretti et al. (2002) and Vakil and Agmon-Ashkenazi (1997) who found that older participants were able to acquire the TT task procedure in spite of a deleterious effect of age on performance levels.

Comparison of the mean length of the learning phase in the two groups showed that the cognitive and the associative phases were significantly longer in the older group and that autonomous phase was therefore shorter, suggesting that the autonomous phase may be delayed for 15 trials in the older participants. These results confirm that despite their improvement, older participants were slowed down in the cognitive procedural

dynamics. More precisely, there may be a lengthening of the two first phases of learning with age, deferring but not jeopardising the autonomous phase.

With reference to Ackerman's (1988) model, we then studied the extent to which nonverbal intelligence and psychomotor functions determined procedural performance levels, and confirmed the boundaries of the learning phases in both groups. The results of the 50 younger participants were, as expected, similar to those reported by Beaunieux et al. (2006) in 100 participants (including these 50), showing three distinct phases in cognitive procedural learning. Psychomotor abilities mainly determined procedural performance levels during the blocks 3 and 4, suggesting that these two last blocks may correspond to the autonomous phase. These data seem to fit perfectly with the boundaries defined by the first analysis (trials 19–40, i.e., blocks 3 and 4). The cognitive phase of the young participants covered trials 1–4 but our results did not reveal a greater contribution of nonverbal intellectual abilities than psychomotor abilities in block 1. These findings might be accounted for by the shortness of the cognitive phase in the younger group: they were already in the associative phase at the end of the first block, and the aggregate of the data by block hampered us in conducting correlations strictly during the cognitive phase.

With regard to the older group, the first analysis suggested that the cognitive phase covered trials 1–13 (block 1), the associative phase trials 14–33 (blocks 2, 3, and 4), and the autonomous phase trials 34–40 (block 4). Correlational analysis showed that in block 1 the differences between intellectual and psychomotor abilities tended to be significant, suggesting that this block may correspond to the cognitive phase in concordance with the first analysis. The associative phase, corresponding to the absence of any difference between the two determinants, may correspond to the last blocks (2–4) as was suggested by the first analysis. The absence of greater involvement of psychomotor abilities compared with nonverbal intelligence in block 4 contradicts the predictions of Ackerman's model but may be explained by the same factors as those mentioned for the younger participants. Older participants were still in the associative phase at the beginning of the last block and the aggregate of the data by block may mask the significant contribution of the psychomotor abilities at the end of the last block. We have to take these methodological limitations into consideration and interpret these data with caution. Further studies with larger samples would allow correlational analysis "trial by trial" as was done by Beaunieux et al. (2006), and therefore permit a more refined comparison between these two modes of analysis of the cognitive procedural dynamics.

The comparison of the two groups on the basis of the two main determinants of the learning process showed that the two groups differed solely regarding the psychomotor component, mainly during blocks 3 and 4 in accordance with the comparison of the mean length of the learning phases. These differences, observed over two blocks, confirm the slowdown in the dynamics of cognitive procedural learning of the older participants compared with the younger ones.

The characterisation of the different learning phases highlighted the contribution of episodic memory in the younger group especially at the beginning of the learning process (Wilson, Baddeley, Evans, & Shiel, 1994), i.e., during the cognitive phase. On the contrary, our results suggest that the older participants did not invoke episodic memory during the cognitive and the associative phase, but rather working memory, suggesting therefore different learning strategies in the two groups. The slowdown in the learning abilities of the older participants may be explained by the episodic memory alteration, which hampers the procedural learning process by preventing an effective correction of errors (Baddeley & Wilson, 1994). They seemed to solve the problem all along the learning blocks without trying to explicitly remember the strategies previously used. The automation of the procedure may be delayed because of these episodic difficulties in older participants who rely, perhaps by compensation, on their working memory capacities. Thus the use of different learning strategies in the two groups may account for the slowdown in the cognitive procedural learning in the older participants (Hubert et al., in press), as has already been described in alcoholic patients (Pitel et al., 2007). In contrast with our older participants, alcoholic patients were characterised by a late involvement of both episodic and working memory. These results were also considered as reflecting compensatory mechanisms to generate the cognitive procedure in spite of episodic deficits. Further studies should allow exploration of this compensatory role of working memory.

CONCLUSION

To conclude this experiment, our findings highlight the interest in jointly analysing improvement capacities with performance levels to examine the effect of age on cognitive procedural learning. Furthermore, the study of the cognitive determinants allows unravelling of the fine-grained differences in the processes underlying automation of a cognitive procedure in normal ageing and thus provides a better understanding of the various conclusions from the literature. Our findings suggest that older participants improve their procedural performances but at a lower level, owing to less involvement of episodic memory which delayed the automation of the cognitive procedure. Assessment of the strategies invoked by the two groups emphasises the "optimiser" role of episodic memory in cognitive procedural learning. In effect, in the presence of episodic deficits, cognitive procedural learning is not impossible, but slows down. It would be relevant to use such experimental methods to better understand the remaining procedural abilities in amnesic patients.

REFERENCES

Ackerman, P. L. (1988). Determinants of individual differences during skill acquisition: Cognitive abilities and information processing. *Journal of Experimental Psychology: General, 117,* 288–318.

Ackerman, P. L. (1990). A correlation analysis of skill specificity: Learning, abilities, and individual differences. *Journal of Experimental Psychology: Learning, Memory Cognition, 16,* 883–901.

Ackerman, P. L., & Cianciolo, A. T. (2000). Cognitive, perceptual speed, and psychomotor determinants of individual differences during skill acquisition. *Journal of Experimental Psychology: Applied, 6,* 259–290.

Anderson, J. R. (2000). Skill acquisition. In J. R. Anderson (Ed.), *Learning and memory* (2nd ed., pp. 304–337). New York: Wiley.

Baddeley, A. (1996). The fractionation of working memory. *Proceedings of the National Academy of Sciences of the United States of America, 93,* 13468–13472.

Baddeley, A. (2000). The episodic buffer: A new component of working memory? *Trends in Cognitive Sciences, 4,* 417–423.

Baddeley, A. (2003). Working memory: Looking back and looking forward. *Nature reviews. Neuroscience, 4,* 829–839.

Baddeley, A., & Wilson, B. A. (1994). When implicit learning fails: Amnesia and the problem of error elimination. *Neuropsychologia, 32*, 53–68.

Beaunieux, H., Hubert, V., Witkowski, T., Pitel, A. L., Rossi, S., Danion, J. M., et al. (2006). Which processes are involved in cognitive procedural learning? *Memory, 14*, 521–539.

Davis, H. P., & Bernstein, P. A. (1992). Age-related changes in explicit and implicit memory. In L. R. Squire & N. Butters (Eds.), *Neuropsychology of memory* (pp. 249–261). New York: Guilford Press.

Deltour, J. J. (1998). *Echelle de vocabulaire de Mill Hill. Adaptation française* [Mill Hill Vocabulary Scale. French-language adaptation]. Paris: EAP.

Fisher, R. A. (1921). On the probable error of a coefficient of correlation deduced from a small sample. *Metron, 1*, 3–32.

Head, D., Raz, N., Gunning-Dixon, F., Williamson, A., & Acker, J. D. (2002). Age related differences in the course of cognitive skill acquisition: The role of regional cortical shrinkage and cognitive resources. *Psychology and Ageing, 17*, 72–84.

Hubert, V., Beaunieux, H., Chételat, G., Platel, H., Landeau, B., Danion, J. M., et al. (2007). The dynamic network subserving the three phases of cognitive procedural learning. *Human Brain Mapping, 28*, 1415–1429.

Hubert, V., Beaunieux, H., Chételat, G., Platel, H., Landeau, B., Viader, F., et al. (in press). Age-related changes in the cerebral substrates of cognitive procedural learning. *Human Brain Mapping.* [Epub ahead of print].

Ishihara, S. (1997). *Tests for colour blindness.* Tokyo: Kanehara Shuppan Co. Ltd.

Peretti, C. H., Danion, J. M., Gierski, F., & Grange, D. (2002). Cognitive skill learning and ageing. A component process analysis. *Archives of Clinical Neuropsychology, 17*, 445–459.

Pitel, A. L., Witkowski, T., Vabret, F., Guillery-Girard, B., Desgranges, B., Eustache, F., et al. (2007). Effect of episodic and working memory impairments on semantic and cognitive procedural learning at alcohol treatment entry. *Alcoholism, Clinical and Experimental Research, 31*, 238–248.

Steiger, J. H. (1980). Tests for comparing elements of a correlation matrix. *Psychological Bulletin, 87*, 245–251.

Tulving, E. (2001). Episodic memory and common sense: How far apart? *Philosophical transactions of the Royal Society of London. Series B, Biological sciences, 29*, 1505–1515.

Vakil, E., & Agmon-Ashkenazi, D. (1997). Baseline performance and learning rate of procedural and declarative memory tasks: Younger versus older adults. *Journal of Gerontology: Psychological Sciences, 52*, 229–234.

Wechsler, D. (2001). *Wechsler Adult Intelligence Scale – Third Edition (WAIS III)* (French version). Paris: EAP.

West, R. L. (1996). An application of prefrontal cortex function theory to cognitive aging. *Psychological Bulletin, 120*, 272–292.

Wilson, B. A., Baddeley, A. D., Evans, J. J., & Shiel, A. (1994). Errorless learning in the rehabilitation of memory impaired people. *Neuropsychological Rehabilitation, 4*, 307–326.

MEMORY, 2009, 17 (2), 208–219

How emotion affects older adults' memories for event details

Elizabeth A. Kensinger

Boston College, Chestnut Hill, MA, USA

As adults age, they tend to have problems remembering the details of events and the contexts in which events occurred. This review presents evidence that emotion can enhance older adults' abilities to remember episodic detail. Older adults are more likely to remember affective details of an event (e.g., whether something was good or bad, or how an event made them feel) than they are to remember non-affective details, and they remember more details of emotional events than of non-emotional ones. Moreover, in some instances, emotion appears to narrow the age gap in memory performance. It may be that memory for affective context, or for emotional events, relies on cognitive and neural processes that are relatively preserved in older adults.

Keywords: Affect; Aging; Emotion; Episodic memory; Source memory.

Episodic memory complaints are frequent among older adults, even those who are ageing successfully (reviewed by Kausler, 1994; Kensinger & Corkin, 2003b; Light, 1991). However, the magnitude of the deficits can vary widely depending on the mnemonic demands placed on participants. Older adults have particular difficulty remembering the spatiotemporal context in which an event occurred or the precise details that comprised the event. Thus, although older adults may remember that they ate dinner at a restaurant last week, they may be unable to remember the restaurant's name, the layout of the restaurant, or the particular meal that they ordered.

Dissociations between older adults' memories for general event information and their memories for event details have been demonstrated in a plethora of studies. For example, older adults tend to be relatively unimpaired at distinguishing which items have been presented previously and which items are new (as required on standard recognition tasks; Bastin & Van der Linden, 2003). By contrast, they often show marked impairments when they must indicate not only which items they have seen previously, but also in what context they studied those items (e.g., which experimenter read the sentence or in what font the words were written). This difficulty remembering the context in which items are presented (termed "source memory") has been associated with the ageing process in a number of studies (reviewed by Spencer & Raz, 1995). Older adults also tend to show impairments when they must remember not only whether single items were presented (e.g., were "pig" and "fork" on the study list?) but also whether items were paired together earlier (e.g., were "pig" and "fork" presented at the same time?; Castel & Craik, 2003; Naveh-Benjamin, 2000). They are similarly impaired when they must remember not only the general type of item that was presented (e.g., that an image of a fork was shown) but also the

Address correspondence to: Elizabeth A. Kensinger PhD, McGuinn Hall, Rm. 510, 140 Commonwealth Ave., Chestnut Hill, MA 02467, USA. E-mail: elizabeth.kensinger@bc.edu

Preparation of this article was supported by the National Science Foundation (grant BCS 0542694) and by the American Federation for Ageing Research.

DOI:10.1080/09658210802221425

specific details of that item (e.g., when they must distinguish the studied fork from other, non-studied ones; e.g., Adams, Labouvie-Vief, Hobart, & Dorosz, 1990; Bayen, Nakamura, Dupois, & Yang, 2000; Gould, Trevithick, & Dixon, 1991; Koutstaal, 2003).

These studies make clear that older adults' memory impairments are often most notable when they are attempting to retrieve precise episodic details. What has been less certain is whether there are circumstances in which older adults' deficits in remembering these sorts of episodic details are reduced, or even eliminated. In this review I will present evidence that emotion can enhance older adults' abilities to remember detail. Moreover, although older adults' mnemonic benefit from emotion does not always exceed that derived by young adults, in some instances memories for emotional information seem to be less affected by ageing than memories for information without emotional content. I will describe findings from two somewhat distinct literatures that support these conclusions. The first line of research examines whether older adults are better able to remember the emotional aspects of an event (e.g., how the event made them feel) as compared to other aspects (e.g., the perceptual details of the event). Thus, this section focuses on older adults' memories for the affective *context* in which information is encountered. The second line of research examines whether older adults remember more contextual details about emotional events than they do about non-emotional events. Therefore this section focuses on how the emotional *content* of an event influences older adults' memories for non-emotional contextual details of that event. The critical questions asked in each of these sections are whether older adults receive mnemonic benefits from emotion, and if so, whether these conferred benefits close the age gap in memory performance.

REMEMBERING AFFECTIVE CONTEXT

When we think back to a prior experience, we can remember any number of aspects of that experience. Thinking back to a dinner that we ate at a restaurant, we can remember the perceptual context (e.g., what the restaurant looked like or what the food tasted like), we can remember the semantic context (e.g., what we discussed over the meal), and we can remember the affective context (e.g., how we felt as we ate the food or as we

talked with others at our table). Not everyone will remember each type of detail; some people may remember the semantic context well but little about the perceptual context, whereas the reverse may be true for others.

A number of studies have investigated whether ageing influences the types of contextual details remembered about events, with particular emphasis on examining whether ageing influences the proportion of remembered details that are affective in tone. There is reason to expect that a lot of what older adults remember may be affective in nature. With ageing, emotion-related[1] goals become particularly salient and older adults become more focused on emotional information in their environment (e.g., Carstensen, Fung, & Charles, 2003; Gross et al., 1997). Thus, older adults place more importance on their personal values than young adults (Hasher & Zacks, 1988; Labouvie-Vief, 1982) and they are more likely than young adults to prefer spending time with close social partners who bring them emotional fulfilment (e.g., Fredrickson & Carstensen, 1990). This affective shift with ageing appears to have important consequences for memory. Older adults tend to remember more information when it is presented to them with an affective tone (e.g., they are more likely to remember advertisement slogans with emotional connotations such as "capture those special moments" than they are to remember slogans that focus on expansion of world knowledge such as "capture the unexplored world"; Fung & Carstensen, 2003). They also tend to remember the thoughts or feelings elicited by previous experiences far better than they remember other types of event details, such as the perceptual or semantic features of an event (Comblain, D'Argembeau, Van der Linden, & Aldenhoff, 2004; Hashtroudi, Johnson, & Chrosniak, 1990; Schaefer & Philippot, 2005), and they remember proportionally more emotional information from prose passages than do young adults (Carstensen & Turk-Charles, 1994; Yoder & Elias, 1987).

More broadly, older adults seem to show a particular benefit for remembering affect-relevant source information over other types of

---

[1] In this paper I use the term "emotion" to refer to short-lived cognitive and somatic reactions to specific environmental or cognitive events (e.g., Scherer, 2000) and the term "affect" to refer more broadly to either the short-lived emotional reaction elicited by an event or to a more sustained mood state felt during an event.

contextual details. Thus, older adults can remember whether a name is associated with a "good person" or a "bad person", whereas they have difficulty remembering whether the name was read by a male or female voice (Rahhal, May, & Hasher, 2002). Age deficits in memory for source information can even be eliminated when the source detail is emotionally relevant. For example, May, Rahhal, Berry, and Leighton (2005) asked young and older adults to remember whether food was "safe" or "unsafe" to eat (i.e., whether or not it was spoiled) and also to remember other, non-affective, characteristics of the food (e.g., whether it should be served hot or cold). They found that older adults were much better at remembering the affective context (i.e., whether food was safe to eat) than they were at remembering the other contexts (e.g., the temperature at which the food was to be served). Importantly, the benefit for the affective context exhibited by the older adults was not mirrored in the young adults; thus, the age-related decline in contextual memory was eliminated for the affective context.

As described earlier, affective information takes on additional meaning for older adults, giving it a salience above and beyond that perceived by young adults (Carstensen, Isaacowitz, & Charles, 1999). It would be logical that older adults would be best at remembering the contextual details that had the most salience and personal relevance to them, and this factor is likely to have a strong influence on their enhanced ability to remember the affective context in which information was studied. Indeed, older adults' memory benefit for the affective seems intricately linked to the way in which they process and rehearse the experienced information. If older adults are encouraged to focus on the facts rather than on the affective tone of information, their source monitoring generally improves, and they no longer show a bias to remember affective information (Hashtroudi, Johnson, Vneck, & Ferguson, 1994). Thus it appears that the way in which older adults process incoming information has predictable effects in terms of the types of details most likely to be remembered.

Older adults' affective focus, however, is likely to be influenced by their retrieval orientation as well as their encoding focus. At a cognitive level, it may take less effort to retrieve emotional information than to retrieve non-emotional information (Zajonc, 1980), making emotional information easier to retrieve than other types of information. Because older adults tend to show the most difficulties on tasks with high retrieval demands (Kausler, 1994; Light, 1991), emotional information may make up a greater proportion of their recalled memories simply because that affective information is easier for them to retrieve (see Burke & Light, 1981, for further discussion). Thus, remembering the affective tone of information may be just another example of older adults' reliance on memory for gist-based or schematic information, rather than on memory for precise details (Buchanan & Adolphs, 2002). This hypothesis aligns with the claims of Adams et al. (1990), who described how older adults may remember the moral or the gist of a story because memory for those aspects requires fewer information-processing resources than memory for the story's specific details. However, the causal link could be in the opposite direction: It is possible that good memory for affective information does not arise from older adults' reliance on memory for gist-based information but rather that their memory for affective information *causes* their focus on the gist. Indeed, there is some evidence to suggest that any adult (young or old) who focuses on the affective meaning of information is more likely to extract the gist and is less likely to remember the details (Hashtroudi et al., 1994). Thus older adults' affective focus may lead them to extract the gist of an event easily but to fail to retrieve the details. Further research is needed to clarify the extent, and directionality, of the links between older adults' reliance on schematic processing and their enhanced memory for affective details.

Although the results described so far have suggested that older adults' enhanced memory for affective context may result from a relative preservation of affect-related processing, an alternate possibility is that this affective focus arises as a consequence of older adults' failure to inhibit processing of information that is less relevant to the ongoing experience (Hasher, Stolzfus, Zacks, & Rypma, 1991; Hasher & Zacks, 1988). In many circumstances, attending to the affective tone of information will be counterproductive to remembering the content or broader context of the presented information. It is possible that older adults' preserved memory for affective information, and reduced memory for other types of details, reflects the fact that older adults are less likely to filter out the task-irrelevant affective details. In other words, perhaps both young and older adults initially focus on affective context, but perhaps young adults soon realise that this information is not the only information that they should be remembering. They may therefore switch strategies in order to boost their encoding of other types of details. Given the difficulties that older adults have with flexible deployment of attention (Braver & Barch, 2002; Gutchess et al., 2007) and with inhibition of task-irrelevant information (Zacks & Hasher, 1997), it is plausible that older adults cannot strategically redirect their attention once it is focused on the affective context.

Some evidence to support this hypothesis has come from studies examining the ease with which young and older adults are able to shift their attention from affective aspects of scenes or sentences to non-affective aspects. Even for young adults it appears difficult to disengage attention from affective information; for example, if young adults are shown a scene depicting a snake in the forest, participants will look longer at the snake than they will at the forest (Loftus, Loftus, & Messo, 1987), and they will be more likely to remember the snake than the forest (reviewed by Reisberg & Heuer, 2004). However, when young adults are encouraged to process the non-affective elements of the scene (either by warning them that their memories will be tested for the non-affective context or by giving them encoding tasks—such as telling a story about the scene—that force them to attend to all aspects), they are able to do so (Kensinger, Garoff-Eaton, & Schacter, 2007b; Kensinger, Piguet, Krendl, & Corkin, 2005). They no longer show impaired memory for non-affective details, such as the forest; rather, they appear to be able to effectively disengage attention from the emotional elements (e.g., the snake) and to direct their processing resources towards the non-emotional elements (e.g., the forest scene). Older adults, in contrast, do not enjoy this flexibility in attentional deployment. Regardless of the encoding instructions given to them, older adults appear to maintain focus on the emotional elements in the scenes, leading them to have good memory for those aspects, but poor memory for the non-affective details (Kensinger, Gutchess, & Schacter, 2007c; Kensinger et al., 2005). This focus on the affective occurs even when such a focus impedes successful performance on the encoding task (Kensinger, O'Brien, Swanberg, Garoff-Eaton, & Schacter, 2007d).

Indeed, across a range of paradigms older adults' memory for the affective has seemed to come at a cost for memory for other types of details. For example, Comblain, D'Argembeau, and Van der Linden (2005) found that while older adults remembered a lot of thoughts and feelings elicited by pictures that they had viewed, they remembered little perceptual or semantic detail. Kensinger, Brierley, Medford, Growdon, and Corkin (2002) also found that while older adults were good at remembering the affective words within a sentence, they did poorly at remembering the non-affective words. Young adults, in contrast, showed good memory not only for the affective words but also for the non-affective ones. Thus it seems that older adults' focus on the affective can lead to decrements in memory for other types of details. Although young adults remember the perceptual and semantic details of many of life's experiences just as well as they remember the affective details (e.g., May et al., 2005), for older adults the non-affective details may never be attended to, or may not be the target of retrieval processes, leaving them primarily with a sense for the affective tinge of an event. Thus, in thinking back to a dinner with friends, young adults may remember the taste of the food, the topics discussed, or the layout of the restaurant; older adults, in contrast, may primarily remember the calm feeling elicited as they enjoyed the meal.

REMEMBERING DETAILS OF EMOTIONAL EVENTS

The research described above has suggested that older adults are more likely than young adults to process incoming information in an affect-relevant way, and that they are more likely to remember the affective qualities of prior experiences. A related line of research has examined whether older adults remember more contextual details about emotional events than they do about non-emotional events. When an event elicits significant emotional reactions, do older adults continue to display memory only for the general affective tone of these events, or is there something about emotionally evocative events that may cause older adults to remember other types of contextual details as well?

Most investigations of this issue have focused on older adults' abilities to form "flashbulb memories" of highly surprising and emotional public events. Because the hallmark of a flashbulb memory is the vividness with which people remember contextual details that are not inherently affective in nature (e.g., what they were wearing or what they were doing when they learned of an event's occurrence), assessing the frequency of these memories across the adult lifespan provides a way to examine whether older adults, like young adults, are likely to remember contextual details about emotional events.

Initial reports were fairly inconclusive regarding the effects of ageing on flashbulb memory: Although some studies revealed that older adults retained flashbulb memories at least as frequently as young adults (e.g., Christianson, 1989; Otani et al., 2005; Wright, Gaskell, & O'Muircheartaigh, 1998), other studies revealed that older adults demonstrated these vivid memories significantly less often than young adults (e.g., Cohen, Conway, & Maylor, 1994; Tekcan & Peynircioglu, 2002; Yarmey & Bull, 1978). Because these studies differed in methodologies—including differences in how memory was tested, in how flashbulb memory was defined, and in how long a delay there was between memory assessments—there were a number of possible reasons for the mixed findings. For example, Wright et al. (1998), who found no age effects on the frequency of flashbulb memory formation, measured memory via a marketing phone interview, asking participants simply to respond "yes" or "no" to a series of questions. By contrast, Cohen et al. (1994) and Tekcan and Peynircioglu (2002), who found age-related declines in the frequency of flashbulb memories, used written questionnaires to assess participants' memories, suggesting that age deficits may be most apparent when memory is assessed via free recall of details. Whether age differences in recall are revealed may also depend on whether the consistency of a memory is taken into consideration: Tekcan and Peynircioglu (2002), who found age differences, considered any detailed memory to be indicative of a flashbulb memory, whereas Otani et al. (2005), who found no age differences, required flashbulb memories to be consistent over time. Taken together, these results suggest that age differences may be reduced when consistency of free recall is considered. However, Cohen et al. (1994), who required strict consistency of free recall, found that older adults formed flashbulb memories less often than young adults, drawing into question the generality of this conclusion. Thus, no simple explanation emerged from these studies to account for when older adults do, and do not, form flashbulb memories as frequently as young adults.

A further difficulty with interpreting these studies arose because they did not include a control event to which memory for the emotional event could be compared. Without a non-emotional control event, general effects of ageing on memory for all experiences could not be distinguished from specific effects of ageing on memory for emotional events. An age difference could arise from global age-related decline in the amount of detail recorded about any event or from a specific difficulty that older adults have in forming detailed memories about emotional events—although Tekcan and Peynircioglu (2002) did reveal that older adults were able to retrieve more information about emotional events than non-emotional events that had occurred when the participants were young adults, demonstrating that ageing does not eliminate the memory enhancement for retrieval of emotional events.

To circumvent this problem, three recent studies have directly compared young and older adults' memories of an emotional event to their memories for a non-emotional event that occurred within a similar time period. Davidson and Glisky (2002) asked participants about the deaths of Princess Diana and Mother Theresa, and about a personal event that had occurred over Labor Day weekend (a weekend that occurred in close temporal proximity to the two deaths). Davidson, Cook, and Glisky (2006) asked older adults to remember the details of the September 11 terrorist attack and a control event from that same week. Kensinger, Krendl, and Corkin (2006b) asked young and older adults to recall details about two public events that occurred in close temporal proximity to one another: the *Columbia* Shuttle explosion, which all participants rated as a highly emotional event, and the SuperBowl game. Because participants were not avid fans of either team, they rated the game as having little emotional importance to them. Each of these studies converged on the same conclusions; in each study, older adults formed flashbulb memories as frequently as young adults and, like young adults, older adults remembered far more contextual details about emotional events than about non-emotional events. In fact, Kensinger et al. (2006b) found that age-related deficits in memory for contextual detail were greatly reduced for the emotional event as compared to the non-emotional one, suggesting that ageing has less of an impact on the ability to remember the details associated with emotional events.

Notably, all of these studies of "flashbulb memories" have assessed memory for negative events. There has yet to be a study comparing young and older adults' memories for a highly positive public event, but recent investigations in young adults suggest that the likelihood that details are remembered accurately may be critically impacted by the valence of the event. Levine and Bluck (2004) asked young adults who were either pleased or displeased with the verdict in the O.J. Simpson trial to indicate whether or not particular events had occurred during the trial. They found that the young adults who were pleased with the verdict were more lenient in endorsing that something had occurred during the trial than were individuals who were displeased with the verdict. Thus, individuals pleased about the verdict falsely endorsed more statements than individuals upset by the verdict. Young adults who were happy about the verdict were also more confident in their inaccurate endorsements than were individuals who were unhappy about the outcome. Kensinger and Schacter (2006) assessed baseball fans' memories of the 2004 American League Championship series, in which the Red Sox defeated the Yankees. They found that Red Sox fans (who found the event positive) had less-consistent memories than Yankees' fans, yet the Red Sox' fans were more confident in the accuracy of their memories. Thus, these studies both converged on the same general conclusion that—for young adults—events that evoke negative emotional responses may lead to more accurate memories, and a more realistic perception of memory accuracy, than events that elicit positive affect.

Although no study has directly examined the effect of valence on young and older adults' memories for autobiographical experiences, a retrospective study by Bohn and Berntsen (2007) suggests that negative valence may confer a memory accuracy advantage for adults of all ages. The authors asked individuals from former East and West Germany to recall the details of the fall of the Berlin Wall; some of these individuals had found the event to be a highly positive one, and others had experienced it as a highly negative event. Just as in Levine and Bluck (2004) and Kensinger and Schacter (2006), those individuals who had found the event to be negative remembered it with more accuracy than those who had found it to be positive. Because the mean age of Bohn and Berntsen's participants was 55 (and ages ranged from 29–82), their data suggest that the benefit that negative emotion confers on memory accuracy may be preserved across the adult lifespan.

A couple of laboratory studies have provided further evidence that the divergent effects of negative versus positive valence on the detail with which information is remembered may be maintained in older adulthood. In one set of studies (Kensinger, Garoff-Eaton, & Schacter, 2006a; Kensinger, Garoff-Eaton, & Schacter, 2007), young and older adults were asked to distinguish *same* items (identical to those that they'd studied) from *similar* items (sharing the same verbal label as a studied item, but differing in visual details) and *new* items (not related to a studied item). One-third of the items were positive (e.g., a sundae, a dollar bill), one-third of the items were negative (e.g., a snake, a grenade), and one-third of the items were neutral (e.g., a cabbage, a barometer). Both young and older adults were more accurate at distinguishing *same* from *similar* items when those items were negative than when they were positive or neutral. These results suggest that across the adult lifespan, negative information may be more likely to be remembered with details than other types of information. A similar pattern of results was revealed in a reality-monitoring study that required young and older adults to distinguish items they'd seen from those they'd only imagined. Young adults showed better reality monitoring for negative information than for positive or neutral information (Kensinger & Schacter, 2006; Kensinger, O'Brien, Swanberg, Garoff-Eaton, & Schacter, 2007d); similarly, older adults showed better reality monitoring only for negative items (not positive items) compared to neutral ones.

These findings suggest that older adults, like young adults, may be particularly good at extracting details about a negative event. Indeed, there is some evidence that older adults' memories for negative events may be even more vivid than young adults' memories, whereas the two age groups may not differ in the subjective vividness for positive events (Comblain et al., 2005). These findings follow logically from a vast literature suggesting that positive and negative affect lead to differences in the ways in which information is processed. Whereas negative information is processed in a detail-oriented and analytical fashion, positive information is processed in a more heuristic or schematic fashion (e.g., Bless et al., 1996; Gasper & Clore, 2002). This difference in processing seems to have widespread effects on memory, with negative information remembered with more vividness and contextual detail than positive or neutral information (e.g., Kensinger &

Corkin, 2003a; Ochsner, 2000), and with negative events remembered with less distortion (e.g., Kensinger & Schacter, 2006; Kensinger & Corkin, 2004b; Storbeck & Clore, 2005). It appears that this difference in how negative versus positive information is remembered remains consistent across the adult lifespan.

These findings are particularly interesting in light of evidence suggesting that older adults are more likely than young adults to focus on positive information and that older adults retain proportionally more positive information in their memories than young adults (reviewed by Mather & Carstensen, 2005). It might have been expected that because older adults attend more to positive information than young adults, they would also show a greater advantage in remembering the details of positive events. However, the extant data suggest that despite age-related changes in the salience of positive compared to negative information, older adults do not show an advantage for extracting contextual details of positive items' presentations. It is likely that older adults, like young adults, process positive information in a more heuristic fashion than negative information; thus, devoting more attention towards positive items (perhaps leading to additional, heuristic processing) does not lead to benefits in memory for those positive items' details. Thus, young and older adults are no more likely to remember the details of a sundae (its exact visual details, or whether it was seen or imagined) than they are to remember the details of a cabbage.

Positive items are associated with some mnemonic advantages unique to older adults, however. In particular, when memory for the general theme of presented information—regardless of memory for the details—is assessed, young adults often show a memory advantage only for negative items as compared to neutral ones, whereas older adults sometimes show a broader memory advantage extending to negative and positive items as compared to neutral ones. For example, whereas young adults were no more likely to remember that positive items (e.g., a sundae) had been presented than that neutral items (e.g., a cabbage) had been presented, older adults were more likely to remember the positive items (Kensinger et al., 2007a, 2007d; see also Charles, Mather, & Carstensen, 2003, and Comblain et al., 2005, for evidence of this age-related broadening of emotional memory enhancement). These results emphasise that the mnemonic influence of age-related changes in the processing of emotional information can differ depending on the way in which memory is assessed. Although older adults sometimes show a broader emotional memory enhancement in terms of item recognition, this broadening does not seem to extend to memory for details of the item's presentation. Thus, ageing does not impact the types of events that are most likely to be remembered with rich detail: Across the adult lifespan, negative events seem to be remembered with more contextual detail than positive or neutral ones.

WHY EMOTION MAY HELP OLDER ADULTS TO REMEMBER THE DETAILS

As the sections above have highlighted, older adults' ability to remember the details of an event is linked to the event's affective importance. In the case of information studied in different contexts, older adults appear better able to remember the affective context in which information was presented, while they have greater impairments in remembering non-affective details. Part of these influences may arise from encoding processes: older adults' natural tendency to focus on (or failure to inhibit the processing of) affective information may help them to remember the affective context in which information was studied, although this affective focus may come at the cost of remembering other, non-affective details (discussed by Comblain et al., 2005 Kensinger et al., 2007c; Schaefer & Philippot, 2005). It also may be that retrieval of affective context requires fewer resources than retrieval of other types of details, thereby reducing age-related deficits.

At a neural level, it may be that the encoding and retrieval of affective context relies on distinct neural processes from the encoding and retrieval of other types of contextual details, and the neural processes that support memory for affective context may be relatively spared with ageing. For example, the amygdala, orbitofrontal cortex, and medial prefrontal cortex are regions often implicated in the encoding and retrieval of self-relevant and emotional information (Dolan & Morris, 2000; LaBar & Cabeza, 2006; Phelps & LeDoux, 2005). These regions are relatively spared in ageing, showing rates of decline no greater than that of the whole brain (reviewed by Chow & Cummings, 2000; Salat, Kaye, & Janowsky, 2001; Tisserand, Visser, van Boxtel, & Jolles, 2000). In contrast, the lateral prefrontal regions often implicated in the encoding and retrieval of non-affective context (Paller & Wagner, 2002; Ranganath & Knight, in press) tend to undergo more significant structural and functional changes with ageing (Rajah & D'Esposito, 2005; Raz et al., 2004; Salat et al., 2004). Thus, it is plausible that older adults' abilities to retrieve affective context relate to a relative preservation of the neural processes recruited for such retrieval.

A recent neuroimaging study conducted in young adults (Smith, Stephan, Rugg, & Dolan, 2006) has lent some support to this hypothesis, providing evidence for dissociable processes corresponding with retrieval of affective context versus non-affective context. In particular, Smith and colleagues demonstrated that when young adults were asked to determine whether information had been studied in an affective context (i.e., to decide whether information had been presented in a negative or neutral context) there was increased connectivity between the orbitofrontal cortex and the amygdala as compared to a condition in which participants were asked to discriminate in which of two non-affective contexts information had been studied (i.e., to decide whether information had been presented in a context with people or without people; Smith et al., 2006; see also Somerville, Wig, Whalen, & Kelley, 2006 for evidence that the amygdala is involved in retrieval of whether someone is a "good" or "bad" person). To the extent that orbitofrontal and amygdalar processing is relatively preserved with ageing (Salat et al., 2001; Wright, Dickerson, Feczko, Negeira, & Williams, 2007), it would follow that older adults might be better at remembering affective contexts compared to non-affective ones.

In the case of emotional events, it appears that contextual details—even those not inherently affective in nature (e.g., what the weather was like on the day an emotional event occurred)—can be remembered well by older adults, and that age declines in remembering these details are reduced for emotional events as compared to non-emotional ones (e.g., Davidson & Glisky, 2002; Kensinger et al., 2006b). Davidson and Glisky (2002), and more recently Davidson et al. (2006), have shed light on why there may be this relative preservation with ageing. Whereas memory for source information typically correlates strongly with older adults' performance on measures of frontal lobe function and executive ability (Glisky, Rubin, & Davidson, 2001; Spencer & Raz, 1995), memory for the contextual details associated with a highly emotional event does not. In other words, older adults with low frontal function are just as likely to form "flashbulb memories" as are individuals with high frontal function. This result led Davidson and colleagues to suggest that the processes that allow individuals to remember the details of emotional events may be different from those that allow individuals to remember the details of non-emotional ones; in other words, memory for the details of emotional events may be a special form of source memory that is less reliant on the typical lateral prefrontal mechanisms.

Neuroimaging data gathered in young adults provide evidence in support of Davidson and colleagues' hypothesis. In one study, Kensinger and Corkin (2004a) revealed that non-arousing items that were vividly remembered were associated with enhanced lateral prefrontal and hippocampal activity during encoding, consistent with the results revealed in a number of subsequent-memory neuroimaging studies (Paller & Wagner, 2002). By contrast, vivid remembering of arousing information was associated with enhanced amygdalar and hippocampal activity during encoding, and was not influenced by the magnitude of prefrontal engagement during encoding. Although this study did not examine memory for source information specifically, the results suggest that vivid memories for emotional events may be supported by encoding processes independent of those mediated by lateral prefrontal regions.

More broadly, a large number of neuroimaging studies examining the neural processes involved in the successful encoding and retrieval of emotional information have implicated the amygdala and the hippocampus, as well as medial and orbital prefrontal regions (reviewed by Hamann, 2001; LaBar & Cabeza, 2006; Phelps, 2004). By contrast, studies of emotional memory have not typically implicated the lateral prefrontal regions traditionally associated with memory for the details of non-emotional information. These results provide tantalising evidence for a separation between the processes that support memory for the details of emotional events and those that support memory for the details of non-emotional events. Although it remains to be seen whether such a process dissociation will explain the pattern of results demonstrated in older adults, given the widespread age-related changes in the engagement of lateral prefrontal regions during the encoding and retrieval of episodic detail (Cabeza, 2002; Rajah & D'Esposito, 2005), it seems a promising avenue for further research.

FUTURE DIRECTIONS

The study of emotional memory in older adults is still at an early stage of inquiry, leaving open many questions. A couple of gaps in our knowledge have been alluded to in the sections above. As discussed in the first part of this review, there is reason to believe that older adults' focus on the "gist" of information may be tied to their tendency to focus on the affective meaning of information. However, the basis for such a link— if one does exist—is not known. Because the affective tone of material often is tied to the gist of the information, gist-based processing could lead a person to be good at remembering the affective qualities. Conversely, the fact that older adults focus on the affective nature of an experience could lead them to process its gist at the expense of other event details. It also is possible that older adults' ability to remember affective and gist-based information is linked to slowed memory decay rates for these sorts of information. Even in young adults, gist information decays more slowly than detailed information (e.g., Bransford & Franks, 1971; Friedman & deWinstanley, 1998) and affective information is associated with a shallower forgetting curve than other types of information (LaBar & Phelps, 1998; Sharot & Phelps, 2004; Sharot & Yonelinas, 2008). Therefore it is possible that older adults' memories for many contextual details quickly degrade, whereas their memory for the affective gist remains intact over time. It will be important for future research to examine the basis for older adults' focus on the affective and the extent to which it stems from affect-specific processes versus domain-general processes that underlie memory for all gist information.

More broadly, and as pointed out in the third section of this review, future research will do well to examine whether the encoding or retrieval of affective information (e.g., whether a name refers to someone good or bad) relies on distinct processes from the encoding or retrieval of non-affective information (e.g., whether a name refers to someone old or young). There is suggestive evidence of such a dissociation (e.g., Smith et al., 2006). However the nature of this distinction, and the extent to which it explains older adults' relatively preserved ability to remember affective information, remain to be seen. This issue may turn out to be a fundamental one, by informing whether older adults focus on affectively mean-

ingful information because of motivational shifts (i.e., older adults attend to the affective information because it has additional meaning for them) or because of age-related declines in other processes (i.e., older adults cannot bind or retain other details as readily, and therefore retain affective information).

In order for a complete understanding of age-related changes in emotional memory to be achieved, future research must also consider not only the affect–memory ties that hold across groups of older adults but also the potential importance of individual differences. It is likely that not all older adults are equally affectively focused, and important insights may be gained by understanding what cognitive, affective, or personality variables influence the degree to which a person focuses on affectively meaningful information. It would seem particularly worthwhile to examine ties between older adults' cognitive control ability, emotion regulation ability, and memory for affective information. One explanation for older adults' good memory for affective information is that they are less good at emotion regulation than young adults and therefore have more affective details that they can remember. This hypothesis makes sense in light of older adults' generally reduced cognitive control ability (see recent reviews by Buckner, 2004; Verhaeghen & Cerella, 2002) and the reliance of emotion regulation on those control processes (reviewed by Ochsner & Gross, 2005). However, in spite of this intuitive link, there is extensive evidence to suggest that older adults may be *better* at regulating their emotions than young adults (reviewed by Mather & Carstensen, 2005). Based on these findings, an alternate explanation for older adults' good memory for affective information is that they devote more of their cognitive resources towards emotion regulation and fewer resources towards processing or binding together other event attributes, thereby leading to particularly good memory for affective information. Future research could adjudicate between these alternatives by taking an individual-differences approach to examining the links between an older adult's emotion regulation ability, cognitive control ability, and ability to remember affective versus non-affective details.

These avenues for future research are likely to intersect. For example, the alternatives just described for possible ties between emotion regulation, cognitive control, and memory link back to the question of whether older adults' affective focus stems from their enhanced motivation to process affective information or from their diminished ability to process other sorts of information. Thus, it seems likely that future research will benefit from combining rigorous assessment of group differences with neuroimaging investigations and with careful considerations of individual differences. This combined approach may hold the key to answering outstanding questions regarding how emotion affects older adults' memories for event details.

REFERENCES

Adams, C., Labouvie-Vief., G., Hobart, C. J., & Dorosz, M. (1990). Adult age group differences in story recall style. *Journal o f Gerontology, 45*, P17–P27.

Bastin, C., & van der Linden, M. (2003). The contribution of recollection and familiarity to recognition memory: a study of the effects of test format and ageing. *Neuropsychology, 17*, 14–24.

Bayen, U. J., Nakamura, G. V., Dupuis, S. E., & Yang, C. L. (2000). The use of schematic knowledge about sources in source monitoring. *Memory and Cognition, 28*, 480–500.

Bless, H., Clore, G. L., Schwarz, N., Golisano, V., Rabe, C., & Wolk, M. (1996). Mood and the use of scripts: Does a happy mood really lead to mindlessness? *Journal of Personality and Social Psychology, 71*, 665–679.

Bohn, A., & Berntsen, D. (2007). Pleasantness bias in flashbulb memories: Positive and negative flashbulb memories of the fall of the Berlin Wall among East and West Germans. *Memory & Cognition, 35*, 565–577.

Bransford, J. D., & Franks, J. J. (1971). The abstraction of linguistic ideas. *Cognitive Psychology, 2*, 331–350.

Braver, T. S., & Barch, D. M. (2002). A theory of cognitive control, ageing, cognition, and neuromodulation. *Neuroscience and Biobehavioral Reviews, 26*, 809–817.

Buchanan, T., & Adolphs, R. (2002). The role of the human amygdala in emotional modulation of long-term declarative memory. In: S. Moore & M. Oaksford (Eds.), *"Emotional cognition: From brain to behavior"*. London: John Benjamins.

Buckner, R. L. (2004). Memory and executive function in ageing and AD: multiple factors that cause decline and reserve factors that compensate. *Neuron, 44*, 195–208.

Burke, D., & Light, L. (1981). Memory and ageing: The role of retrieval processes. *Psychological Bulletin, 90*, 513–554.

Cabeza, R. (2002). Hemispheric asymmetry reduction in older adults: The HAROLD model. *Psychology and Ageing, 17*, 85–100.

Carstensen, L. L., Fung, H., & Charles, S. (2003). Socioemotional selectivity theory and the regulation of emotion in the second half of life. *Motivation and Emotion, 27*, 103–123.

Carstensen, L. L., Isaacowitz, D. M., & Charles, S. T. (1999). Taking time seriously: A theory of socioemotional selectivity. *American Psychologist, 54*, 165–181.

Carstensen, L. L., & Turk-Charles, S. (1994). The salience of emotion across the adult life course. *Psychology and Ageing, 9*, 259–264.

Castel, A. D., & Craik, F. I. (2003). The effects of ageing and divided attention on memory for item and associative information. *Psychology and Ageing, 18*, 873–885.

Charles, S. T., Mather, M., & Carstensen, L. L. (2003). Ageing and emotional memory: The forgettable nature of negative images for older adults. *Journal of Experimental Psychology: General, 132*, 310–324.

Chow, T. W., & Cummings, J. L. (2000). The amygdala and Alzheimer's disease. In J. P. Aggleton (Ed.), *The amygdala: A functional analysis* (pp. 656–680). Oxford, UK: Oxford University Press.

Christianson, S. A. (1989). Flashbulb memories: Special, but not so special. *Memory and Cognition, 17*, 435–443.

Cohen, G., Conway, M. A., & Maylor, E. A. (1994). Flashbulb memories in older adults. *Psychology and Ageing, 9*, 454–463.

Comblain, C., D'Argembeau, A., & Van der Linden, M. (2005). Phenomenal characteristics of autobiographical memories for emotional and neutral events in older and younger adults. *Experimental Ageing Research, 31*, 173–189.

Comblain, C., D'Argembeau, A., Van der Linden, M., & Aldenhoff, L. (2004). The effect of ageing on the recollection of emotional and neutral pictures. *Memory, 12*, 673–684.

Davidson, P. S., Cook, S. P., & Glisky, E. L. (2006). Flashbulb memories for September 11th can be preserved in older adults. *Neuropsychological Development and Cognition, Series B: Ageing, Neuropsychology, and Cognition, 13*, 196–206.

Davidson, P. S. R., & Glisky, E. L. (2002). Is flashbulb memory a special instance of source memory? Evidence from older adults. *Memory, 10*, 99–111.

Dolan, R. J., & Morris, J. S. (2000). The functional anatomy of innate and acquired fear: Perspectives from neuroimaging. In R. D. Lane & L. Nadel (Eds.), *Cognitive neuroscience of emotion* (pp. 225–241). New York: Oxford University Press.

Fredrickson, B. L., & Carstensen, L.L. (1990). Choosing social partners: How old age and anticipated endings make us more selective. *Psychology and Ageing, 5*, 335–347.

Friedman, W. J., & deWinstanley, P. A. (1998). Changes in the subjective properties of autobiographical memories with the passage of time. *Memory, 6*, 367–381.

Fung, H. H., & Carstensen, L. L. (2003). Sending memorable messages to the old: Age differences in preferences and memory for advertisements. *Journal of Personality & Social Psychology, 85*, 163–178.

Gasper, K., & Clore, G. L. (2002). Attending to the big picture: Mood and global versus local processing of visual information. *Psychological Science, 13*, 34–40.

Glisky, E. L., Rubin, S. R., & Davidson, P. S. (2001). Source memory in older adults: An encoding or retrieval problem? *Journal of Experimental Psychology: Learning, Memory, and Cognition, 27*, 1131–1146.

Gould, O. N., Trevithick, L., & Dixon, R. A. (1991). Adult age differences in elaborations produced during prose recall. *Psychology and Ageing, 6*, 93–99.

Gross, J. J., Carstensen, L. L., Pasupathi, M., Tsai, J., Skorpen, C. G., & Hsu, A. Y. C. (1997). Emotion and ageing: Experience, expression, and control. *Psychology and Ageing, 12*, 590–599.

Gutchess, A. H., Hebrank, A., Sutton, B., Leshikar, E., Chee, M. W. L., Tan, J. C., et al. (2007). Contextual interference in recognition memory with age. *Neuroimage, 35*, 1338–1347.

Hamann, S. B. (2001). Cognitive and neural mechanisms of emotional memory. *Trends in Cognitive Sciences, 5*, 394–400.

Hasher, L., Stoltzfus, E. R., Zacks, R. T., & Rypma, B. (1991). Age and inhibition. *Journal of Experimental Psychology: Learning, Memory, and Cognition, 17*, 163–169.

Hasher, L., & Zacks, R. T. (1988). Working memory, comprehension, and ageing: A review and a new view. In G. H. Bower (Ed.), *The psychology of learning and motivation: Advances in research and theory* (Vol. 22 (pp. 193–225)). San Diego, CA: Academic Press, Inc.

Hashtroudi, S., Johnson, M. K., & Chrosniak, L. D. (1990). Ageing and qualitative characteristics of memories for perceived and imagined complex events. *Psychology and Ageing, 5*, 119–126.

Hashtroudi, S., Johnson, M. K., Vnek, N., & Ferguson, S. A. (1994). Ageing and the effects of affective and factual focus on source monitoring and recall. *Psychology and Ageing, 9*, 160–170.

Kausler, D. H. (1994). *Learning and memory in normal ageing*. San Diego, CA: Academic Press.

Kensinger, E. A., Brierley, B., Medford, N., Growdon, J. H., & Corkin, S. (2002). Effects of normal ageing and Alzheimer's disease on emotional memory. *Emotion, 2*, 118–134.

Kensinger, E. A., & Corkin, S. (2003a). Memory enhancement for emotional words: Are emotional words more vividly remembered than neutral words? *Memory and Cognition, 31*, 1169–1180.

Kensinger, E. A., & Corkin, S. (2003b). Neural changes in ageing. In L. Nadel (Ed.), *Encyclopedia of cognitive science*. London: Macmillan Ltd.

Kensinger, E. A., & Corkin, S. (2004a). The effects of emotional content and ageing on false memories. *Cognitive, Affective, and Behavioral Neuroscience, 4*, 1–9.

Kensinger, E. A., & Corkin, S. (2004b). Two routes to emotional memory: Distinct neural processes for valence and arousal. *Proceedings of the National Academy of Sciences, USA, 101*, 3310–3315.

Kensinger, E. A., Garoff-Eaton, R. J., & Schacter, D. L. (2006a). Memory for specific visual details can be enhanced by negative arousing content. *Journal of Memory and Language, 54*, 99–112.

Kensinger, E. A., Garoff-Eaton, R. J., & Schacter, D. L. (2007a). Effects of emotion on memory specificity in young and older adults. *Journal of Gerontology, 62*, 208–215.

Kensinger, E. A., Garoff-Eaton, R. J., & Schacter, D. L. (2007b). Effects of emotion on memory specificity: Memory trade-offs elicited by negative visually arousing stimuli. *Journal of Memory and Language, 56*, 575–591.

Kensinger, E. A., Gutchess, A. H., & Schacter, D. L. (2007c). Effects of ageing and encoding instructions on emotion-induced memory trade-offs. *Psychology and Ageing, 22*, 781–795.

Kensinger, E. A., Krendl, A. C., & Corkin, S. (2006b). Memories of an emotional and a non-emotional event: Effects of ageing and delay interval. *Experimental Ageing Research, 32*, 23–45.

Kensinger, E. A., O'Brien, J., Swanberg, K., Garoff-Eaton, R. J., & Schacter, D. L. (2007d). The effects of emotional content on reality-monitoring performance in young and older adults. *Psychology and Ageing, 22*, 752–764.

Kensinger, E. A., Piguet, O., Krendl, A. C., & Corkin, S. (2005). Memory for contextual details: Effects of emotion and ageing. *Psychology and Ageing, 20*, 241–250.

Kensinger, E. A., & Schacter, D. L. (2006). When the Red Sox shocked the Yankees: Comparing negative and positive memories. *Psychonomic Bulletin and Review, 13*, 757–763.

Koutstaal, W. (2003). Older adults encode – but do not always use – perceptual details: Intentional versus unintentional effects of detail on memory judgments. *Psychological Science, 14*, 189–193.

LaBar, K. S., & Cabeza, R. (2006). Cognitive neuroscience of emotional memory. *Nature Neuroscience Reviews, 7*, 54–56.

LaBar, K. S., & Phelps, E. A. (1998). Arousal-mediated memory consolidation: Role of the medial temporal lobe in humans. *Psychological Science, 9*, 490–493.

Labouvie-Vief, G. (1982). Growth and ageing in life span perspective. *Human Development, 25*, 65–79.

Levenson, R. W., Friesen, W. V., Ekman, P., & Carstensen, L. L. (1991). Emotion, physiology, and expression in old age. *Psychology and Ageing, 6*, 28–35.

Levine, L. J., & Bluck, S. (2004). Painting with broad strokes: Happiness and the malleability of event memory. *Cognition and Emotion, 18*, 559–574.

Light, L. L. (1991). Memory and ageing: Four hypotheses in search of data. *Annual Review of Psychology, 42*, 333–376.

Loftus, E. F., Loftus, G. R., & Messo, J. (1987). Some facts about weapon focus. *Law and Human Behavior, 11*, 55–62.

Mather, M., & Carstensen, L. L. (2005). Ageing and motivated cognition: The positivity effect in attention and memory. *Trends in Cognitive Sciences, 9*, 296–502.

May, C. P., Rahhal, T., Berry, E. M., & Leighton, E. A. (2005). Ageing, source memory, and emotion. *Psychology of Ageing, 20*, 571–578.

Naveh-Benjamin, M. (2000). Adult age differences in memory performance: Tests of an associative deficit hypothesis. *Journal of Experimental Psychology: Learning, Memory, and Cognition, 26*, 1170–1187.

Ochsner, K. N. (2000). Are affective events richly "remembered" or simply familiar? The experience and process of recognizing feelings past. *Journal of Experimental Psychology: General, 129*, 242–261.

Ochsner, K. N., & Gross, J. J. (2005). The cognitive control of emotion. *Trends in Cognitive Science, 9*, 242–249.

Otani, H., Kusumi, T., Kato, K., Matsuda, K., Kern, R. P., Widner, R. Jr., et al. (2005). Remembering a nuclear accident in Japan: Did it trigger flashbulb memories? *Memory, 13*, 6–20.

Paller, K. A., & Wagner, A. D. (2002). Observing the transformation of experience into memory. *Trends in Cognitive Sciences, 6*, 93–102.

Phelps, E. A. (2004). Human emotion and memory: Interactions of the amygdala and hippocampal complex. *Current Opinion in Neurobiology, 14*, 198–202.

Phelps, E. A., & LeDoux, J. E. (2005). Contributions of the amygdala to emotion processing: From animal models to human behavior. *Neuron, 48*, 175–187.

Rahhal, T., May, C. P., & Hasher, L. (2002). Truth and character: Sources that older adults can remember. *Psychological Science, 13*, 101–105.

Rajah, M. N., & D'Esposito, M. (2005). Region-specific changes in prefrontal function with age: A review of PET and fMRI studies on working and episodic memory. *Brain, 128*, 1964–1983.

Ranganath, C., & Knight, R. T. (in press). Prefrontal cortex and episodic memory: Integrating findings from neuropsychology and functional brain imaging. In A. Parker, E. Wilding, & T. Bussey (Eds.), *Memory encoding and retrieval: A cognitive neuroscience perspective*. New York: Psychology Press.

Raz, N., Gunning-Dixon, F., Head, D., Rodrigue, K. M., Williamson, A., & Acker, J. D. (2004). Ageing, sexual dimorphism, and hemispheric asymmetry of the cerebral cortex: Replicability of regional differences in volume. *Neurobiology of Ageing, 25*, 377–396.

Reisberg, D., & Heuer, F. (2004). Remembering emotional events. In D. Reisberg & P. Hertel (Eds.), *Memory and emotion* (pp. 3–41). New York: Oxford University Press.

Salat, D. H., Buckner, R. L., Snyder, A. Z., Greve, D. N., Desikan, R. S. R., Busa, E., et al. (2004). Thinning of the cerebral cortex in ageing. *Cerebral Cortex, 14*, 721–730.

Salat, D. H., Kaye, J. A., & Janowsky, J. S. (2001). Selective preservation and degeneration within the prefrontal cortex in ageing and Alzheimer's disease. *Archives of Neurology, 58*, 1403–1408.

Schaefer, A., & Philippot, P. (2005). Selective effects of emotion on the phenomenal characteristics of autobiographical memories. *Memory, 13*, 148–160.

Scherer, K. R. (2000). Psychological models of emotion. In J. C. Borod (Ed.), *The neuropsychology of emotion* (pp. 137–162). New York: Oxford University Press.

Sharot, T., & Phelps, E. A. (2004). How arousal modulates memory: Disentangling the effects of attention and retention. *Cognitive, Affective, Behavioral Neuroscience, 3*, 294–306.

Sharot, T., & Yonelinas, A. P. (2008). Differential time-dependent effects of emotion on recollective experience and memory for contextual information. *Cognition, 106*, 538–547.

Smith, A. P., Stephan, K. E., Rugg, M. D., & Dolan, R. J. (2006). Task and content modulate amygdala-hippocampal connectivity in emotional retrieval. *Neuron, 49*, 631–638.

Somerville, L. H., Wig, G. S., Whalen, P. J., & Kelley, W. M. (2006). Dissociable medial temporal lobe contributions to social memory. *Journal of Cognitive Neuroscience, 18*, 1253–1265.

Spencer, W. D., & Raz, N. (1995). Differential effects of ageing on memory for content and context: A meta-analysis. *Psychology and Ageing, 10*, 527–539.

Storbeck, J., & Clore, G. L. (2005). With sadness comes accuracy; with happiness, false memory: Mood and the false memory effect. *Psychological Science, 16*, 785–791.

Tekcan, A. I., & Peynircioglu, Z. F. (2002). Effects of age on flashbulb memories. *Psychology and Ageing, 17*, 416–422.

Tisserand, D. J., Visser, P. J., van Boxtel, M. P. J., & Jolles, J. (2000). The relation between global and limbic brain volumes on MRI and cognitive performance in healthy individuals across the age range. *Neurobiology of Ageing, 21*, 569–576.

Tsai, J. L., Levenson, R. W., & Carstensen, L. L. (2000). Autonomic, subjective, and expressive responses to emotional films in older and younger Chinese Americans and European Americans. *Psychology and Ageing, 15*, 684–693.

Verhaeghen, P., & Cerella, J. (2002). Ageing, executive control, and attention: A review of meta-analyses. *Neuroscience and Biobehavioral Reviews, 26*, 849–857.

Wright, C.I., Dickerson, B.C., Feczko, E., Negeira, A., & Williams, D. (2007). A functional magnetic resonance imaging study of amygdala responses to human faces in ageing and mild Alzheimer's disease. *Biological Psychiatry, 62*, 1388–1395.

Wright, D. B., Gaskell, G. D., & O'Muircheartaigh, C. A. (1998). Flashbulb memory assumptions: Using national surveys to explore cognitive phenomena. *British Journal of Psychology, 89*, 103–121.

Yarmey, A. D., & Bull, M. P. (1978). Where were you when President Kennedy was assassinated? *Bulletin of the Psychonomic Society, 11*, 133–135.

Yoder, C. Y., & Elias, J. W. (1987). Age, affect, and memory for pictorial story sequences. *British Journal of Psychology, 78*, 545–549.

Zacks, R., & Hasher, L. (1997). Cognitive gerontology and attentional inhibition: A reply to Burke and McDowd. *Journal of Gerontology: Psychological Sciences, 52B*, 274–283.

Zajonc, R. B. (1980). Feeling and thinking. Preferences need no inferences. *American Psychologist, 35*, 151–175.

MEMORY, 2009, 17 (2), 220–232

Adult age differences in memory for name–face associations: The effects of intentional and incidental learning

Moshe Naveh-Benjamin

Department of Psychological Sciences, University of Missouri, MO, USA

Yee Lee Shing

Centre for Lifespan Psychology, Max Planck Institute for Human Development, Berlin, Germany

Angela Kilb

Department of Psychological Sciences, University of Missouri, MO, USA

Markus Werkle-Bergner, Ulman Lindenberger, and Shu-Chen Li

Centre for Lifespan Psychology, Max Planck Institute for Human Development, Berlin, Germany

Previous studies have indicated that older adults have a special deficit in the encoding and retrieval of associations. The current study assessed this deficit using ecologically valid name–face pairs. In two experiments, younger and older participants learned a series of name–face pairs under intentional and incidental learning instructions, respectively, and were then tested for their recognition of the faces, the names, and the associations between the names and faces. Under incidental encoding conditions older adults' performance was uniformly lower than younger adults in all three tests, indicating age-related impairments in episodic memory representations. An age-related deficit specific to associations was found under intentional but not under incidental learning conditions, highlighting the importance of strategic associative processes and their decline in older adults. Separate analyses of hits and false alarms indicate that older adults' associative deficit originated from high false alarm rates in the associative test. Older adults' high false alarm rates potentially reflect their reduced ability to recollect the study-phase name–face pairs in the presence of intact familiarity with individual names and faces.

Keywords: Ageing; Episodic memory; Associative memory; Learning instructions.

Old age has been shown to be associated with a decline in episodic memory performance (e.g., Craik, 1999; Light, 1991; Zack, Hasher, & Li, 2000). However, this decline is differential and depends on various factors, including whether the information to be remembered comprises indivi-

Address correspondence to: Moshe Naveh-Benjamin, Department of Psychological Sciences, University of Missouri, 106 McAlester Hall, Columbia, MO 65211, USA. E-mail: NavehbenjaminM@missouri.edu

We thank Jenny Flatt for her help in collecting the data for Experiment 1, as well as the student assistants of Project FOR 448 in collecting the data for Experiment 2. Part of this work was funded by the German Research Foundation (DFG), Research Group FOR 448: "Binding: Functional architecture, neuronal correlates, and ontogeny". Additionally, the second and fourth author would like to express gratitude to the support of the International Max Planck Research School "The Life Course: Evolutionary and Ontogenetic Dynamics (LIFE)".

http://www.psypress.com/memory   DOI:10.1080/09658210802222183

dual pieces of information (item memory) or the relationships among these pieces (associative memory).

Previous studies have indicated that older adults tend to perform worse on tests of memory for associations relative to memory for items. For example, Chalfonte and Johnson (1996) showed no age-related deficits in memory for individual objects or individual colours. However, older adults showed poorer memory for colours in combination with specific objects. These researchers suggested that this deficit reflects an age-related decline in the ability to bind different components together (see also Mitchell, Johnson, Raye, Mather, & D'Esposito, 2000). In this vein, Naveh-Benjamin (2000) suggested an associative deficit hypothesis (ADH), which attributes age-related declines in associative memory to older adults' inability to encode and retrieve the relationships between single units of information. Several studies have since supported these suggestions by demonstrating that older adults tend to show poorer associative than item memory for word pairs (Castel & Craik, 2003; Light, Patterson, Chung, & Healy, 2004; Naveh-Benjamin, 2000), word–font pairs (Naveh-Benjamin, 2000), picture pairs (Naveh-Benjamin, Hussain, Guez, & Bar-On, 2003b), and face–spatial-location pairs (Bastin & Van der Linden, 2006; see also a meta-analysis by Old & Naveh-Benjamin, 2008a).

In the current studies we aimed to replicate and extend existing tests of the ADH. First, we wanted to assess whether older adults exhibit an associative deficit under conditions in which the information presented is meaningful and has high ecological validity. To this end, we used face–name associations that are prevalent in daily life, as numerous everyday situations require people to interact with others whose names must be both remembered and mentally linked to the corresponding faces. Older adults tend to report problems in this domain, specifically in retrieving the name of a person they have met or seen before (Cohen & Faulkner, 1984), although it is not yet clear whether older adults actually possess a specific deficit in retrieving proper names as opposed to names of objects (e.g., Maylor, 1997).

Most previous research on memory for faces and names has employed a cued-recall test, which presents participants with a series of faces, each paired with a proper name, and later requires them to report the correct name in response to a given face (e.g., Crook, Larrabee & Younjohn,

1993; Evrard, 2002). The problem with such cued-recall tasks is that it is often not clear whether older adults' performance in them reflects a deficit in memory for names (i.e., an item deficit) or for the associations between names and faces (an associative deficit).

In an attempt to tease apart these age-related item deficits from associative deficits, Naveh-Benjamin, Guez, Kilb, and Reedy (2004) presented younger and older adults with name–face pairs under intentional learning instructions. These instructions explicitly required participants to learn the pairs in preparation for three memory tests, for names, faces, and their associations, respectively. The subsequent recognition tests showed only small age-related differences in memory for names and faces, but large age-related differences in memory for the associations between names and faces. In support of the ADH, these results indicated a unique deficit in older adults' memory for associations, above and beyond their deficits (if any) in item memory.

The major purpose of our current experiments was to further examine the extent to which an age-related associative deficit was related to intentions to learn the information. Previous research using word–colour or word–spatial-location pairs (Chalfonte & Johnson, 1996) or word pairs (Naveh-Benjamin, 2000) had shown that older adults exhibit an associative deficit under both incidental (i.e., learn the pairs as single items) and intentional (i.e., learn the pairs as pairs) learning instructions. In general, the functioning of episodic memory can be conceived as operated and affected by two interacting components, one associative and one strategic (Moscovitch, 1992; Simons & Spiers, 2003). The associative component refers to mechanisms occurring during encoding, storage, and retrieval that bind different aspects of an event into a cohesive episode (Treisman, 1996; Zimmer, Mecklinger, & Lindenberger, 2006). The strategic component refers to the elaboration and organisation of memory features. Most importantly, these two components undergo declines in functioning in ageing (Brehmer, Li, Müller, v. Oertzen, & Lindenberger, 2007; Shing, Werkle-Bergner, Li, Lindenberger, in press a). The above pattern of results can be interpreted to mean that the associative deficit of older adults is driven by decline in the associative component (under incidental learning instructions), and even more drastic decline in the strategic component, as the deficit was larger under intentional learning instructions.

In the present experiments we wanted to assess how these two components of episodic memory would operate with ecologically relevant materials, such as associations between names and faces. Also, in the past the associative deficit has been shown under incidental learning instructions of associative information in which participants were told to pay attention only to item (word) information. Such instructions might have made participants pay more attention to item memory (the words), leaving them with fewer attentional resources to associate the two words. Older adults, who have been shown to possess reduced attentional resources (e.g., Craik, 1986; Craik & Byrd, 1982), might be particularly affected by such instructions, leading to an associative deficit even under incidental learning instructions. To rectify this issue, in the current experiments, in addition to intentional learning instructions, we also used incidental learning instructions in which we did not inform participants in advance of any subsequent memory test on the name, the face, or the name–face pairs.

In addition, we designed the current studies to extend Naveh-Benjamin et al.'s (2004) findings and to address methodological issues of that study by using a different type of memory test. In the Naveh-Benjamin et al. study, recognition tests were presented in a forced-choice format. For each given test (for faces, for names, or their associations), participants were asked to select from among two choices, one of which had been presented during the study phase. In contrast, in the current studies we employed a yes–no procedure, presenting participants with separate targets (previously presented events) and distractors (newly presented events) during a given test, asking them to identify the targets. The yes–no task, in addition to potentially broadening the ADH applicability to a different format of test, permitted us to study the deficit more analytically. Whereas the forced-choice procedure provided only a single accuracy index of performance (e.g., percentage correct responses), the yes–no test procedure provided separate measures of hits and false alarms. These separate measures may point to a possible source for any emerging associative deficit, by indicating whether the deficit is due to a relatively low hit rate (reflecting an inability to identify previously presented name–face pairs), a high false alarm rate (reflecting a tendency to falsely identify an association among previously unpaired names and faces), or both. If manifested, such a differential pattern might also have practical implications, such as, for example, for eyewitness testimony situations, indicating whether older adults tend to make more errors in correctly identifying felons, in falsely implicating innocent people, or in both (see Memon, Bartlett, Rose, & Gray, 2003; Wells & Olson, 2003).

Since the original results in the context of memory for name–face associations (Naveh-Benjamin et al., 2004) were reported for intentional learning, we first describe Experiment 1 in which participants were aware of the three upcoming tests during study. Once this deficit is established under intentional learning instructions, we proceed to describe Experiment 2 where we assessed the associative deficit involved in name–face associations under incidental instructions that withheld information of the subsequent memory tests from the participants.

Overall, these experiments investigated the role of strategic and automatic processes in the age-related associative deficit in memory for name–face pairs, assessing whether the deficit is mostly due to a decline in hit rates, an increase in false alarm rates, or both. A list of name–face pairs were presented during study to groups of younger and older adults followed by three separate yes–no recognition tests, one on the names, one on the faces, and one on the associations between the names and the faces.

EXPERIMENT 1

Method

Participants. Participants in this experiment were 24 young adults (ages 18–21), and 23 older adults (ages 65–81). The young adults were undergraduate students enrolled in an introductory psychology course at the University of Missouri who received course credit for their participation. All older adults were community dwellers who reported no major health problems and were each paid $15 for their participation. The two age groups were equated on levels of formal education ($p > .10$). A summary of all participants' demographic information appears in Table 1.

Design. The experiment used a 2 (age: older, younger; between participants) × 3 (test: face, name, associative; within participants) design.

TABLE 1
Demographic information for participants in Experiments 1 and 2

	n	*Age*	*Education*	*Proportion male*
Experiment 1				
Young	24	18.9 (0.80)	12.8 (0.93)	.45
Old	23	72.7 (5.07)	13.4 (1.60)	.32
Experiment 2				
Young	42	23.2 (1.65)	15.6 (1.87)	.52
Old	42	73.2 (1.67)	16.1 (3.71)	.50

Age and education are measured in years; means are presented, with standard deviations in parentheses.

Materials. Study materials comprised three sets, each consisting of 27 name–face pairs. The faces were chosen from diverse sources such as online school yearbooks, with half the faces belonging to younger adults (ages 18–25) and half to older ones (ages 65–80), with equal male and female representation. The names (first and last, half male and half female) were sampled randomly from a phone directory. For each set, two versions of 27 name–face pairings were created, matching faces and names to gender. A given display contained a face at the top of the screen with the name below it. Two random orders were created for each of these pairings, for a total of four versions; five or six participants in each age group were run in each version. The order of the sets was counterbalanced for each group. For the name and face recognition tests, distractors that did not appear during the study phase were chosen with similar characteristics of the targets.

Procedure. For each set, individually tested participants saw a succession of 27 name–face pairs on a computer monitor, at a rate of 3 seconds per pair with a .25 second interval between pairs. Study conditions were intentional, and participants were told that they must pay attention not only to each face and name, but also to the name–face pairs, because their memory for the name, the face, and their pairings would be tested. The first two pairs and the last pair were used as buffers to eliminate primacy and recency effects and were not analysed.

For each set, after the study phase and an interpolated activity of 60 seconds, three memory tests, two for the components and one for their associations, were administered to all participants. The order of the tests was counterbalanced across all participants in each age group, and any given name or face appeared on only one of the tests.

The stimuli in each test appeared for 4 seconds each, during which the participant responded by saying "yes" or "no" to each stimulus presented.

Before the name test participants were told they would see a succession of 16 names, 8 that had appeared in the study phase and 8 that had not. They were instructed to say "yes" for names they remembered and "no" for those they thought were new. Likewise, prior to the face test participants were told they would see 16 human faces, 8 that had appeared in the study phase and 8 that had not. They were instructed to say "yes" to faces they have recognised from the study phase and "no" to those they did not recognise. Finally, prior to the associative test participants were told that they would see a face from the study phase with a name from the study phase, but that only half of the time would the face and name be a pair from the study phase, whereas in the other half the name would be mismatched with a face that had been part of a different pair at study. They were asked to say "yes" for "intact" pairs and "no" for "recombined" pairs. Each test was preceded by a practice test to permit clarification of participants' questions before the experimental tests began.

Results

Measures of proportion of hits minus false alarms[1] were computed for each participant and then averaged over each age group for each test (see Figure 1). This equated the component and the associative recognition tests with respect to the scale used (from chance level performance at

---

[1] All analyses were also run using the *d′* measure of signal detection theory (Snodgrass & Corwin, 1988). There was no difference in findings.

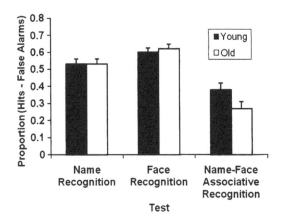

Figure 1. Memory performance under intentional learning in the name, face, and name–face association tests for younger and older adults in Experiment 1. Error bars represent standard errors around the mean.

0.0 to the highest possible score at 1.0). In addition, because a preliminary analysis of variance indicated no interaction effect of the order of the administration of the tests with any of the independent variables, in all analyses reported below (for this and the following experiment), performance was collapsed across the different orders. Performance of each group on each of the tests was better than chance ($p < .05$, using one-sample t-tests).

The first analysis conducted was a two-way analysis of variance (ANOVA): 2 (Age: young, old) $\times$ 3 (Test: face, name, associative). This analysis revealed no significant main effect of age, $F(1, 45) = 0.35$, $MSe = .035$, ns, with younger participants ($M = .50$, $SD = .11$) performing at the same level as older participants ($M = .48$, $SD = .12$). The effect of test was significant, $F(2, 90) = 46.29$, $MSe = .022$, $p < .001$. Performance on the face test was highest ($M = .61$, $SD = .18$), followed by that on the name test ($M = .53$, $SD = .21$) and the association test ($M = .33$, $SD = .22$). Impor-

tantly, the two-way interaction was significant, $F(2, 90) = 3.14$, $MSe = .022$, $p < .05$. Two additional two-way ANOVAs, each including age (young vs old) and one of the component tests (name or face) vs the associative one, showed similar patterns of interaction, with older adults performing more poorly on the associative test than on each of the component tests, $F(1, 45) = 4.81$, $MSe = .027$, $p < .05$, when the face and the associative tests were used, and, $F(1, 45) = 3.12$, $MSe = .025$, $p = .08$, when the name and the associative tests were used. To directly assess age-related differences in component and associative memory, a follow-up interaction comparison with age as one variable and the average performance on the component tests (name and face) vs the associative test as the other variable, showed a significant interaction, $F(1, 45) = 4.63$, $MSe = .029$, $p < .05$. Follow-up contrasts showed that whereas older adults performed as well as younger ones on the average of the component tests ($M = .56$, $SD = .12$, and $M = .59$, $SD = .10$, for young and old, respectively), $F(1, 45) = 0.63$, $MSe = .023$, ns, older adults performed more poorly than did young adults on the associative test ($M = .38$, $SD = .21$, and $M = .27$, $SD = .20$, for young and old, respectively) and this difference approached significance, $F(1, 45) = 3.23$, $MSe = .041$, $p = .07$. This finding provides evidence of an age-related associative deficit.

In order to further assess the associative deficit of older adults, the proportion of hits and false alarms were examined separately. These data are presented in Table 2. Name and face tests were again averaged into one overall "component" test measure. In terms of hits, a 2 (age) $\times$ 2 (test: component, associative) ANOVA did not reveal a significant main effect of age, $F(1, 45) = 1.33$, $MSe = .022$, ns, with similar hit rates by the

TABLE 2
Mean proportion hits and false alarms, Experiment 1 and Experiment 2

Group	Name test		Face test		Associative test	
	Hits	*FAs*	*Hits*	*FAs*	*Hits*	*FAs*
Experiment 1						
Young	.69 (.16)	.16 (.11)	.72 (.14)	.13 (.10)	.68 (.16)	.30 (.15)
Old	.69 (.13)	.16 (.10)	.78 (.13)	.15 (.12)	.72 (.13)	.45 (.14)
Experiment 2						
Young	.72 (.17)	.16 (.09)	.76 (.12)	.22 (.10)	.70 (.13)	.31 (.14)
Old	.54 (.22)	.24 (.17)	.76 (.14)	.42 (.17)	.61 (.17)	.49 (.21)

Standard deviations in parentheses. FAs = false alarms.

younger ($M = .70$, $SD = .14$) and the older ($M = .73$, $SD = .11$) adults. The effect of test was also not significant, $F(1, 45) = 1.05$, $MSe = .012$, ns, with similar hit rates on the component ($M = .72$, $SD = .14$) and the associative ($M = .70$, $SD = .12$) measures. Finally, the ANOVA did not reveal a significant interaction, $F(1,45) = 0.05$, $MSe = .012$, ns.

A similar two-way ANOVA was conducted with false alarm rates as the dependent variable; name and face tests were again averaged into one overall "component" test measure. The analysis yielded a significant main effect of age, $F(1, 45) = 7.63$, $MSe = .018$, $p < .01$, with older adults showing higher false alarm rates ($M = .30$, $SD = .11$, and $M = .22$, $SD = .12$) for old and young, respectively. This effect is qualified by the two-way interaction reported below. The effect of test was also significant, $F(1, 45) = 115.64$, $MSe = .010$, $p < .01$, with higher false alarm rate in the associative than in the component test ($M = .38$, $SD = .14$, and $M = .15$, $SD = .08$, respectively). Interestingly, the analysis yielded a significant interaction, $F(1, 45) = 11.33$, $MSe = .010$, $p < .01$. Further contrasts showed that while older adults produced similar proportions of false alarms as did the younger adults on the component test measure ($M = .14$, $SD = .09$, and $M = .15$, $SD = .08$, for young and old, respectively), $F(1, 45) = .07$, $MSe = .015$, ns, age differences were significant on the associative measure, $F(1, 45) = 12.16$, $MSe = .02$, $p < .01$, with older adults showing higher false alarm rates ($M = .30$, $SD = .15$, and $M = .45$, $SD = .14$, for young and old, respectively). Thus, it appears that the associative deficit of the older adults in this experiment stemmed from high rates of false alarms on the associative test.

Discussion

The results of this experiment show that the ADH applies to associations between a face and a name. Older adults under intentional learning instructions exhibited a deficit in memory for names bound to faces, while showing similar memory performance to that of young adults in memory for faces or names. These results replicate those reported by Naveh-Benjamin et al. (2004) and extend it to situations when a yes–no recognition procedure is used. Furthermore, in contrast to most previous studies in which the age-related associative deficit was accompanied

by some decline in component memory, the age-related associative deficit shown here was accompanied by intact component memory in older adults, as indicated by their equivalent performance to young adults in the separate tests of memory for names and faces. This pattern appears to rule out any age-related deficit in component memory as the source for the associative deficit of older adults in the current experiment.

Furthermore, whereas previous studies on the ADH have generally analysed only an overall accuracy measure of performance on each test, the current results suggest that such a method may be missing important information about the mechanisms behind the associative deficit. The results of the current experiment indicate that older adults' associative deficit was entirely due to their increased false alarms but not to a decrease in hit rates. According to the dual-process account (Jacoby, 1991; Yonelinas, 2002), memory for past events can be based on retrieval accompanied by specific contextual details (recollection) or on the feeling of knowing that an event is old or new without necessarily recollecting specific details (familiarity). In the ageing literature, converging evidence indicates that ageing disrupts recollection to a greater extent than does familiarity (Healy, Light, & Chung, 2005; Jacoby & Hay, 1998; Souchay, Moulin, Clarys, Taconnat, & Isingrini, 2007). Given that the distractors of our associative test comprised familiar stimuli that were presented at study but rearranged in pairing only at test, the ability to reject them is essentially a test of recollection (a recall-to-reject notion; Gallo, Sullivan, Daffner, Schacter, & Budson, 2004). In this light, the increase in false alarms of older adults in identifying the relationships between a name and a face could be due to their over-reliance on the familiarity of the components— the name or the face—that they remembered equally as well as did young adults, combined with a deficit in the recollection of the exact name–face associations. This issue is discussed further in the General Discussion.

Older adults' different patterns of hits and false alarms in the associative test are related to eyewitness studies wherein older adults were shown to perform almost as well as young adults in identifying culprits when the culprit was present in a given line-up, but tended to commit false identifications at high rates when the culprit did not appear in the line-up (Wells & Olson, 2003).

EXPERIMENT 2

The results of Experiment 1 indicated that older adults exhibit a deficit in memory of name–face associations under intentional learning instructions. In Experiment 2 we assess whether older adults will show a similar deficit under incidental learning conditions. Such results will indicate that at least part of the age-related associative deficit is related to the operation of automatic processes. However, if the deficit is not demonstrated under incidental learning conditions, it would point to the predominantly strategic origins of the deficit.

Method

Participants. Data were collected from 42 older adults between 70 and 76 years of age and 42 younger adults between 20 and 26 years of age. All participants were residents of Berlin, Germany. The older adults lived independently in the community and travelled to the laboratory by themselves for testing. Participants were again roughly equated on their level of education ($p > .05$). In order to optimise the incidental nature of the memory test, none of the participants in this experiment had taken part in other experiments similar to Experiment 1 and none of the younger adults was a psychology major. All participants received 17 Euros for their participation. Additional demographic information is provided in Table 1.

Design. This experiment consisted of a 2 (age: younger, older; between participants) × 3 (test: face, name, associative, within participants) design.

Materials and procedure. The materials and procedure for the memory task were similar to those used in Experiment 1, except for a number of minor changes. First, a set of 48 name–face pairs were used (for references of face stimuli, see Ebner, 2008; Minear & Park, 2004). Each pair was presented for 3 seconds with .5 seconds of a blank slide before the next pair appeared. Each test included 32 stimuli with 16 targets and 16 distractors. The nature of stimuli was the same as in Experiment 1. However, in contrast to Experiment 1, participants were not made aware of the upcoming tests until the testing session began. Instead, before study they were instructed to respond with "fit" or "fit very well" to each name–face pair to indicate subjective evaluations

of whether the name and the face fitted together. They were further told that there were no correct or wrong answers on this task and the aim of the test was to examine subjective perception of how names and faces match together. Post-test informal inquiries indicated that overall, during the study phase, participants did not anticipate the upcoming memory tests.

Results

As in Experiment 1, memory performance was measured in terms of the proportion of hits minus the proportion of false alarms produced by each participant. Figure 2 presents memory performance for each age group for each of the tests. Performance of each group on each of the tests was better than chance ($p < .05$, using one-sample t-tests).

The first ANOVA performed was 2 (age) × 3 (test: name, face, associative). There was a significant main effect of age, $F(1, 82) = 105.78$, $MSe = .036$, $p < .01$. Specifically, younger adults ($M = .50$, $SD = .11$) performed better than did older adults ($M = .25$, $SD = .11$). There was also a significant main effect of test, $F(2, 164) = 39.64$, $MSe = .024$, $p < .001$, with scores on the name ($M = .43$, $SD = .22$) and the face ($M = .44$, $SD = .19$) tests similar to each other, $F(1, 82) = 0.17$, $MSe = .025$, ns, and both higher than the scores on the associative ($M = .25$, $SD = .21$) test, $F(1, 82) = 57.46$, $MSe = .024$, $p < .01$ and $F(1, 82) = 63.80$, $MSe = .024$, $p < .01$, respectively. The interaction between age and test was not significant, $F(2, 164) = 1.36$, $MSe = .024$, ns. To assess the

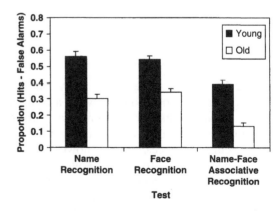

Figure 2. Memory performance under incidental learning in the name, face, and name–face association tests for younger and older adults in Experiment 2. Error bars represent standard errors around the mean.

associative deficit hypothesis, a follow-up interaction comparison with age as one variable, and the average performance on the component tests (name and face) vs the associative test as the other variable, was carried out and showed no significant interaction, $F(1, 82) = 1.60$, $MSe = .022$, ns. Younger and older adults reduced their performance in the associative test relative to the component test to a similar degree. Specifically, hit minus false alarm measures were .39 and .11 for younger and older adults on the associative test, and .55 and .31 for younger and older adults on the component test, respectively.

As in Experiment 1, the proportion of hits and false alarms were examined separately. These data are presented in Table 2. In terms of hits, a 2 (age) × 2 (test: component, associative) ANOVA revealed a significant main effect of age, $F(1, 82) = 13.49$, $MSe = .026$, $p < .01$, where younger adults ($M = .72$, $SD = .13$) performed better than did older adults ($M = .63$, $SD = .16$). There was also a significant main effect of test, $F(1, 82) = 4.34$, $MSe = .015$, $p < .05$, with scores on the component test ($M = .70$, $SD = .14$) higher than those on the associative test ($M = .65$, $SD = .15$). Finally, there was no significant interaction between age and type of test, $F(1, 82) = .02$, $MSe = .015$, ns, reflecting the fact that hit rate was lower in the associative test ($M = .70$, and $M = .61$, for young and old, respectively) than in the component test ($M = .74$, and $M = .65$, for young and old, respectively) to the same degree in the younger and older participants. These results are similar to those obtained in Experiment 1.

A 2 (Age) × 2 (test; component vs associative) ANOVA with proportion of false alarms as the dependent measure was also conducted. The analysis revealed a significant main effect of age, $F(1, 82) = 38.06$, $MSe = .029$, $p < .01$, where younger adults ($M = .25$, $SD = .10$) had lower false alarm rates than did older adults ($M = .41$, $SD = .18$). There was also a significant main effect of test, $F(1, 82) = 52.29$, $MSe = .016$, $p < .01$, with false alarm scores on the component test ($M = .26$, $SD = .14$) lower than those on the associative test ($M = .40$, $SD = .18$). Finally, the interaction between age and test was not significant, $F(1, 82) = 1.43$, $MSe = .016$, ns, indicating that although older adults had higher false alarm rates, these were similar for the component test ($M = .18$ and $M = .33$ for young and old, respectively) and for the associative test ($M = .31$ and $M = .49$, for young and old, respectively).

Discussion

The results of Experiment 2 showed that although older adults' overall memory performance was lower than that of the young adults, older adults did not exhibit a specific associative deficit on any of the measures used (including hits minus false alarms, as well as separate measures of hits and false alarms) when they learned the information incidentally. This result is different from a couple of past studies (e.g., Chalfonte & Johnson, 1996; Naveh-Benjamin, 2000) that have shown the existence of such a deficit under incidental learning conditions. One possibility is that this result is related to the specific stimuli used in this experiment. In particular, since associations of names and faces happen frequently in daily life, older adults have considerable practice and experience with this type of binding, which they eventually may process automatically (e.g., Hasher & Zacks, 1979). The studies by Chalfonte and Johnson (1996) and Naveh-Benjamin (2000), in contrast, employed stimuli that people do not need to bind as often in everyday life, like words and colours, colours and spatial locations, or two unrelated words. The binding of these components is not automatic, possibly explaining why older adults' associative deficit emerged with such stimuli in these studies even under incidental learning instructions.

Another possible reason for the difference in the current findings from previous literature concerns methodological issues. Specifically, in previous research (e.g., Naveh-Benjamin, 2000) the incidental associative learning condition was one in which participants did not expect an associative memory test, but were told about the upcoming item memory test. The focus on the item information in the incidental associative learning condition might have helped participants improve their item memory performance while degrading their encoding of associative information. This could have been especially true for older adults who were shown to have fewer cognitive resources (e.g., Craik, 1986; Craik & Byrd, 1982), leading to their associative deficit under incidental learning conditions. In contrast, in the current experiment the participants in the incidental learning condition were not required to intentionally encode either item or associative information. Therefore, both were likely encoded incidentally, and in this case older adults showed no deficit in automatic binding processes.

A second methodological aspect that is different from previous studies is the specific cover task required to be carried out by the participants during encoding. Participants were asked to subjectively rate whether the name and face of each pair fitted together, an assessment that could have led to a processing of the relationships between the two components, thus reducing age differences in the relative cost of the associative test.

Finally, another potential reason for the lack of an interaction between age and test in this experiment is the relatively poor performance of older adults on the associative test. To assess whether a potential floor effect might be involved here in preventing an age × test interaction, we conducted the analysis on the overall measure of accuracy (proportion hits minus proportion false alarms) while excluding participants who performed close to floor (less than 0.1 in any of the tests). The results of this analysis replicated those performed on the full sample, and in particular did not indicate an interaction between age and test, $F(2, 122) = 0.07$, $MSe = .024$, ns. This lends further support to our interpretation of the current results as indicating that older adults do not have a specific associative deficit in binding names and faces under incidental learning conditions.

GENERAL DISCUSSION

The two experiments reported here both replicate and extend previous results reported in the literature. Older adults have difficulty in memory for bound information, in this case for the associations between a name and a face when learning is intentional (see Naveh-Benjamin et al., 2004). Interestingly, this deficit was not found under incidental learning instructions when participants did not anticipate the subsequent memory tasks, despite the fact that the performance of older adults was lower in all three types of memory tests (face, name, and associative tests). An additional contribution of the current study is in pointing analytically to potential factors underlining the associative deficit of older adults. As mentioned in the Introduction, most studies of age-related differences in memory for items and associations that employed recognition tests looked only at a general accuracy measure, either proportion correct in forced-choice tests (e.g., Bastin & Van der Linden, 2006; Naveh-Benjamin

et al., 2004) or proportion of hits minus false alarms (e.g., Naveh-Benjamin, 2000). The current study indicated an interesting pattern when the age-related associative deficit shown under intentional learning instructions was analysed further. In particular, when responses were analysed separately in terms of hits and false alarms, specific deficits emerged in older adults' performance. The results of Experiment 1 show that the associative deficit exhibited by the older adults was due exclusively to their tendency to falsely remember distractor pairs; that is, they produced especially high rates of false alarms on the associative test, but not particularly low hit rates (see also Shing et al., in press a, in press b).

As mentioned above, researchers generally agree that the effective operation of episodic memory requires interactions between the strategic and associative components of memory (Miller & Cohen, 2001; Moscovitch, 1992; O'Reilly & Norman, 2002; Prull, Gabrieli, & Bunge, 2000; Simons & Spiers, 2003). Furthermore, these two components show age-related changes in functioning (Brehmer et al., 2007; Shing et al., in press a). One possible explanation of our findings concerns older adults' deficit in employing strategic processes to encode associative information. In the present study the relative contribution of effortful strategic processes was manipulated across two experiments. The fact that an age-related associative deficit was found under intentional but not under incidental learning is in line with suggestions that older adults do not do as well as younger ones in initiating and efficiently using appropriate strategies to encode associations, in this case between names and faces. This conclusion is supported by a recent study employing a direct manipulation of strategies (Naveh-Benjamin, Keshet Brav, & Levy, 2007; see also Shing et al., in press a, for a lifespan comparison).

At the same time, in the absence of intentional learning older adults showed a general decline in their ability to remember information by mere exposure. Both empirical evidence (e.g., Eichenbaum, 2004) and computational theories (e.g., McClelland, McNaughton, & O'Reilly, 1995) suggest that the hippocampus supports fast, incidental episodic memory processes. Ageing compromises the hippocampus and related regions (Raz et al., 2005; Wilson, Gallagher, Eichenbaum, & Tanila, 2006), which in turn may negatively affect the binding of information. Furthermore, neurocomputational modelling results concerning cognitive ageing in general (Li, Lindenberger, & Sikström, 2001) and older adults' associative deficit in particular (Li, Naveh-Benjamin, & Lindenberger, 2005) suggest that ageing-related declines in neuromodulation could result in less distinctive memory representations. Similarly, the hippocampal ageing model (Wilson et al., 2006) suggests that ageing-related memory decline could arise from a lack of distinction between newly learned information and existing memory traces, possibly due to deteriorating functional connectivity between the entorhinal cortex and the hippocampus. Less distinctive memory representations due to one or both of these reasons may underlie illusory familiarity, resulting in older adults' higher false alarm rates. Overall, the differential age-related decline in associative memory, which was shown only under intentional encoding instructions and only for types of retrieval involving distractor pairs, increases the likelihood that the origin of the associative deficit is a result of age-related differences in the interaction between encoding and retrieval processes.

Taken together, while older adults' decline in the associative component may be a consequence of reduced distinctiveness of internal memory representations, they also suffer from a declining contribution of the strategic processes. The latter may be used by younger adults to increase the distinctiveness of memory representations, possibly by biasing the competition between memory representations via signals from prefrontal areas (Miller & Cohen, 2001). Future studies need to make use of paradigms that vary the relative contributions of both sets of processes to better understand their interactions (cf. Werkle-Bergner, Müller, Li, & Lindenberger, 2006).

Another potential explanation of the current results involves the importance of a reduction in attentional resources in older adults' episodic memory decline (e.g., Craik & Byrd, 1982). It might be that in Experiment 1, where participants were instructed to study names, faces, and associations among them, older adults were not able to allocate enough attentional resources to all three features, so after attending to the name and face separately, the creation of associations was neglected. Although this is a plausible explanation, several studies indicate that whereas general memory decline may be related to a decrease in attentional resources with age, older adults' differential decline in associative memory is not

necessarily related to such a decrease in attentional resources (e.g., Naveh-Benjamin, Guez, & Marom, 2003a; Naveh-Benjamin et al., 2003b, 2004; but see different results by Castel & Craik, 2003).

As mentioned before, the pattern of differentially high false alarms in older adults' performance in the associative test in Experiment 1 is in line with the distinction made in the literature between familiarity, a sense of "knowing" without conscious awareness of relevant contextual information, and recollection, conscious retrieval accompanied by contextual information (e.g., Light, Prull, La Voie, & Healy, 2000; Yonelinas, 2002; see also Jacoby, 1991). Previous research has provided evidence that, whereas familiarity remains mostly unaffected in old age, recollection is strongly impaired in older adults (e.g., Light et al., 2000; Prull, Dawes, Martin, Rosenberg, & Light, 2006). Using these terms, it is possible that older adults' tendency to erroneously accept repaired associations as intact (resulting in a high false alarm rate) is related to the age-related changes in the mechanism of familiarity and recollection. In particular, whereas the item memory tests may have been at least partially performed based on familiarity, the associative tests required recollection; together with an inability to recollect the originally studied pairs, older adults' high levels of familiarity with individual items might have led them to high rates of incorrect recognition of recombined pairs (cf. Daselaar, Fleck, Dobbins, Madden, & Cabeza, 2006). Furthermore, older adults' disproportionally higher false alarm rates on the associative test in Experiment 1 but not in Experiment 2 could have been due to the higher levels of familiarity with item information in Experiment 1 where they intentionally tried to encode the name and the face components, relative to Experiment 2, when learning of the components was incidental. This could have led to older adults' higher false alarms rates in the associative test of Experiment 1 but not Experiment 2 (see similar results by Old & Naveh-Benjamin, 2008b, under intentional learning conditions for person–action associations). The current findings are also compatible with the notion that older adults tend to be "captured" by misleading information such that they may forgo engaging in recollection (Jacoby & Rhodes, 2006). Such deficits may reflect a decline in strategic processes that underlie cognitive control at retrieval (Rugg & Wilding, 2000).

An applied implication of the current results arises from the fact that while older adults show a deficit in remembering the associations between names and faces, this deficit seems to happen mostly under intentional learning conditions. Given that, in daily life, such learning often happens incidentally (e.g., when people are introduced to each other in a social situation), the current results may indicate that, in general, older adults may not have a specific problem in learning the name–face associations, although their overall memory performance in terms of the name, the face, and the association (as indicated in Experiment 2) may be relatively poor in comparison to that of younger adults. Second, older adults, at least under intentional learning conditions, may not have as much of a problem correctly recognising that a given person's name is actually what it is, but may have problems such as attributing a wrong name to a given face. As mentioned earlier, this finding is somewhat similar to results reported in eyewitness research, which show that older adults generally perform nearly as well as do young adults at identifying culprits when the culprit is present in a given line-up, but tend to commit false identifications at high rates when the culprit does not appear in the line-up (Wells & Olson, 2003). Finally, in terms of intervention studies, the current results indicate that in order to improve older adults' memory for associations between names and faces, specific strategies could be employed to promote relationships between the name and the face. However, these interventions do not necessarily need to promote the familiarity of the name or the face, as this might increase false memory for the associations.

In summary, the current experiments extend the ADH to memory for ecologically relevant stimuli, showing that older adults have a specific deficit in memory for name–face associations. However, this deficit was exhibited under intentional but not under incidental learning instructions. This finding highlights the role of strategic processes in the associative deficit, suggesting that older adults may have trouble initiating efficient associative strategies when trying to intentionally encode information. Furthermore, employing a yes–no recognition paradigm, which allowed the separate analysis of hits and false alarms, facilitated the identification of the locus of the age-related associative deficit of older adults in the current experiments, which seems to be driven more by high false alarm rates than by low hit rates.

REFERENCES

Bastin, C., & Van der Linden, M. (2006). The effects of aging on the recognition of different types of associations. *Experimental Aging Research, 32,* 61–77.

Brehmer, Y., Li, S-C., Müller, V., v. Oertzen, T., & Lindenberger, U. (2007). Memory plasticity across the lifespan: Uncovering children's latent potential. *Developmental Psychology, 43*(2), 465–478.

Castel, A. D., & Craik, F. I. M. (2003). The effects of aging and divided attention on memory for item and associative information. *Psychology and Aging, 18,* 873–885.

Chalfonte, B. L., & Johnson, M. K. (1996). Feature memory and binding in young and older adults. *Memory & Cognition, 24,* 403–416.

Cohen, G., & Faulkner, D. (1984). Memory in old age: "Good in parts". *New Scientist, 11,* 49–51.

Craik, F. I. M. (1986). A functional account of age differences in memory. In F. Klix & H. Hagendorf (Eds.), *Human memory and cognitive capabilities, mechanisms and performance* (pp. 409–422). Amsterdam: North-Holland and Elsevier.

Craik, F. I. M. (1999). Age-related changes in human memory. In D. C. Park & N. Schwarz (Eds.), *Cognitive aging: A primer* (pp. 75–99). Philadelphia, PA: Psychology Press.

Craik, F. I. M., & Byrd, M. (1982). Aging and cognitive deficits: The role of attentional resources. In F. I. M. Craik & S. E. Trehub (Eds.), *Advances in the study of communication and affect: Vol. 8. Aging and cognitive processes* (pp. 191–211). New York: Plenum.

Crook, T. H., Larrabee, G. J., & Youngjohn, J. (1993). Age and incidental recall for a simulated everyday memory task. *The Journals of Gerontology: Psychological Sciences, 48,* P45–47.

Daselaar, S. M., Fleck, M. S., Dobbins, I. G., Madden, D. J., & Cabeza, R. (2006). Effects of healthy aging on hippocampal and rhinal memory functions: An event-related fMRI study. *Cerebral Cortex, 16,* 1771–1782.

Eichenbaum, H. (2004). Hippocampus: Cognitive processes and neural representations that underlie declarative memory. *Neuron, 44,* 109–120.

Ebner, N. C. (2008). Age of face matters: Age-group differences in ratings of young and old faces. *Behavior Research Methods, 40*(1), 130–136.

Evrard, M. (2002). Ageing and lexical access to common and proper names in picture naming. *Brain & Language, 81,* 174–179.

Gallo, D. A., Sullivan, A. L., Daffner, K. R., Schacter, D. L., & Budson, A. E. (2004). Associative recognition in Alzheimer's disease: Evidence for impaired recall-to-reject. *Neuropsychology, 18,* 556–563.

Hasher, L., & Zacks, R. T. (1979). Automatic and effortful processes in memory. *Journal of Experimental Psychology: General, 108*, 356–388.

Healy, M. R., Light, L. L., & Chung, C. (2005). Dual-process models of associative recognition in young and older adults: Evidence from receiver operating characteristics. *Journal of Experimental Psychology: Learning, Memory, and Cognition, 31*(4), 768–788.

Jacoby, L. L. (1991). A process dissociation framework: Separating automatic from intentional uses of memory. *Journal of Memory and Language, 30*, 513–541.

Jacoby, L. L., & Hay, J. F. (1998). Age-related deficits in memory: Theory and application. In M. A. Conway, S. E. Gathercole, & C. Cornoldi (Eds.), *Theories of memory* (pp. 111–134). Hove, UK: Psychology Press.

Jacoby, L. L., & Rhodes, M. G. (2006). False remembering in the aged. *Current Directions in Psychological Science, 15*(2), 49–53.

Li, S-C., Lindenberger, U., & Sikström, S. (2001). Aging cognition: From neuromodulation to representation. *Trends in Cognitive Sciences, 5*(11), 479–486.

Li, S-C., Naveh-Benjamin, M., & Lindenberger, U. (2005). Aging neuromodulation impairs associative binding: A neurocomputational account. *Psychological Science, 16*(6), 445–450.

Light, L. L. (1991). Memory and aging: Four hypotheses in search of data. *Annual Review of Psychology, 43*, 333–376.

Light, L. L., Patterson, M. M., Chung, C., & Healy, M. R. (2004). Effects of repetition and response deadline on associative recognition in young and older adults. *Memory & Cognition, 32*, 1182–1193.

Light, L. L., Prull, M. W., La Voie, D. J., & Healy, M. R. (2000). Dual-process theories of memory in old age. In T. J. Perfect & E. A. Maylor (Eds.), *Models of cognitive aging* (pp. 238–300). New York: Oxford University Press.

Maylor, E. A. (1997). Proper name retrieval in old age: Converging evidence against disproportionate impairment. *Aging Neuropsychology & Cognition, 4*, 211–226.

McClelland, J. L., McNaughton, B. L., & O'Reilly, R. C. (1995). Why there are complementary learning-systems in the hippocampus and neocortex: Insights from the successes and failures of connectionist models of learning and memory. *Psychological Review, 102*(3), 419–457.

Memon, A., Bartlett, J., Rose, R., & Gray, C. (2003). The aging eyewitness: Effects of age on face, delay, and source-memory ability. *Journal of Gerontology: Psychological Sciences, 58B*, P338–P345.

Miller, E. K., & Cohen, J. D. (2001). An integrative theory of prefrontal cortex function. *Annual Reviews Neuroscience, 24*, 167–202.

Minear, M., & Park, D. C. (2004). A lifespan database of adult facial stimuli. *Behavior Research Methods. Instruments, & Computers, 36*(4), 630–633.

Mitchell, K. J., Johnson, M. K., Raye, C. L., Mather, M., & D'Esposito, M. (2000). Aging and reflective processes of working memory: Binding and testload deficits. *Psychology and Aging, 15*, 527–541.

Moscovitch, M. (1992). Memory and working-with-memory: A component process model based on

modules and central systems. *Journal of Cognitive Neuroscience, 4*, 257–267.

Naveh-Benjamin, M. (2000). Adult age differences in memory performance: Tests of an associative deficit hypothesis. *Journal of Experimental Psychology: Learning, Memory, and Cognition, 26*, 1170–1187.

Naveh-Benjamin, M., Guez, J., Kilb, A., & Reedy, S. (2004). The associative memory deficit of older adults: Further support using face–name associations. *Psychology and Aging, 19*, 541–546.

Naveh-Benjamin, M., Guez, J., & Marom, M. (2003a). The effects of divided attention in young adults and adult-age differences in episodic memory: A common associative deficit mechanism? *Memory & Cognition, 31*, 1021–1035.

Naveh-Benjamin, M., Hussain, Z., Guez, J., & Bar-On, M. (2003b). Adult age differences in episodic memory: Further support for an associative-deficit hypothesis. *Journal of Experimental Psychology: Learning, Memory, and Cognition, 29*, 826–837.

Naveh-Benjamin, M., Keshet Brav, T., & Levy, O. (2007). The associative memory deficit of older adults: The role of strategy utilization. *Psychology and Aging, 22*, 202–208.

Old, S., & Naveh-Benjamin, M. (2008a). Differential effects of age on item and associative measures of memory: A meta-analysis. *Psychology and Aging, 23*, 104–118.

Old, S., & Naveh-Benjamin, M. (2008b). Memory for people and their actions: Further evidence for an age-related associative deficit. *Psychology and Aging, 23*, 467–472.

O'Reilly, R., & Norman, K. A. (2002). Hippocampal and neocortical contributions to memory: Advances in complementary learning systems framework. *Trends in Cognitive Sciences, 6*, 505–510.

Prull, M. W., Dawes, L. L. C., Martin, A. M. III, Rosenberg, H. F., & Light, L. L. (2006). Recollection and familiarity in recognition memory: Adult age differences and neuropsychological test correlates. *Psychology and Aging, 21*, 107–118.

Prull, M. W., Gabrieli, J. D. E., & Bunge, S. A. (2000). Age-related changes in memory: A cognitive neuroscience perspective. In F. I. M. Craik & T. A. Salthouse (Eds.), *The handbook of aging and cognition* (pp. 91–153). Mahwah, NJ: Lawrence Erlbaum Associates Inc.

Raz, N. (2000). Aging of the brain and its impact on cognitive performance: Integration of structural and functional findings. In F. I. M. Craik & T. A. Salthouse (Eds.), *Handbook of aging and cognition* (pp. 1–90). Mahwah, NJ: Lawrence Erlbaum Associates Inc.

Raz, N., Lindenberger, U., Rodrigue, K. M., Kennedy, K. M., Head, D., Williamson, A., et al. (2005). Regional brain changes in aging healthy adults: General trends, individual differences, and modifiers. *Cerebral Cortex, 15*(11), 1676–1689.

Rugg, M. D., & Wilding, E. L. (2000). Retrieval processing and episodic memory. *Trends in Cognitive Sciences, 4*(3), 108–115.

Shing, Y. L., Werkle-Bergner, M., Li, S-C., & Lindenberger, U. (in press a). Associative and strategic components of episodic memory: A lifespan dissociation. *Journal of Experimental Psychology: General.*

Shing, Y. L., Werkle-Bergner, M., Li, S-C., & Lindenberger, U. (in press b). Committing memory errors with high confidence: Older adults do but children don't. *Manuscript submitted for publication.*

Simons, J. S., & Spiers, H. J. (2003). Prefrontal and medial temporal lobe interactions in long-term memory. *Nature Reviews Neuroscience, 4,* 637–648.

Snodgrass, J. G., & Corwin, J. (1988). Pragmatics of measuring recognition memory: Applications to dementia and amnesia. *Journal of Experimental Psychology: General, 117,* 34–50.

Souchay, C., Moulin, C. J. A., Clarys, D., Taconnat, L., & Isingrini, M. (2007). Diminished episodic memory awareness in older adults: Evidence from feeling-of-knowing and recollection. *Consciousness and Cognition, 16,* 769–784.

Treisman, A. (1996). The binding problem. *Current Opinions in Neurobiology, 6,* 171–178.

Wells, G. L., & Olson, E. A. (2003). Eyewitness testimony. *Annual Review of Psychology, 54,* 277–295.

Werkle-Bergner, M., Müller, V., Li, S-C., & Lindenberger, U. (2006). Cortical EEG correlates of successful memory encoding: Implications for lifespan comparisons. *Neuroscience and Biobehavioral Reviews, 30,* 839–854.

Wilson, I. A., Gallagher, M., Eichenbaum, H., & Tanila, H. (2006). Neurocognitive aging: Prior memories hinder new hippocampal encoding. *Trends in Neuroscience, 29*(12), 662–670.

Yonelinas, A. P. (2002). The nature of recollection and familiarity: A review of 30 years of research. *Journal of Memory and Language, 46*(3), 441–517.

Zacks, R. T., Hasher, L., & Li, K. Z. H. (2000). Human memory. In T. A. Salthouse & F. I. M. Craik (Eds.), *Handbook of aging and cognition* (2nd ed., pp. 293–357). Mahwah, NJ: Lawrence Erlbaum Associates Inc.

Zimmer, H. D., Mecklinger, A., & Lindenberger, U. (Eds.).(2006). *Handbook of binding and memory: Perspectives from cognitive neuroscience.* Oxford, UK: Oxford University Press.

MEMORY, 2009, 17 (2), 233–244

Goals-feedback conditions and episodic memory: Mechanisms for memory gains in older and younger adults

Robin L. West, Alissa Dark-Freudeman, and Dana K. Bagwell

University of Florida, Gainesville, FL, USA

Research has established that challenging memory goals always lead to score increases for younger adults, and can increase older adults' scores under supportive conditions. This study examined beliefs and on-task effort as potential mechanisms for these self-regulatory gains, in particular to learn whether episodic memory gains across multiple trials of shopping list recall are controlled by the same factors for young and old people. Goals with feedback led to higher recall and strategic categorisation than a control condition. Strategy usage was the strongest predictor of gains over trials for both age groups. Age, goal condition, and effort also predicted scores across the entire sample. Older adults' gains, but not younger adults' gains, were affected significantly by the interaction of self-efficacy beliefs and goal condition, and condition interacted with locus of control to predict younger adult gains. These results emphasise the importance of self-regulatory effort and positive beliefs for facilitating goal-related memory gains.

Keywords: Memory; Goal setting; Self-efficacy; Memory gains; Older adults.

The power of goals to change behaviour has been evident in decades of research showing the application of goal setting in businesses and schools. Specific, challenging goals lead to significantly higher performance, as compared to no-goal or "do your best" instructions (Locke & Latham, 2002; Schunk & Zimmerman, 1994). Although considerable research addresses goal setting on complex problem-solving tasks (e.g., DeShon & Alexander, 1996), until recently little was known about goal setting for memory (cf. Ackerman & Woltz, 1994; Hinsz & Ployhart, 1998; Wegge, Kleinbeck, & Schmidt, 2001) or the impact of ageing on memory goals (Stadtlander & Coyne, 1990). Now we know that younger adults respond more reliably to memory goals and feedback than older adults (West,

Thorn, & Bagwell, 2003; West, Welch, & Thorn, 2001; West & Yassuda, 2004); however, under ideal conditions where older adults can receive positive feedback, all adults show substantial performance gains, motivation, and goal commitment (West, Bagwell, & Dark-Freudeman, 2005). Mechanisms for these effects are unclear. How are goal-related memory gains achieved? Are score gains predicted by the same factors in old and young people? Given the past literature on ageing, memory, and factors that influence goal-related gains, this project focused on two categories of predictors—factors related to on-task effort (including subjective effort indicators as well as specific strategy measures) and factors related to beliefs (including general as well as more specific beliefs about one's memory ability).

Address correspondence to: Robin Lea West PhD, P.O. Box 112250-Psychology, University of Florida, Gainesville, Florida 32611-2250, USA. E-mail: west51@ufl.edu

Special thanks to On Top of the World retirement community and to Alyson Sincavage for invaluable contributions to this project. This research was supported by the Evelyn F. McKnight Brain Research Foundation.

DOI:10.1080/09658210802236407

ON-TASK EFFORT

In past research, self-regulatory changes in duration, direction, and intensity of effort have been investigated as sources for goal-related change (Locke & Latham, 1994). Not only is willingness to make an effort important, but strategy utilisation is also a key factor in putting additional effort to work effectively to reach higher goal attainments for complex tasks (Lee, Locke, & Latham, 1989). On-task effort associated with goal attainment has been assessed in a variety of ways in past research. For example, Bandura and Cervone (1983) found that goals and feedback combined led to exerted force (measured with an ergometer) that was twice as high as force levels under control conditions. Effort has also been measured by changes in rate of work, or number of tasks completed (Audia, Kristof-Brown, Brown, & Locke, 1996; Schunk & Gunn, 1985). More often the dependent variable of choice is subjective effort, because it reflects the extent to which individuals *perceive* work-level changes (Ferrer-Caja & Weiss, 2002; Hinsz & Ployhart, 1998). Given individual differences in skills, perception of higher effort may reflect goal responsiveness more than actual changes in rate or other objective measures.

For complex tasks, the application of strategic effort in particular may be essential to goal achievement: Bandura and Wood (1989) found that individuals with goals performed best on organisational decision making if they employed analytic strategies, such as systematic testing of single variables. Chesney and Locke (1991) found that goals resulted in higher performance on a management task primarily when good strategies were employed. Successful application of goal-directed strategies requires strategy knowledge or training, practice, and willingness to employ strategic effort (Locke & Latham, 1994).

BELIEFS

Beliefs about one's capability may be related to goal responsiveness as well. If a person does not believe he/she has the capacity to score higher, it may seem fruitless to invest additional effort in trying to make score gains (Bandura, 1997). Goals lead, initially, to motivated effort, but persistence is unlikely for individuals with low self-efficacy because they do not expect their efforts to yield

results. This would tend to reduce motivation and commitment to the goals (Klein, Wesson, Hollenbeck, & Alge, 1999). When goals are highly challenging and individuals perceive that their performance is poor, reductions in self-efficacy and commitment to goals, and decreased performance, can occur over time (Locke & Latham, 1994; West et al., 2001). At the same time, positive feedback under ideal learning conditions can sometimes encourage goal-directed behaviour even for those groups with low self-efficacy, such as older adults (West et al., 2005). Thus, beliefs can affect one's response to a goal, but these beliefs may also interact with specific learning conditions to affect goal-related outcomes.

AGEING, EFFORT, AND BELIEFS

Few previous memory and ageing studies have examined goal prediction mechanisms. Nevertheless, some factors posited above are relevant for predicting age differences in response to memory goals and feedback. For instance, older adults show a more limited repertoire of strategies, less consistent strategy usage, and poorer-quality mediators than younger adults (Dunlosky & Hertzog, 1998; Dunlosky, Hertzog, & Powell-Moman, 2005; Verhaeghen & Marcoen, 1996). If strategic processing predicts episodic memory performance after goals, then older adults may be less responsive to a goal if they are unable to initiate the most effective strategies for that task. The best information-processing strategy for recall of partially categorisable lists, like those used in most ageing studies of goals (see West et al., 2005), is likely to involve some combination of categorical clustering and item-specific processing to create distinctive memory traces (Hunt & McDaniel, 1993). Although these strategies show age differences (Kausler, 1994), over a series of trials, older adults could recognise categories, or identify specific associations, and begin to employ strategies spontaneously (Camp, Markley, & Kramer, 1983). Thus strategic younger adults, and older adults who are able to effectively initiate strategy usage, may benefit most from having a goal.

There is a dearth of data in ageing related to other indicators of effort that might predict performance, largely because few studies of ageing and goal setting have been conducted. In previous goal studies older adults have shown higher self-reported subjective effort and willingness to persist on memory tasks, as compared to younger adults (West et al., 2003, 2005). This could be because the memory task is more novel for the older group; alternatively, greater subjective effort by older adults may be a veridical indicator of their greater difficulty on secondary memory tasks (Kausler, 1994). In any case, none of the previous goal studies shed any light on whether indicators of subjective effort will predict performance outcomes, although goal theory would lead to such an expectation (Locke & Latham, 1990).

Self-efficacy beliefs and feelings of control over memory may also be important mechanisms to investigate and understand ageing in relation to memory gains over goal trials (e.g., Miller & Lachman, 1999; West & Yassuda, 2004). Most older adults see memory decline as normative and inevitable (Lineweaver & Hertzog, 1998). They have little confidence in their ability to remember or to modify inexorable memory decline (Berry & West, 1993; Hultsch, Hertzog, & Dixon, 1987; Miller & Lachman, 1999). Furthermore, concerns about memory become more salient with age, as evidenced by studies of beliefs and impairments due to stereotype threat (Berry & West, 1993; Cavanaugh, Feldman, & Hertzog, 1998; Dark-Freudeman, West, & Viverito, 2006; Hess, Hinson, & Hodges, in press; Levy, 2003; O'Brien & Hummert, 2006). In previous goal-setting research, measures of self-efficacy and control have predicted final trial performance (West et al., 2001; West & Yassuda, 2004). That evidence emphasises the impact of beliefs on goal-directed performance; however, the relative influence of beliefs and on-task effort as mechanisms for goal-related change remains unknown because subjective effort and strategies were not evaluated to predict goal-related gains in past studies.

THE PRESENT RESEARCH

In this study participants were given a baseline trial and then randomly assigned to a goal-feedback or control condition for three subsequent trials. Based on goal theory and previous research, we were confident that goal effects would occur—individuals assigned to a goal-feedback condition should show greater performance gains over trials than a no-goal control condition. Hypotheses about relevant predictive

mechanisms were more exploratory in nature. Although other studies have predicted performance after goal setting (West et al., 2005; West & Yassuda, 2004), they did not focus on changes in performance or beliefs over trials, nor were memory strategies assessed. Because this was the first attempt to investigate strategic mechanisms and dynamic belief changes in relation to other potential predictors for goal-related gains, no specific causal model was tested. Instead we examined factors that seemed likely to yield valuable information, based on goal theory and empirical ageing research, including on-task subjective effort and subjective and objective strategy measures, as well as task-specific and general beliefs about memory. Because this is an exploratory investigation, we also examined the impact of several individual difference factors such as education and self-rated health. Together, this series of analyses provided the first overall picture of the way in which on-task effort, beliefs, and individual differences affect goal responsiveness.

Our objective was to determine which factors, if any, predicted the gains made by old and young after memory goals were set. Based on past research we expected strategies to predict gains, and more so for the younger adults because they employ strategies more effectively. Because success on complex tasks requires effective strategies, we anticipated that subjective effort would be less influential in predicting test scores than strategy utilisation. Based on past goal-setting research we expected beliefs to have some influence on responsiveness to the goal-feedback condition. With respect to ageing we anticipated more effective use of strategies by younger adults, and we expected age differences in beliefs about memory. We also anticipated age interactions for self-evaluative beliefs, due to the greater salience of memory beliefs for older adults than for younger adults, such that self-efficacy and related memory beliefs would more strongly predict goal-feedback responses for the older group.

METHOD

Participants

The participants were 85 community-dwelling older adults who were well educated and healthy, and 96 younger college students. Sample details

TABLE 1
Means and standard deviations (in parentheses) for sample characteristics

Age*	
Younger adults	18.9 (1.4)
Older adults	68.5 (5.9)
Years of Education*	
Younger adults	13.0 (1.2)
Older adults	13.9 (2.5)
Vocabulary*	
Younger adults	29.6 (3.2)
Older adults	33.2 (4.2)
Self-rated Health*	
Younger adults	2.7 (1.4)
Older adults	3.1 (1.7)

*$p < .01$ for age differences.

are noted in Table 1. Data from five participants were dropped due to experimental error. Seven adults were excluded due to stroke or use of anticholinergic medications. Participants were interviewed in groups varying in size from 4 to 14, with an average group size of 8.

Materials and procedures

Memory beliefs. Memory beliefs were examined with three scales from the Metamemory in Adulthood questionnaire (MIA; Dixon, Hultsch, & Hertzog, 1988), the General Memory Efficacy scale (GME; West et al., 2003), and four scales from the Memory Self-Efficacy Questionnaire (MSEQ-4; see West et al., 2005). In previous research the order of presentation of the MSEQ and other memory self-evaluation measures did not affect scores (West et al., 2001); all participants received these questionnaires in the order specified above. The MIA and GME measures were included in order to examine whether individual differences in baseline beliefs predicted responses to goal conditions.

Broadly, individuals were asked to keep in mind "how they used their memory and how they felt about it" when answering the MIA. Three of the MIA subscales were presented: Need for Achievement (Cronbach's $\alpha = .77$); Locus of Control (Cronbach's $\alpha = .70$); and Anxiety (Cronbach's $\alpha = .88$). Negatively worded items were reversed for final scoring. The dependent measure was the average value for each subscale, on a 1–5 Likert scale.

On the GME individuals assessed "your memory performance in the last month or so" for three items, each on a 1–7 Likert scale (West et al., 2003). The dependent measure for the GME was a summed score for three items concerning satisfaction with performance, performance evaluation, and performance compared to peers (range = 3–21). This scale had good internal consistency reliability (Cronbach's $\alpha = .84$).

On the MSEQ-4 individuals indicated whether they could perform a specific memory task by indicating their confidence level on a scale from 0% to 100% confident, where 0% indicated that the individuals could not perform the memory task specified. Four memory subscales are assessed on the MSEQ-4: location recall, shopping list recall, name recall, and story recall. For each one there were five questions, ordered hierarchically from high performance (all items remembered correctly) to low performance (only two items remembered correctly). The dependent measure at baseline and final trial was self-efficacy strength, representing an overall indicator of memory self-efficacy, calculated as the individual's average level of confidence across the 20 items (range = 0–100). This measure had good internal consistency reliability on the baseline assessment (Cronbach's $\alpha = .91$) and on the final assessment (Cronbach's $\alpha = .94$).

Anxiety scale. The state section of the State-Trait Anxiety Scale (STAI; Spielberger, 1983) was administered before baseline to measure arousal in anticipation of memory testing as an individual difference variable. State anxiety scores ranged from 20 to 80 (Cronbach's $\alpha = .90$)

Memory tests. From a pool of over 1000 items (see West et al., 2003), two matched versions of a 48-item shopping list were constructed and each was assigned randomly to half of the participants. Approximately half of the items on each list were categorisable. Using standard procedure for studies of memory goals (see West et al., 2005), all groups studied a relatively short baseline list first (15 items), and a challenging list on Trials 2–4 (48 items), with 1 minute for study and 4 minutes for written recall per trial. The same list was used across trials and participants were given the entire list to examine during the study period. Allowing participants to study the same list for three trials enabled participants to directly observe the new learning that occurred as a function of repeated studying, and helped to maintain motivation. The dependent measures were number correct on each trial, and score gains from baseline to final trial.

Strategy measures. With no previous research on goals and memory strategy usage, a large number of objective and subjective strategy variables were included to identify those with the strongest impact on goal-related gains. Several objective strategy measures were available, including measures of categorical organisation and subjective organisation, both of which have shown age declines (e.g., West & Thorn, 2001; Witte, Freund, & Sebby, 1990). Objective strategy measures included number of categories retrieved, number of items recalled adjacently from the same category (category repetitions), and clustering. Ratio of repetition (RR) was chosen as the clustering measure because it is independent of recall levels and because RR can be calculated even when recall is low (Murphy & Puff, 1982), as it may be for some older adults. Application of appropriate strategies may take time, and goal gains will generally increase over trials as strategy modifications are made. Due to the presence of these lag effects (Audia et al., 1996), gains were evaluated in relation to final-trial strategy variables.

Because half of the list items were not categorisable, it was important to also evaluate measures of subjective organisation; that is, the extent to which a recall protocol was similar from trial to trial. Subjective organisation reflects use of associations by examining the extent to which specific pairs are recalled adjacently across trials, e.g., a point would be given for subjective organisation if an individual recalled "spoon" and "grapefruit" together on two consecutive trials. Subjective organisation measures count both categorical associations and non-categorical associations. Subjective organisation measures included: the number of items recalled both on Trial t and Trial t + 1, the number of pairs of items recalled together on Trial t and Trial t + 1 (order is irrelevant as long as the items are recalled adjacently), and ITR2, (a calculation of bi-directional inter-trial repetitions as an overall indicator of subjective organisation). ITR2 was selected for the overall subjective organisation measure because it correlates best with recall for both older and younger adults (Witte et al., 1990).

Participants also completed a subjective strategy checklist after the final trial (see Camp et al., 1983). They selected their strategies from a list of 14 common techniques, including "I concentrated on each word", "I looked away from the list and tested myself", and "I grouped items into categories". The strategies represented both simple and higher-order strategies (e.g., "in my mind, I pictured items interacting in an active video"). Participants were permitted to check "other" and describe additional strategies. They also indicated which two strategies they used most. Dichotomous strategy usage variables were created for each listed strategy, to reflect its selection (yes or no) as one of the top two strategies. A dichotomous "high category usage" (HCU) variable was included in the analyses.[1] Approximately 55% of participants in both age groups reported that categorisation was one of their most utilised strategies. The total number of endorsed strategies was also examined because flexible utilisation of several strategies is likely to be related positively to performance on mixed lists.

Goal conditions. Using counterbalancing, groups were assigned to the control condition (C) or a goal-feedback condition (GF). Generally speaking, goal-feedback conditions are more likely to yield significant goal-related gains, so that type of goal condition was selected for this investigation (Locke & Latham, 1990). After each trial experimenters reviewed protocols and counted correctly recalled words. Participants in GF received feedback and a goal "to achieve a 50% improvement in your score". Feedback (e.g., "good job—that's a great score", "keep working for the goal") was handwritten on a goal sheet that also listed individuals' scores. To control for the possible impact of experimenter review, experimenters in both conditions checked each protocol; however, participants in the control condition received neither feedback nor a goal.

Final questions. Participants completed final items, each on a 7-point Likert scale: "Did you achieve your goals today?" "How much effort did you make on the memory tasks today?" and "If you had an opportunity to work on another list, to improve your performance, would you do it?" Finally, a standard vocabulary measure (Shipley, 1940) was presented.

---

[1] For each of the strategies selected as "used most often" on the checklist, a dichotomous variable was created, indicating whether the individual had primarily used that strategy or not. We analysed the impact of each of these dichotomous variables on recall scores. None of these variables showed significant effects except for categorisation. The data for categorisation are reported in the paper (details for other strategies are available on request).

RESULTS

Preliminary findings

Preliminary analyses were designed to test whether there were condition differences or interactions of age with condition assignment at baseline. Baseline data were evaluated for age and condition effects on education, health, vocabulary, and baseline recall, and the self-report baseline measures (MIA scales, GME, MSEQ-4, STAI), and total number of strategies utilised. As expected, age differences were present on most measures. Older adults ($M = 3.2$, $SD = .76$) had higher metamemory anxiety than younger adults ($M = 2.9$, $SD = .60$), $F(1, 177) = 9.7$, $p < .005$, $\eta^2 = .05$ but there were no age differences in baseline STAI scores. Older adults ($M = 3.9$, $SD = .45$) cared more about memory achievement than the younger adults ($M = 3.8$, $SD = .43$), $F(1, 177) = 3.8$, $p < .05$, $\eta^2 = .02$. Younger adults ($M = 3.5$, $SD = .48$) had lower locus of control scores than the older adults ($M = 3.7$, $SD = .52$), $F(1, 177) = 4.9$, $p < .05$, $\eta^2 = .03$. Younger adults reported using significantly more strategies than older adults, $F(1, 177) = 23.1$, $p < .001$, $\eta^2 = .12$. There were no age differences on the GME but younger adults had significantly higher MSEQ-4 scores than older adults, $F(1, 176) = 18.5$, $p < .001$, $\eta^2 = .10$. There were no differences based on condition, and no significant interactions of age and condition, indicating a balanced condition assignment.

Goal effects on memory performance

Goal effects were examined in a mixed design with between-participants factors of age (younger, older), HCU (endorsed high or low category usage), and condition (C, GP), and a repeated trial factor. The presence of goal effects would be supported by significant interactions of trial and condition, showing that GF improved performance significantly more than C across trials. Recall showed significant age, $F(1, 172) = 96.1$, $p < .001$, $\eta^2 = .36$, HCU, $F(1, 172) = 13.1$, $p < .001$, $\eta^2 = .07$, and condition effects, $F(1, 172) = 5.3$, $p < .025$, $\eta^2 = .03$, as well as trial-by-trial gains, $F(3, 516) = 1225.3$, $p < .001$, $\eta^2 = .88$ (see Table 2). Age differences were present on all trials, and both age groups showed significant

goal gains, but the younger adults gained more across trials than the older adults, $F(3, 516) = 67.4$, $p < .001$, $\eta^2 = .28$. There were no differences between GF and C at baseline, but there were significant differences on all other trials, resulting in a significant interaction, $F(3, 516) = 8.4$, $p < .001$, $\eta^2 = .05$, with higher performance in GF than C on Trials 2 through 4.

Objective measures of strategy use were examined in a multivariate analysis showing significant effects of age, $F(3, 174) = 24.8$, $p < .001$, $\eta^2 = .30$, condition, $F(3, 174) = 3.9$, $p < .01$, $\eta^2 = .06$, and trial, $F(9, 168) = 377.3$, $p < .001$, $\eta^2 = .95$, with significant interactions of trial by age, $F(9, 168) = 5.0$, $p < .001$, $\eta^2 = .21$, trial by condition, $F(9, 168) = 3.0$, $p < .005$, $\eta^2 = .14$, and trial by condition by age group, $F(9, 168) = 2.7$, $p < .01$, $\eta^2 = .12$. Univariate follow-up analyses confirmed that trial effects were significant for clustering, $F(3, 528) = 30.4$, $p < .001$, $\eta^2 = .15$, number of repetitions, $F(3, 528) = 115.2$, $p < .001$, $\eta^2 = .40$, and number of categories used, $F(3, 528) = 785.2$, $p < .001$, $\eta^2 = .82$. Younger adults recalled more categories than older adults, $F(3, 528) = 38.7$, $p < .001$, $\eta^2 = .18$, and had more repetitions, $F(3, 528) = 9.5$, $p < .005$, $\eta^2 = .05$, but did not show greater clustering. This suggests that clustering was not the sole strategy accounting for younger adults' higher scores (as expected for partially categorisable lists). More categories were recalled by GF than C, $F(3, 528) = 11.6$, $p < .001$, $\eta^2 = .06$. These main effects were qualified by significant interactions of age by trial, for repetitions, $F(3, 528) = 8.4$, $p < .001$, $\eta^2 = .05$, and categories, $F(3, 528) = 9.0$, $p < .005$, $\eta^2 = .05$, due to larger improvements over time by the young participants. Trial by condition interactions were significant for repetitions, $F(3, 528) = 4.2$, $p < .01$, $\eta^2 = .02$, and categories, $F(3, 528) = 3.5$, $p < .05$, $\eta^2 = .02$, due to larger trial-by-trial gains for GF than C. The three-way interaction of age, condition, and trial was significant only for clustering, $F(3, 528) = 2.9$, $p < .05$, $\eta^2 = .02$. The interaction occurred because the younger group showed no difference in clustering between GF and C, whereas older adults' clustering scores in C were significantly lower than GF on Trials 2 and 3. No other effects were significant.

Subjective organisation measures were examined separately from the other clustering indicators because they were assessed only three times; each subjective organisation measure was the result of a comparison of two trials—trials 1 and 2,

TABLE 2
Baseline and final trial means and standard error values (in parentheses) for all repeated measures

	Baseline		*Final trial*	
	Goal	*No Goal*	*Goal*	*No Goal*
Recall				
Younger adults	11.05 (.30)	10.97 (.38)	32.81 (.75)	29.76 (.94)
Older adults	9.24 (.32)	9.76 (.43)	22.98 (.77)	21.48 (1.06)
Number of categories				
Younger adults	2.31 (.06)	2.22 (.08)	5.85 (.08)	5.78 (.10)
Older adults	2.14 (.06)	2.28 (.09)	5.59 (.08)	5.07 (.11)
Category repetitions				
Younger adults	2.36 (.22)	2.16 (.28)	6.22 (.41)	5.24 (.52)
Older adults	2.00 (.23)	2.52 (.32)	4.29 (.42)	4.00 (.59)
Clustering				
Younger adults	.24 (.02)	.20 (.03)	.19 (.01)	.17 (.02)
Older adults	.22 (.02)	.26 (.03)	.19 (.01)	.19 (.02)
Self-efficacy strength				
Younger adults	56.60 (1.85)	58.46 (2.37)	56.37 (2.07)	60.28 (2.66)
Older adults	47.34 (1.90)	49.76 (2.64)	47.30 (2.13)	48.45 (2.96)
State anxiety				
Younger adults	31.54 (1.14)	33.41 (1.44)	33.90 (1.20)	34.35 (1.52)
Older adults	31.64 (1.17)	35.00 (1.62)	34.39 (1.23)	39.21 (1.71)

trials 2 and 3, and trials 3 and 4. Repeated measures analysis, examining the three measures as a function of age and condition, showed significant effects for age, with greater subjective organisation by the younger adults, $F(1, 176) = 7.78$, $p < .01$, $\eta^2 = .04$. These scores also increased across trials, $F(2, 352) = 12.9$, $p < .001$, $\eta^2 = .07$. There was a significant interaction of Trial × Age group × Condition, due to the fact that the older adults in the control condition showed no change over trials in subjective organisation, whereas the young adults in both conditions, and the older adults in the goal condition, showed significant improvements across trials in use of subjective organisation, $F(2, 352) = 3.6$, $p < .05$, $\eta^2 = .02$.

Mechanisms for change

All variables were entered simultaneously in this exploratory investigation of potential mechanisms for goal-related gains. For significant predictors, we have reported standardised Betas and adjusted R^2 values. Tests of multicollinearity were conducted for all analyses; all tolerance values were within acceptable limits. The de-

pendent variable was gain scores, indicating the number of additional recalled words from baseline to final trial. We conducted separate analyses of older and younger adults, hypothesising that predictive factors might vary with age, and also conducted analyses on the full sample.

The gain score represents change over and above baseline test scores, thus it takes into account basic ability variations. Nevertheless, individual differences at baseline might predict subsequent gain in response to goal setting. Thus, we first examined baseline data to see if a priori individual differences—in education, health, vocabulary, state anxiety, metamemory, self-efficacy strength, and general memory self-efficacy—would predict gains. These results were negative. For older adults, no individual difference variables were significant, $F(9, 74) < 1.0$, $p > .50$, $R^2 = .06$, and the same was true for the young adults, $F(9, 85) = 1.7$, $p > .10$, $R^2 = .06$.

We then tested the final trial assessments of on-task effort and beliefs to identify those factors that predicted final trial success. For this analysis we included condition (goal vs control, as a dummy variable), and final trial measures for self-efficacy, subjective effort, willingness to work more, number of strategies used, category repetitions, age, and HCU.[2] For older adults, this regression yielded a strong prediction of gains, $R^2 = .40$, $F(8, 76) = 7.8$, $p < .001$. Significant predictors were repetitions ($B = .59$, $p < .001$), HCU ($B = -.21$, $p < .05$), and age ($B = -.23$, $p < .01$). Subjective effort and condition approached significance ($ps < .10$). For the younger adults, $F(8, 86) = 5.6$, $p < .001$, $R^2 = .28$, the predictors were repetitions ($B = .42$, $p < .001$), and condition ($B = .24$, $p < .01$). Subjective effort, number of strategies, and HCU all approached significance ($ps < .10$). There was considerable overlap in significant predictors for young and old. To understand factors at work for both populations we then repeated the same regression with the entire sample and found that 60% of gains were predicted by condition and on-task effort variables along with age, $F(8, 171) = 34.3$, $p < .001$, $R^2 = .60$. Gains were significantly predicted by age ($B = -.53$, $p < .001$), repetitions ($B = .39$, $p < .001$), HCU ($B = -.14$, $p < .01$), subjective effort ($B = .12$, $p < .05$), and condition ($B = .15$, $p < .005$).

Even though baseline individual differences in beliefs did not, by themselves, predict gains, another series of regressions considered the possibility that the interaction of condition and pre-existing beliefs might contribute to the prediction of gains. Along with the predictors noted above, we added five interactions with condition to the regression: the MIA metamemory scales, self-efficacy strength, and GME score (each of these measures was centred; see Jaccard, Turrisi, & Wan, 1990). Due to reduced degrees of freedom with so many variables we used backward elimination. Backward elimination removes factors, step-by-step, whose predictive value does not approach significance ($p < .10$), starting with the

weakest predictor, to identify a final parsimonious set of predictors.

With the full sample, none of the interactions of beliefs and condition contributed to the final model; the significant factors reported above remained the same, and the Betas had approximately the same order of magnitude. When the older and younger adults were examined separately, however, condition interacted significantly with some baseline individual differences to predict gains. For the older adults, a strong prediction of gains, $F(5, 79) = 13.0$, $p < .001$, $R^2 = .42$, was based on four variables: repetitions ($B = .52$, $p < .001$), condition ($B = .19$, $p < .05$), age ($B = -.22$, $p < .01$), and the interaction of GME and condition ($\beta = .19$, $p < .05$). Follow-up analyses for this interaction examined older adults in the control condition separately, and showed no effect of GME scores in that condition, whereas older adults in the goal-feedback condition with higher GME performed better than those with lower GME scores. For the younger adults the prediction of gain scores, $F(5, 88) = 10.6$, $p < .001$, $R^2 = .34$, was based on significant coefficients for repetitions ($B = .43$, $p < .001$), condition ($B = .24$, $p < .01$), number of strategies ($B = .24$, $p < .01$), HCU ($B = -.19$, $p < .05$), and the interaction of locus of control and condition ($B = -.18$, $p < .05$). Following up this interaction we found no impact of locus of control on younger adults in the training condition, but younger adults in the control condition performed better if they had higher locus of control for memory.

DISCUSSION

Our research confirmed that goal setting in the domain of memory motivates people to increase their performance significantly over conditions without goals. The impact of goals was significant for both older and younger adults, although the response to goals was stronger for the younger adults, as in previous studies (West et al., 2005). The purpose of this research was to identify some possible mechanisms for goal-related gains. The factors examined as possible mechanisms included measures of on-task effort and memory beliefs, looking at baseline individual differences for both old and young participants, as well as final trial assessments.

The primary mechanism for gains was strategy usage, which affected performance along with

---

[2] Because we had numerous subjective and objective indicators of strategy usage, all of the strategy measures available for final trial performance were included in an initial regression analysis to predict gains over trials. To increase the power for the final analysis by reducing the number of indicators, gains were regressed on all of these strategy indicators, using backward elimination to identify the strongest subset of significant predictors from among the strategy variables. This analysis yielded three strategy measures (number of category repetitions, total number of strategies, and HCU) that were not highly correlated with each other, and together predicted the most variance in gain scores. These three variables were then included in all subsequent regressions (details for this preliminary analysis are available on request).

goal condition. Although the specific strategy predictors varied with age, both age groups showed high predictive power for repetitions and categorisation. Clearly, individuals making an effort to utilise categories showed the highest score gains. This result mirrors decades of work in the developmental literature showing the relationship between knowledge of strategies, strategy usage, and episodic memory performance (e.g., Neimark, 1976; Pressley, Borkowski, & Schneider, 1987). In this study the number of strategies was also a predictor, but for younger adults only. These effects were significant over and above the impact of age and condition. This evidence for a strategic advantage confirmed literature in other cognitive domains showing that strategies reflect action plans motivated by goals (Boekaerts, 1997; Brown & Pressley, 1994; DeShon & Alexander, 1996). Adults seek out a means to accomplish their goals, and strategies are clearly a key means to achieve success (Locke & Latham, 1994).

The interesting finding here is that strategies were a predictor for older adults. This was surprising given episodic memory deficits in ageing (e.g., Bäckman, Small, & Wahlin, 2001) and related age differences in strategy usage (Kausler, 1994). Recently there has been considerable discussion of older adult strategy usage (Dunlosky et al., 2005), building on previous research showing that older adults did not spontaneously utilise episodic memory strategies (Kausler, 1994), and had difficulty employing strategies effectively, even when instructed to do so (e.g., Verhaeghen & Marcoen, 1996). Here, the older adults did use strategies effectively to raise performance. Along with the younger adults, the older adults showed significantly higher use of repetitions and categories in the goal condition. They were able to spontaneously activate this strategic processing with no instruction. Even though strategy variations do not appear to account for age differences in performance, they do account for increased performance in previous studies (Dunlosky & Hertzog, 1998). It may be that some kind of motivational incentive, such as having a goal, is key to the effective activation of strategies by older adults. It may also be the case that categorisation is an easier strategy for older adults to initiate than the more complex mediational strategies needed for other types of memory tasks (West, Bagwell, & Dark-Freudeman, 2008), especially with a more familiar episodic memory task such as shopping list recall. The

value of self-generated strategies for older adults' performance may vary with task requirements (Derwinger, Stigsdotter Neely, Persson, Hill, & Bäckman, 2003; Verhaeghen & Marcoen, 1996). One interesting question for future exploration is whether older adults would successfully employ strategies, and achieve goal-related gains, on more complicated memory tasks such as name recall or story recall, where their lack of familiarity with higher-level strategy alternatives might impair their ability to respond to goals.

Our analysis of gain mechanisms may shed light on age differences in previous studies. First, we know that clustering at retrieval does not account for age differences; younger adults gained more over trials even though older adults used clustering as much as younger adults. It could still be the case, however, that age variations in the effectiveness of strategy usage could explain greater gains made by the young (e.g., Dunlosky et al., 2005). The quality of strategic associations may be as important as quantity in predicting memory outcomes (Hertzog, Lineweaver, & McGuire, 1999; Verhaeghen & Marcoen, 1996). It is interesting to note that, for younger adults only, the attempt to employ an array of strategies was a significant predictor. The most likely interpretations are that younger adults had a larger repertoire of strategies available to them, or were more likely to notice that many items were uncategorisable. When older adults were motivated by goals, they activated relatively simple strategies—concentrate and organise items into categories. When the younger adults were similarly motivated they used organisation, but they also flexibly utilised other strategies, such as imagery and association. It is not clear whether the older adults were unfamiliar with strategy alternatives, due to past lack of training or lack of usage of complex strategies; if their inability to employ multiple strategies reflected processing limitations (Dunlosky & Hertzog, 1998; Dunlosky et al., 2005; Verhaeghen & Marcoen, 1994); or if failure to use more strategies could be related to lack of confidence in their memory skills (Touron & Hertzog, 2004).

Interestingly, those younger adults with a low sense of control over memory were less likely to show gains in the control condition than younger adults with a high sense of control. This finding confirmed the results of West and Yassuda (2004) who examined the impact of control beliefs (using a very different measure of control) on performance under goal conditions. In the control condition in that investigation, individuals with feelings of high control over memory at baseline had higher performance than those with feelings of low control, and this effect occurred for both age groups. The low-control groups performed well only when given a goal (West & Yassuda, 2004).

As expected, memory self-efficacy played a stronger role for the older than for the younger participants. The results suggested that beliefs can act as an impediment to goal activation for older adults—the lower-self-efficacy participants showed weaker goal effects than the high-self-efficacy participants. High-self-efficacy older adults had greater initial confidence in their abilities, and were more likely to show consistent gains on the task when given a goal. Self-efficacy was not a significant predictor for the total sample or for the young adults alone. Mixed findings in the past, about the relationship between self-efficacy and performance, may be related to the use of combined samples (cf. Berry, West, & Dennehy, 1989; Hertzog, Dixon, & Hultsch, 1990; West, Dennehy-Basile, & Norris, 1996; West et al., 2001, 2008). Attitudes towards one's own memory capabilities are more salient for older adults than younger adults, due to age-related deficits (Bandura, 1997). These findings reinforced the notion that self-efficacy has value as a predictor of performance for older adults more so than for the young (Berry & West, 1993; Cavanaugh et al., 1998; Hultsch et al., 1987).

Some possible mechanisms for goal gains, such as changes in speed of processing or attentional shifts, could not be examined in the group-interview paradigm employed here; these may be important mechanisms to examine in future research. Strategy usage could be related to speed of processing (Verhaeghen & Marcoen, 1996) or it could be the case that individuals who showed higher gains selectively allocated their encoding time to unlearned items. Another potentially important factor, strategic persistence, was not examined (see Borkowski & Thorpe, 1994); successful individuals could have worked to identify memorable distinctive connections between the uncategorisable items. Even with these limitations, the approach used here represents an important contribution because no other studies, to our knowledge, have examined the relative value of strategies to predict gains, in relation to other self-regulatory factors.

These results suggest that a strategy checklist, completed immediately after a memory task, is a valuable method for assessing strategy usage. Two of our significant predictors—number of strategies and HCU—derived from that checklist, were stronger predictors of gains than more objective measures such as clustering. This does not necessarily mean that all self-report strategy indicators will be veridical (see Dunlosky & Hertzog, 2001). However, successful prediction of gain scores by variables taken from the checklist confirms that self-reports of strategy usage can yield important results (cf. deFrias, Dixon, & Bäckman, 2003; Dunlosky & Hertzog, 1998; Hill, Allen, & Gregory, 1990).

A growing set of literature in memory ageing documents the positive influence of goals on memory performance, and the greater responsiveness to goals on the part of younger adults, suggesting an association between youth and self-regulatory control. This research replicated those common findings and went beyond the basic outcomes to explore some possible mechanisms for goal-related gains. Across a wide age range, the key factors predicting gains were condition differences (goals or no goals), strategy use, and age, although other factors played a significant role only for the older adults (self-efficacy) or the younger adults (locus of control). Analysis of a number of other potential mechanisms for goal-related change (e.g., faster speed of processing; attentional changes), and investigation of the generalisability of these mechanisms to other types of memory tasks (e.g., prose recall, delayed recall), await further research.

REFERENCES

Ackerman, P. L., & Woltz, D. J. (1994). Determinants of learning and performance in an associative memory/ substitution task: Task constraints, individual differences, volition, and motivation. *Journal of Educational Psychology, 86*, 487–515.

Audia, G., Kristof-Brown, A., Brown, K. G., & Locke, E. A. (1996). Relationship of goals and microlevel work processes to performance on a multipath manual task. *Journal of Applied Psychology, 81*, 483–497.

Bäckman, L., Small, B. J., & Wahlin, Å. (2001). Aging and memory: Cognitive and biological perspectives. In J. E. Birren & K. W. Schaie (Eds.), *Handbook of the psychology of aging* (5th ed., pp. 349–377). San Diego, CA: Academic Press.

Bandura, A. (1997). *Self-efficacy: The exercise of control*. New York: Freeman.

Bandura, A., & Cervone, D. (1983). Self-evaluative and self-efficacy mechanisms governing the motivational effects of goal systems. *Journal of Personality and Social Psychology, 45*, 1017–1028.

Bandura, A., & Wood, R. (1989). Effect of perceived controllability and performance standards on self-regulation of complex decision making. *Journal of Personality and Social Psychology, 56*, 805–814.

Berry, J. M., & West, R. L. (1993). Cognitive self-efficacy in relation to personal mastery and goal setting across the life span. *International Journal of Behavioural Development, 16*, 351–379.

Berry, J. M., West, R. L., & Dennehey, D. M. (1989). Reliability and validity of the Memory Self-Efficacy Questionnaire. *Developmental Psychology, 25*, 701–713.

Boekaerts, M. (1997). Self-regulated learning: A new concept embraced by researchers, policy makers, educators, teachers, and students. *Learning and Instruction, 7*, 161–186.

Borkowski, J. G., & Thorpe, P. K. (1994). Self-regulation and motivation: A life-span perspective on underachievement. In D. H. Schunk & B. J. Zimmerman (Eds.), *Self-regulation of learning and performance* (pp. 45–73). Hillsdale, NJ: Lawrence Erlbaum Associates Inc.

Brown, R., & Pressley, M. (1994). Self-regulated reading and getting meaning from text: The transactional strategies instruction model and its ongoing validation. In D. H. Schunk & B. J. Zimmerman (Eds.), *Self-regulation of learning and performance* (pp. 155–179). Hillsdale, NJ: Lawrence Erlbaum Associates Inc.

Camp, C. J., Markley, R. P., & Kramer, J. J. (1983). Spontaneous use of mnemonics by elderly individuals. *Educational Gerontology, 9*, 57–71.

Cavanaugh, J. C., Feldman, J. M., & Hertzog, C. (1998). Memory beliefs as social cognition: A reconceptualization of what memory questionnaires assess. *Review of General Psychology, 2*, 48–65.

Chesney, A. A., & Locke, E. A. (1991). Relationships among goal difficulty, business strategies, and performance on a complex management simulation task. *Academy of Management Journal, 34*, 400–424.

Dark-Freudeman, A., West, R. L., & Viverito, K. M. (2006). Future selves and ageing: Older adults' memory fears. *Educational Gerontology, 32*, 85–109.

deFrias, C. M., Dixon, R. A., & Bäckman, L. (2003). Use of memory compensation strategies is related to psychosocial and health indicators. *Journal of Gerontology: Psychological Sciences, 58B*, P12–P22.

Derwinger, A., Stigsdotter Neely, A., Persson, M., Hill, R. D., & Bäckman, L. (2003). Remembering numbers in old age: Mnemonic training versus self-generated strategy training. *Aging, Neuropsychology, and Cognition, 10*, 202–214.

DeShon, R. P., & Alexander, R. A. (1996). Goal setting effects on implicit and explicit learning of complex tasks. *Organisational Behaviour and Human Decision Processes, 65*, 18–36.

Dixon, R. A., Hultsch, D. F., & Hertzog, C. (1988). The Metamemory in Adulthood (MIA) Questionnaire. *Psychopharmacology Bulletin, 24*, 671–688.

Dunlosky, J., & Hertzog, C. (1998). Ageing and deficits in associative memory: What is the role of strategy production? *Psychology and Aging, 13*, 597–607.

Dunlosky, J., & Hertzog, C. (2001). Measuring strategy production during associative learning: The relative utility of concurrent versus retrospective reports. *Memory & Cognition, 29*, 247–253.

Dunlosky, J., Hertzog, C., & Powell-Moman, A. (2005). The contribution of mediator-based deficiencies to age differences in associative learning. *Developmental Psychology, 41*, 389–400.

Ferrer-Caja, E., & Weiss, M. R. (2002). Cross-validation of a model of intrinsic motivation with students enrolled in high school elective courses. *Journal of Experimental Education, 71*, 41–65.

Hertzog, C., Dixon, R. A., & Hultsch, D. F. (1990). Relationships between metamemory, memory predictions, and memory task performance in adults. *Psychology and Aging, 5*, 215–227.

Hertzog, C., Lineweaver, T. T., & McGuire, C. L. (1999). Beliefs about memory and aging. In T. M. Hess & F. Blanchard-Fields (Eds.), *Social cognition and aging* (pp. 43–68). San Diego, CA: Academic Press.

Hess, T. M., Hinson, J. T., & Hodges, E. A. (in press). Moderators of and mechanisms underlying stereotype threat effects on older adults' memory performance. *Experimental Aging Research.*

Hill, R. D., Allen, C., & Gregory, K. (1990). Self-generated mnemonics for enhancing free recall performance in older learners. *Experimental Aging Research, 16*, 141–145.

Hinsz, V. B., & Ployhart, R. E. (1998). Trying, intentions, and the processes by which goals influence performance: An empirical test of the theory of goal pursuit. *Journal of Applied Social Psychology, 28*, 1051–1066.

Hultsch, D. F., Hertzog, C., & Dixon, R. A. (1987). Age differences in metamemory: Resolving the inconsistencies. *Canadian Journal of Psychology, 41*, 193–208.

Hunt, R. R., & McDaniel, M. A. (1993). The enigma of organisation and distinctiveness. *Journal of Memory and Language, 32*, 421–445.

Jaccard, J., Turrisi, R., & Wan, C. K. (1990). Implications of behavioural decision theory and social marketing for designing social action programs. In J. Edwards & R. S. Tindale (Eds.), *Social influence processes and prevention* (pp. 103–142). New York: Plenum Press.

Kausler, D. H. (1994). *Learning and memory in normal aging.* San Diego, CA: Academic Press.

Klein, H. J., Wesson, M. J., Hollenbeck, J. R., & Alge, B. J. (1999). Goal commitment and the goal-setting process: Conceptual clarification and empirical synthesis. *Journal of Applied Psychology, 84*, 885–896.

Lee, T. W., Locke, E. A., & Latham, G. P. (1989). Goal setting theory and job performance. In L. A. Pervin (Ed.), *Goal concepts in personality and social psychology* (pp. 291–326). Hillsdale, NJ: Lawrence Erlbaum Associates Inc.

Levy, B. R. (2003). Mind matters: Cognitive and physical effects of ageing self-stereotypes. *Journal of Gerontology: Psychological Sciences, 58B*, P203–P216.

Lineweaver, T. T., & Hertzog, C. (1998). Adults' efficacy and control beliefs regarding memory and ageing: Separating general from personal beliefs. *Aging, Neuropsychology, and Cognition, 5*, 264–296.

Locke, E. A., & Latham, G. P. (1990). *A theory of goal setting and task performance.* Englewood Cliffs, NJ: Prentice-Hall.

Locke, E. A., & Latham, G. P. (1994). Goal setting theory. In H. F. J. O'Neil & M. Drillings (Eds.), *Motivation: Theory and research* (pp. 13–29). Hillsdale, NJ: Lawrence Erlbaum Associates Inc.

Locke, E. A., & Latham, G. P. (2002). Building a practically useful theory of goal setting and task motivation: A 35-year odyssey. *American Psychologist, 57*, 705–717.

Miller, L. M. S., & Lachman, M. E. (1999). The sense of control and cognitive ageing: Toward a model of mediational processes. In T. M. Hess & F. Blanchard-Fields (Eds.), *Social cognition and aging* (pp. 17–41). San Diego, CA: Academic Press.

Murphy, M. D., & Puff, C. R. (1982). Free recall: Basic methodology and analyses. In C. R. Puff (Ed.), *Handbook of research methods in human memory and cognition* (pp. 99–128). New York: Academic Press.

Neimark, E. D. (1976). The natural history of spontaneous mnemonic activity under conditions of minimal experimental constraint. In A. D. Pick (Ed.), *Minnesota symposium on child psychology Vol. 10.* Minneapolis, MN: University of Minnesota Press.

O'Brien, L. T., & Hummert, M. L. (2006). Memory performance of late middle-aged adults: Contrasting self-stereotyping and stereotype threat accounts of assimilation to age stereotypes. *Social Cognition, 24*, 338–358.

Pressley, M., Borkowski, J. G., & Schneider, W. (1987). Cognitive strategies: Good strategy users coordinate metacognition and knowledge. In R. Vasta & G. Whitehurst (Eds.), *Annals of child development* (Vol. 4 (pp. 89–129)). Greenwich, CT: JAI Press.

Schunk, D. H., & Gunn, T. P. (1985). Modeled importance of task strategies and achievement beliefs: Effect on self-efficacy and skill development. *Journal of Early Adolescence, 5*, 247–258.

Schunk, D. H., & Zimmerman, B. J. (1994). *Self-regulation of learning and performance: Issues and educational applications.* Hillsdale, NJ: Lawrence Erlbaum Associates Inc.

Shipley, W. C. (1940). A self-administering scale for measuring intellectual impairment and deterioration. *Journal of Psychology: Interdisciplinary & Applied, 9*, 371–377.

Spielberger, C. D. (1983). *State-Trait Anxiety Inventory for adults.* Palo Alto, CA: Mind Garden.

Stadtlander, L. M., & Coyne, A. C. (1990). The effect of goal-setting and feedback on age differences in secondary memory. *Experimental Ageing Research, 16*, 91–94.

Touron, D. R., & Hertzog, C. (2004). Distinguishing age differences in knowledge, strategy use, and confidence during strategic skill acquisition. *Psychology and Aging, 19*, 452–466.

Verhaeghen, P., & Marcoen, A. (1994). Production deficiency hypothesis revisited: Adult age differences in strategy use as a function of processing resources. *Aging, Neuropsychology, and Cognition, 1*, 323–338.

Verhaeghen, P., & Marcoen, A. (1996). On the mechanisms of plasticity in young and older adults after instruction in the method of loci: Evidence for an amplification model. *Psychology and Aging, 11*, 164–178.

Wegge, J., Kleinbeck, U., & Schmidt, K-H. (2001). Goal setting and performance in working memory and short-term-memory tasks. In M. Erez & U. Kleinbeck (Eds.), *Work motivation in the context of a globalizing economy* (pp. 49–72). Mahwah, NJ: Lawrence Erlbaum Associates Inc.

West, R. L., Bagwell, D. K., & Dark-Freudeman, A. (2005). Memory and goal setting: The response of older and younger adults to positive and objective feedback. *Psychology and Aging, 20*, 195–201.

West, R. L., Bagwell, D. K., & Dark-Freudeman, A. (2008). Self-efficacy and memory aging: The impact of a memory intervention based on self-efficacy. *Aging Neuropsychology and Cognition, 15*, 302–329.

West, R. L., Dennehy-Basile, D., & Norris, M. P. (1996). Memory self-evaluation: The effects of age and experience. *Aging and Cognition, 3*, 67–83.

West, R. L., & Thorn, R. M. (2001). Goal-setting, self-efficacy, and memory performance in older and younger adults. *Experimental Aging Research, 27*, 41–65.

West, R. L., Thorn., R. M., & Bagwell, D. K. (2003). Memory performance and beliefs as a function of goal setting and aging. *Psychology and Aging, 18*, 111–125.

West, R. L., Welch, D. C., & Thorn, R. M. (2001). Effects of goal-setting and feedback on memory performance and beliefs among older and younger adults. *Psychology and Aging, 16*, 240–250.

West, R. L., & Yassuda, M. S. (2004). Ageing and memory control beliefs: Performance in relation to goal setting and memory self-evaluation. *Journal of Gerontology: Psychological Sciences, 59*, 56–65.

Witte, K. L., Freund, J. S., & Sebby, R. A. (1990). Age differences in free recall and subjective organisation. *Psychology and Aging, 5*, 307–309.

MEMORY, 2009, 245–260

Ageing and the self-reference effect in memory*

Angela H. Gutchess

Harvard University and Massachusetts General Hospital, MA, USA

Elizabeth A. Kensinger

Boston College and Massachusetts General Hospital, MA, USA

Carolyn Yoon

University of Michigan, MI, USA

Daniel L. Schacter

Harvard University and Massachusetts General Hospital, MA, USA

The present study investigates potential age differences in the self-reference effect. Young and older adults incidentally encoded adjectives by deciding whether the adjective described them, described another person (Experiments 1 & 2), was a trait they found desirable (Experiment 3), or was presented in upper case. Like young adults, older adults exhibited superior recognition for self-referenced items relative to the items encoded with the alternate orienting tasks, but self-referencing did not restore their memory to the level of young adults. Furthermore, the self-reference effect was more limited for older adults. Amount of cognitive resource influenced how much older adults benefit from self-referencing, and older adults appeared to extend the strategy less flexibly than young adults. Self-referencing improves older adults' memory, but its benefits are circumscribed despite the social and personally relevant nature of the task.

Studies of young adults demonstrate that relating information to oneself is a successful encoding strategy. Self-reference judgements are associated with increased levels of memory compared to making semantic judgements or relating the information to another person such as one's mother or Johnny Carson (e.g., Rogers, Kuiper, & Kirker, 1977; see Symons & Johnson, 1997, for a review). Although there has been debate over the mechanisms of self-referencing and whether the self is a "special" construct that engages unique organisational and elaborative processes (e.g., Greenwald & Banaji, 1989), functional neuroimaging evidence suggests the self engages a unique module and specialised elaborative processes that are not shared by other "deep", or semantically meaningful, judgements (Kelley et al., 2002).

Because self-referencing benefits memory and operates above and beyond depth of processing manipulations (Craik & Lockhart, 1972; Craik & Tulving, 1975), it is surprising that self-referencing has not been extensively investigated in older adults, who sometimes do not benefit as much as

Address correspondence to: Dr Angela Gutchess, Brandeis University, Department of Psychology, MS 062 P.O. Box 549110, Waltham, MA 02454, USA. E-mail: gutchess@brandeis.edu or gutchess@nmr.mgh.harvard.edu

Support for the research was provided by the National Institutes of Health grants R01 AG008441 (to D.L.S.), F32 AG026920 (to A.H.G.), and MH 070199 (to E.A.K.), University of Michigan UROP Supplementary Research Funding, and the Ross School of Business. The authors gratefully acknowledge the experimental assistance provided by Nick Gonzalez, Ashley Eason, Nicole Williams, Jess DeBartolo, Linyun Yang, and in particular, Emily Nelson, who also contributed through her insights into this research.

*Please note that this paper is a reprint of a paper that was originally published in 2007 in *Memory, 15*(8), 822–837.

http://www.psypress.com/memory   DOI:10.1080/09658210701701394

young from "deep" encoding manipulations (Kausler, 1994). At least three areas of research make the self-reference effect of interest to study in older populations: the self is a personally meaningful construct, and therefore may provide an encoding strategy that effectively can support older adults' memory; the self is linked to motivational and social goals, which take on increased importance with ageing; and self-referential encoding could potentially place reduced demands on cognitive resources. Each of these is discussed in turn.

Ageing is marked by cognitive impairments in a number of domains (e.g., Park et al., 2002; Salthouse, 1996), including long-term memory, but older adults' memory performance is malleable. As is the case for young adults, strategies and orientations that engage "deep" encoding processes benefit older adults (e.g., Erber, Herman, & Botwinick, 1980; Eysenck, 1974). Self-referential processing shares elaborative and organisational properties with other deep encoding strategies (Klein & Loftus, 1988) but the benefits of self-referencing extend beyond a simple depth of processing manipulation (Kelley et al., 2002). It could be that the rich structure of the self constitutes a familiar and natural encoding strategy. These properties may be particularly important for older adults' encoding success (Castel, 2005) and could mitigate difficulties with self-initiating encoding strategies with age (Hultsch, 1969). For example, older adults exhibit increased recall when using self-generated strategies that rely on personally relevant information (e.g., important birthdates) relative to other mnemonic strategies (Derwinger, Neely, MacDonald, & Bäckman, 2005). The self-concept is relatively stable throughout the lifespan, with adults undergoing modest changes in personality (Terracciano, McCrae, Brant, & Costa, 2005) and there is a large overlap in self-schema across the age groups (Mueller & Johnson, 1990; Mueller, Wonderlich, & Dugan, 1986). Thus, the highly familiar and meaningful structure of the self could support accurate memory.

Because older adults do not always benefit from "deep", or semantic, encoding strategies to the same extent as young adults (Kausler, 1994), it is all the more important to consider the additional mnemonic benefits that are offered by self-referencing. Given the inherently social and emotional nature of the self, older adults may benefit disproportionately from self-referential encoding relative to young adults. Socioemotional processing sometimes confers greater benefits to older adults than young adults compared to neutral or negative processes. Older adults may be more motivated than young adults to maintain positive affect and to exercise controlled processing in order to devote attention to positive socioemotional information, which can lead to superior memory for positive information (Charles, Mather, & Carstensen, 2003; Mather & Carstensen, 2005; Mather & Knight, 2005). Beyond memory improvements for positively valenced information, age-related source memory impairments (e.g., Hashtroudi, Johnson, & Chrosniak, 1989; Schacter, Kaszniak, Kihlstrom, & Valdiserri, 1991) can be eliminated when source information is situated as relative to one's safety or potential to be deceived (May, Rahhal, Berry, & Leighton, 2005; Rahhal, May, & Hasher, 2002). Although these preserved pockets of source memory have been discussed in terms of the prioritisation of emotional information in memory, the participant him- or herself is incorporated into the framing of the problem and the memorial benefits could stem, at least in part, from self-referencing. Based on these findings, orienting to the self could boost memory to the same level in older adults as in young adults, which would contrast with older adults' poorer memory for words encoded using a shallow or semantic task.

Self-referencing may place minimal demands on cognitive resources, which would make the strategy particularly beneficial for older adults. Neuroimaging data indicate that self-referential encoding differs from other encoding strategies in that it engages different neural regions. Whereas semantic or "deep" encoding tasks activate inferior prefrontal regions often associated with controlled processing, self-referencing activates medial prefrontal cortex (Kelley et al., 2002; Macrae, Moran, Heatherton, Banfield, & Kelley, 2004). Medial prefrontal cortex has been implicated in social information processing (Mitchell, Macrae, & Banaji, 2005), but it is unknown to what extent the region contributes to *cognitive* processes. It may be the case that processes that engage medial prefrontal cortex are not as cognitively demanding as processes that draw on other prefrontal regions that contribute to controlled processing. This idea is intriguing because medial prefrontal cortex appears to be less prone to age-related decline, in contrast to many other prefrontal regions that are implicated in cognitively demanding processes. Young and older adults similarly engage medial prefrontal cortex during self-referencing decisions (Gutchess, Kensinger, & Schacter, 2007) and structural data suggest that medial prefrontal regions show little decline with age (Salat et al., 2004). Literature on early development also suggests that the self-reference effect may not depend on the availability of cognitive resources; the effect emerges by age 5 (Sui & Zhu, 2005) and is unaffected by further cognitive development between the ages of 7 and 11 (Pullyblank, Bisanz, Scott, & Champion, 1985). While it is possible that self-referencing is not heavily cognitively demanding, the wide extent of encoding deficits with age (Kausler, 1994) and the finding that medial prefrontal cortex is implicated in successful encoding (Macrae et al., 2004) make it likely that the availability of cognitive resources plays at least some part in supporting recognition. Older adults are an ideal population with which to explore the role of cognitive resources in self-referencing because resources can be limited and vary widely across individuals.

Although it is unclear to what extent the benefits of self-referencing require cognitive resources, the task employed in the one existing study of self-referencing with an older population suggests it may be particularly cognitively demanding. Mueller et al. (1986) measured memory with recall, which suffers heavy impairments with age relative to recognition (Craik & McDowd, 1987). They found that while the memorial benefit of self-referencing extends to older adults, older adults recalled less information than young adults. However, it is possible that under conditions that are less cognitively demanding, such as recognition, self-referencing could lead to similar levels of memory in young and older adults. Thus, it is necessary to study self-referencing with tasks other than recall, particularly because recall can be driven by pre-existing associations in which case the words recalled could reflect the self-schema more than the episodic memory trace (Ferguson, Rule, & Carlson, 1983).

The present study investigates potential age differences in the self-reference effect using recognition memory. We investigate young and older adults' memory for self-referenced information and explore the extent to which cognitive resources and socioemotional orientation affect the benefits of self-referencing. We predict that the self-reference effect should extend to older adults and perhaps even be enhanced relative to semantic or shallow processing orientations because older adults prioritise socioemotional

information and the primary neural region implicated in self-referencing (i.e., medial prefrontal cortex) is relatively preserved with age. However, if cognitive resources contribute substantially to the self-reference effect, older adults could benefit less than young adults from self-referencing. Specifically, we investigate (1) whether the magnitude of the self-reference effect is similar for young and older adults, (2) the role of cognitive resources in self-referencing with age, and (3) the contribution of socioemotional orientation to self-referencing benefits with age.

EXPERIMENT 1

Method

Participants. A total of 24 young adults (age range 18–20) from the University of Michigan and 24 older adults (age range 60–82) from the surrounding Ann Arbor community participated in the study and were compensated with either course credit or payment. Characteristics of these samples, including age, gender, years of education, speed of processing, and vocabulary scores, are presented in Table 1.[1] Consistent with samples in the majority of cognitive ageing studies, older adults had significantly more years of education than young adults, $t(46) = 4.05$, $p < .001$, and better vocabulary scores, $t(46) = 4.87$, $p < .001$, suggesting preserved crystallised knowledge. Young adults exhibited greater processing capacity, completing significantly more items than older adults on the speed of processing tasks: digit comparison, $t(46) = 3.03$, $p < .005$, and pattern comparison, $t(46) = 4.54$, $p < .001$.

Materials. A set of 288 adjectives were selected from Craik et al. (1999), drawn primarily from Anderson's (1968) adjective norms. The adjectives were divided into subsets with approximately equal numbers of positive and negative adjectives. Word sets were assigned to three different yes/no judgements: Self (i.e., does this word describe me?), Other Person (i.e., does this word describe Albert Einstein?), or Case (i.e., is this word displayed in upper case?). These conditions are alike in that they require orientation to a specific aspect of the word. They also allow for a contrast of deep (i.e., self and other person)

---

[1] Due to omission of responses, ages are unavailable for one young and one older adult.

TABLE 1
Participant demographics from Experiments 1–3 (means and *SD*)

	Experiment 1		Experiment 2		Experiment 3	
	Young	*Older*	*Young*	*Older*	*Young*	*Older*
Age	19.50 (.79)	68.50 (5.64)	20.46 (2.51)	71.03 (4.60)	19.61 (2.25)	71.11 (5.80)
N	24	24	30	60	18	18
Gender	13M, 11F	9M, 15F	15M, 15F	25M, 35F	8M, 10F	5M, 13F
Years of education	12.96 (1.06)	15.25 (2.56)	13.35 (1.02)	16.17 (2.61)	13.47 (1.74)	17.42 (2.68)
Digit comparison	74.46 (12.63)	62.54 (14.54)	73.83 (10.11)	58.10 (10.04)	76.35 (11.92)	60.06 (12.58)
Pattern comparison	57.33 (11.11)	44.04 (9.06)	58.80 (9.70)	46.17 (9.42)	N/A	N/A
Shipley vocabulary	31.42 (2.47)	35.75 (3.59)	29.37 (5.25)	35.75 (3.44)	34.39 (3.15)	35.65 (4.54)

with shallow (i.e., case) encoding conditions, and the comparison of self with a comparable social condition, as in previous studies (e.g., Craik et al., 1999; Kelley et al., 2002). Words were presented in Arial 24-point font. Half of the words in each condition, including lures, were randomly selected to appear in all upper case letters, whereas the remaining half of the words appeared in all lower case letters. Case was relevant only for the upper case judgement condition, but varied within each condition to control for perceptual characteristics of the stimuli.

Because the self-concept is complex and generally positive (e.g., people endorse more positive than negative items), it is difficult to match a personally unfamiliar other to the self. Pilot ratings from 25 young and 25 older adults suggested that Albert Einstein was a reasonable choice out of a number of famous people rated on nine-point scales (1 = low, 9 = high) because he was regarded as both positive (young $M = 7.20$, $SD = 1.39$; older adults $M = 7.44$, $SD = 1.47$) and familiar (young $M = 6.80$, $SD = 1.52$; older adults $M = 7.12$, $SD = 1.69$) by young and older adults ($ts < 1$).

Procedures. Participants provided written informed consent for a protocol approved by the University of Michigan Behavioral Sciences Institutional Review Board. After receiving instruction and practice on the adjective judgement task, participants incidentally encoded adjectives by making self, other, and case judgements. Adjectives were presented on the computer screen for 4 seconds, during which time the participants pressed a labelled key on a computer keyboard to provide a "yes" (i.e., adjective describes me/Einstein; adjective is displayed in upper case) or "no" (i.e., adjective does not describe me/Einstein; adjective is not displayed in upper case)

response. A total of 144 adjectives were encoded, with 48 adjectives assigned to each of the three conditions (self, other, and case). Three counterbalanced orderings allowed the adjectives to be assigned to each condition across participants, and trials were presented in a random order, unique to each participant.

During a 10-minute retention interval participants completed measures including a digit comparison task (Hedden, Park, Nisbett, Li, & Jing, 2002) and a pattern comparison task (Salthouse & Babcock, 1991) to assess speed of processing. Participants then received instructions for the surprise recognition test, which was self-paced on the computer. Participants responded by pressing keys labelled "yes" to denote a previously studied word or "no" to denote a new word. Recognition was tested for all 144 encoded adjectives and 144 lures. Instructions placed equal emphasis on responding with accuracy and speed. Tasks were presented with E-Prime software (Psychology Software Tools, Pittsburgh, PA). Demographics and vocabulary measures (Shipley, 1986) were administered at the beginning and end of the session, respectively.

Results and discussion

To assess performance we calculated three memory scores for each participant, consisting of the hit rate to studied items (for Self, Other, and Case trials) minus the false alarm rate to new items. Because there was only one pool of lure items at recognition, the false alarm rate was constant across the three hit minus false alarm scores, but provided a correction for potential between-group differences in the false alarm rate.

We conducted a 2×3 mixed analysis of variance (ANOVA) on the hit minus false alarm rates, with Age (Young/Older adults) as the between-groups variable and Condition (Self/Other/Case) as the within-group variable. Results are shown in Figure 1a. Importantly, the Age × Condition interaction did not reach significance, $F(2, 92) = 2.12$, $p = .13$, $\eta_p^2 = .04$. The ANOVA yielded a main effect of Age, with young adults $(M = .34)$ exhibiting more accurate recognition of words than older adults $(M = .21)$, $F(1, 46) = 14.53$, $p < .001$, $\eta_p^2 = .24$. The main effect of Condition was also significant, $F(2, 92) = 64.67$, $p < .001$, $\eta_p^2 = .58$. Follow-up 2×2 ANOVAs with Age (Young/Older adults) and only two levels of the Condition variable (Self/Other or Other/Case) revealed that words encoded in the self condition were remembered better than those encoded in the other person condition, $F(1, 46) = 24.53$, $p < .001$, $\eta_p^2 = .35$, and that, in turn, the other person condition supported better memory than the case condition $F(1, 46) = 51.26$, $p < .001$, $\eta_p^2 = .53$.

The main effect of age emerged primarily due to the false alarm rates (young $M = .19$, older adults $M = .31$), $t(46) = 3.08$, $p < .01$. In an ANOVA of the hit rates alone, neither the main effect of age $(F < 1)$ nor the interaction of age with condition $(F < 2.5)$ reached significance. Compared to older adults, young adults had numerically higher hit rates in the self and other conditions and a lower hit rate in the case condition, but none of the hit rates differed significantly across the age groups $(ts < 1)$.

The pattern of results suggests that the self-referencing effect benefits older adults' memory, much like it does for young adults. However, older adults exhibit lower levels of memory than young adults across the board, and self-referencing does not reduce age differences in memory relative to other types of encoding strategies.

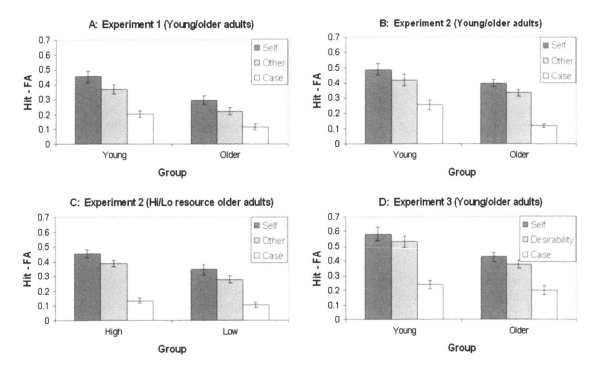

Figure 1. (a) Age comparison for Experiment 1. The graphs display adjective recognition performance for Experiment 1 across the age groups. Although young adults exhibit better memory than the older adults, the pattern is the same across age groups and both samples benefit from self-referencing of information. (b) Age comparison for Experiment 2. The graphs display adjective recognition performance for Experiment 2 across the age groups. Even when judgements are made about a "close other", the findings are identical to those of Experiment 1 with main effects of Age and Condition, but no interaction of Age × Condition. (c) Comparison of high vs low resource older adults for Experiment 2. The graphs display adjective recognition performance for Experiment 2 across the groups of older adults with high and low amounts of cognitive resource. High resource older adults benefit more than low resource older adults from referencing the self or another person. (d) Age comparison for Experiment 3. The graphs display adjective recognition performance for Experiment 3 across the age groups. When judgements are made about desirability, young adults show enhanced encoding relative to older adults for self and desirability trials compared to case trials.

Influence of emotion on age differences. To explore the extent to which self-referencing depended on age-related differences in emotional processing, we examined the influence of adjective valence (positive/negative) and the participants' ratings responses (yes/no) on recognition performance. Using a median split on adjective valence (Anderson, 1968), we divided the adjectives into positive and negative sets. Based on the findings of a positivity bias in older adults' memories (Mather & Carstensen, 2005), we might expect that older adults' memory performance would approach that of young adults for positive words. In a comparison of hit minus false alarm rates using an ANOVA of Age (Young/Older) × Condition (Self/Other/Case) × Valence (Positive/Negative), we did not find evidence that valence differentially affected memory across the age groups (Fs < 2). However, there was a trend overall for negative words ($M = .29$) to be better remembered than positive words ($M = .26$), $F(1, 46) = 2.84$, $p < .10$, $\eta_p^2 = .06$. Although hit rates were higher for positive than negative words for all conditions (ps < .03), the particularly high false alarm rate for positive compared to negative items ($p < .001$) likely contributes to the overall trend for higher corrected recognition scores for negative items. Valence interacted with condition, $F(2, 92) = 4.73$, $p < .02$, $\eta_p^2 = .09$. While corrected recognition scores were higher for negative than positive items in the case condition, the pattern differed significantly from the self condition, in which memory was more balanced for positive and negative words with a slight tendency for positive items to be remembered more accurately than negative items, $F(1, 46) = 8.75$, $p < .01$, $\eta_p^2 = .16$. The other condition ($F < 1$) did not differ significantly from the case condition. Hit and false alarm rates are displayed in Table 2. Across both age groups, higher levels of memory for positive self-relevant items and negative items in the other and case conditions seem to reflect memory processes rather than differences in initial judgements because young and older adults initially endorse similar proportions of positive and negative items as descriptive of self and other (Gutchess et al., 2007).

Influence of self-relevance ratings on age differences. Age differences in reflecting on the self, or the complexity of the self-concept, could be reflected in the initial ratings judgements and impact recognition memory. Young adults show increased recognition for items that are characteristic of themselves (as in Rogers et al., 1977, but not Rogers, Rogers, & Kuiper, 1979); it could be the case that resource limitations with age cause older adults to prioritise information that is most personally relevant at the expense of information that is not self-relevant. One might predict that even though young and older adults remember more items judged as self-descriptive than items that do not describe the self, this benefit will be exaggerated in older adults. Across all participants, the proportion of items rated "yes" that were subsequently recognised was higher than the proportion for those rated "no", $F(1, 45) = 58.14$, $p < .001$, but none of the interactions involving age reached significance (Fs < 2).[2] In addition, the time needed to make the initial judgement did not vary significantly across the age groups. Although there was a main effect of condition, $F(2, 90) = 39.19$, $p < .001$, with the slowest RTs for the "other" condition and the fastest RTs for the case condition, the pattern was the same across both age groups, and did not vary as a function of response (Yes/No). Reaction times are displayed in Table 2. We did not find any evidence for differences in the diversity of the self-concept across age groups. Young and older adults required similar amounts of time to make judgements of self-descriptiveness, relative to the judgements for other conditions, and remembered similar proportions of items rated as self-descriptive.

For self and other person trials, the amount of time spent making the initial rating judgements was unrelated to later memory performance. The contribution of cognitive resources to self-referencing benefits will be addressed further in Experiment 2, but because the other encoding variables (i.e., response speed and yes/no response) did not differentially affect memory across the age groups, these factors will not be considered in subsequent experiments.

Based on Experiment 1, we conclude that self-referential information may support effective encoding by young and older adults, although it does not reduce age-related declines in episodic memory. Encoding information in relation to oneself is a socially meaningful task, which engages successful encoding strategies for older adults.

---

[2] Rating and reaction time data during encoding were unavailable for one young participant.

TABLE 2
Reaction times for ratings and the number of hits (out of 24) and false alarms (out of 72) for positive and negative items in Experiment 1 (means and *SD*)

Hits & false alarms by valence	Self		Other		Case		FA	
	Pos	*Neg*	*Pos*	*Neg*	*Pos*	*Neg*	*Pos*	*Neg*
Young	16.67 (4.31)	14.38 (4.67)	13.79 (4.20)	12.63 (4.60)	9.13 (3.97)	9.67 (3.73)	17.42 (10.96)	10.92 (8.16)
Older	16.96 (4.49)	12.00 (4.32)	14.46 (5.19)	10.83 (5.03)	12.17 (5.19)	8.13 (4.93)	28.79 (14.14)	15.38 (8.87)
Reaction times								
Young	1788 (406)		1811 (427)		1421 (476)		N/A	
Older	1857 (380)		1944 (445)		1632 (479)		N/A	

EXPERIMENT 2

Based on Experiment 1, we found young and older adults both benefit from self-referencing of information beyond the benefit from other-person referencing. However, additional factors could restrict the self-reference benefit for older compared to young adults. First, judgements about highly familiar, intimate others (Bower & Gilligan, 1979; Ferguson et al., 1983) lead to high levels of recognition. These judgements support more modest benefits for self-referencing compared to other-referencing. It is as if there is an incorporation of information regarding both the self and the close other, such that the self does not remain as distinct an entity. Because older adults should generally have longer-lasting relationships with an intimate other person compared to young adults, this could allow for more incorporation of the close other in older adults' concept of self (Aron, Aron, Tudor, & Nelson, 1991). Were this to occur, older adults should have a less distinct self-representation and should not benefit from self-referencing more than other-referencing. Even if an extended relationship selectively affects the representation of the other person, rather than also influencing the representation for self, a highly differentiated and elaborated other would lead to a reduced self-referencing effect due to a smaller memory enhancement for self over other.

The self-reference effect could also be more limited in older adults if self-referential processing places strong demands on cognitive resources. It is unclear whether there would be such a draw on cognitive resources. On the one hand, the child development literature divulges that the self-reference effect can be stable despite changes in cognitive development (Pullyblank

et al., 1985), and thereby suggests that cognitive capacity plays a small role in self-referential encoding. On the other hand, however, cognitive resources likely contribute to the ability to benefit from organisational and elaborative processes engaged by the self (Klein & Kihlstrom, 1986; Klein & Loftus, 1988; McDaniel, Lapsley, & Milstead, 1987), and it would be surprising if older populations were not affected by resource limitations. Older adults often show substantial variability in cognitive resources, and these individual differences can lead to marked differences in performance on a range of cognitive tasks.

Experiment 2 was designed to address potential age-related limitations in the self-reference effect. To examine the extent to which a blending of self and other could reduce the self-reference benefit, we asked young and older adults to make decisions about the self and about a close other person. To address the degree to which the self-reference effect depends on the availability of cognitive resources, we compare older adults with high and low levels of resource using speed of processing measures. Although it is unclear whether speed of processing tasks tap into one fundamental process, such as the speed of neural transmission, or reflect resource availability through the interaction of speed with other higher-order cognitive processes such as working memory, prior research suggests that speed of processing is highly correlated with measures of executive function and memory, and mediates much of the age-related variance in cognitive performance (Park et al., 2002; Salthouse, 1996). We predict that older adults with more cognitive resources available should benefit from self-referencing more than those with limited cognitive capacity.

Method

Participants. A total of 30 young (age range 18–30) and 60 older adults (age range 61–80), drawn from the same samples as Experiment 1, participated in the study. Demographic characteristics and performance on measures of cognitive ability are presented in Table 1.[3] Older adults were significantly more educated than young adults, $t(88) = 5.69$, $p < .001$, slower on the speeded digit comparison, $t(88) = 5.94$, $p < .001$, and pattern comparison, $t(88) = 6.99$, $p < .001$, tasks, and scored higher on the Shipley vocabulary scale, $t(84) = 6.79$, $p < .001$.

Materials and procedures. The experiment was identical to Experiment 1, but participants were cued to make judgements about a "Close Person" rather than Albert Einstein. Participants identified a single personally familiar other to reference for all "Close Person" judgements, and completed a questionnaire about this individual. Both age groups selected close others who were highly familiar (young $M = 8.67$, $SD = .81$; older adults $M = 8.47$, $SD = 1.48$) and well liked (young $M = 8.86$, $SD = .44$; older adults $M = 8.62$, $SD = .92$) as rated on a 9-point scale where a score of 9 indicates "extremely familiar" or "like very much", and there were no significant age differences in these ratings ($ts < 1.5$). Not surprisingly, older adults reported knowing their close other significantly longer ($M = 44.11$ years, $SD = 13.13$) than did young adults ($M = 12.18$ years, $SD = 8.11$); $t(81) = 11.75$, $p < .001$. They also reported more frequent contact with their selected target person, with daily contact for 73% of older adults as opposed to only 24% of young adults. The majority of older adults (72%) selected a spouse or romantic partner as their close other, with a friend/best friend (12%) or family member (child 10%, parent 3%, sibling 2%) selected less often. Young adults' selections were more evenly distributed across romantic partner/spouse (28%), best friend (31%), and family members (24% for siblings and 17% for parents). Both age groups selected close others with similar proportions of each gender (young 62% female; older adults 58% female), although older adults' close other was older ($M = 66.75$ years, $SD = 11.98$) than young adults' ($M = 26.86$ years, $SD = 12.81$); $t(87) = 14.39$, $p < .001$. In sum, older adults

reported more contact and longer experiences, particularly of a romantic nature, with their close other compared to young adults, although both groups selected individuals they held in high regard and had known for a large proportion of their lives.

Subdivision of older adult group. To investigate the role of cognitive resources in the ability to benefit from self-referencing, we divided older adults into high and low resource groups based on the speed of processing measures. Digit and pattern comparison tasks require participants to make perceptual judgements of two strings of characters. We selected these tasks because they represent both verbal and non-verbal judgements, and because they make fewer motor demands than some other speed tasks (such as digit–symbol substitution). We used the combined total number of items correctly completed (minus errors) on the two speed tasks. Thus, high performers, compared to low performers, were significantly faster on both the pattern comparison, $t(58) = 8.81$, $p < .001$, and digit comparison, $t(58) = 5.90$, $p < .001$. Across both measures, high performers completed an average of 117.43 items ($SD = 8.37$) while low performers completed an average of 91.10 items ($SD = 11.72$). Low performers, in comparison to high performers, were significantly older ($M = 72.62$ vs $M = 69.44$), $t(58) = 2.83$, $p < .01$, less educated ($M = 15.48$ vs $M = 16.85$), $t(58) = 2.09$, $p < .05$, and had poorer vocabularies ($M = 34.70$ vs $M = 36.72$), $t(54) = 2.28$, $p < .05$.

To ensure that older adults with high and low amounts of cognitive resource did not differ in the types of close others selected, we conducted independent-sample t-tests on the close person questionnaire responses. The groups did not differ in their ratings of familiarity or liking, or in their length of acquaintance with the target individuals ($ts < 1$). The target individuals did not differ on age ($t < 1.5$), gender (53% female for low resource; 63% for high resource), relationship to the participant (the majority were spouses/romantic partners: 70% low resource; 73% high resource), or frequency of interaction (daily: 73% for both groups).

Results and discussion

Age differences. As in Experiment 1, we calculated hit minus false alarm rates to assess recognition performance for each of the three conditions (Self, Close Other, and Case). We then

---

[3] Ages are unavailable for two young adults and vocabulary scores are unavailable for four older participants.

conducted a 2×3 mixed ANOVA on the hit minus false alarm rates, with Age (Young/Older adults) as the between-groups variable and Condition (Self/Other/Case) as the within-group variable. Results are displayed in Figure 1b. The ANOVA revealed a main effect of Age: $F(1, 88) = 10.97$, $p < .005$, $\eta_p^2 = .11$. As in Experiment 1, young adults remembered more items relative to their false alarm rate than older adults (young $M = .39$; older adults $M = .29$). The main effect of Condition was significant, $F(2, 176) = 121.08$, $p < .001$, $\eta_p^2 = .58$, with the self condition resulting in higher levels of memory than the other person condition, $F(1, 88) = 34.51$, $p < .001$, $\eta_p^2 = .28$, and the other person condition supported higher levels of memory than did the case condition, $F(1, 88) = 103.88$, $p < .001$, $\eta_p^2 = .54$. The Age $\times$ Condition interaction did not approach significance: $F(2, 176) = 1.30$, $p = .28$, $\eta_p^2 = .02$. Thus, the results converge with those of Experiment 1 to demonstrate that older adults' memory benefits from referencing the self or a familiar person, relative to the case condition. Memory is poorer across all conditions with age; even referencing an intimately close individual with whom older adults have extensive life experience does not afford any advantage relative to young adults. Young and older adults exhibit self-reference effects of a similar magnitude in comparison to a personally familiar close companion.

The main effect of age emerges through the combination of the hit and false alarm rates. Older adults ($M = .27$) make more false alarms than young adults ($M = .23$), but this difference is not significant, $t(88) = 1.04$, $p = .30$. Young adults had significantly more hits in the case condition, $t(88) = 2.56$, $p < .02$, and marginally more in the self, $t(88) = 1.53$, $p = .13$, and other, $t(88) = 1.36$, $p = .18$, conditions. Although a different pattern emerged in Experiment 1, which yielded significant age differences in false alarms rates but not the hit rates, inspection of the means reveals substantial similarity across the two conditions. The patterns of results for the age groups are identical across the two studies, with the sole exception of the hit rate for the case condition.

The results of Experiment 2 converge with those of Experiment 1 to suggest that although recognition performance is impaired for older adults relative to young adults, self- and other-referencing of information at encoding leads to higher levels of memory compared to a shallow condition for both young and older adults.

Referencing a close other person did not substantially change the pattern of results compared to the use of a personally unfamiliar other in Experiment 1. This result is in contrast to previous literature (Bower & Gilligan, 1979), which suggests that personally familiar others engage the same elaborative encoding processes as the self. Even though the close other was much more familiar and possibly incorporated into the construct of "self" (Aron et al., 1991) for older more than young adults, the relative differences between the young and older adults were similar across the conditions and similar to the pattern exhibited in Experiment 1. If anything, the poorer performance of older adults was exaggerated for the case condition. Another factor to consider is that the large number of trials in this experiment may have maximised the difference between conditions. A meta-analysis shows that the self-reference effect is larger under conditions of high memory load and distraction during the retention interval (Symons & Johnson, 1997), both of which were present in our design.

Resource-based differences for older adults. To compare the effect of self-referencing across high and low resource groups of older adults,[4] we conducted a 2×3 mixed ANOVA with Group (High/Low resource) as a between-subjects variable and Condition (Self/Other/Case) as a within-subjects variable on the corrected recognition (hit minus false alarm) scores. There was a main effect of Group, $F(1, 58) = 7.44$, $p < .01$, $\eta_p^2 = .11$, such that high resource older adults ($M = .33$) exhibited better memory than low resource older adults ($M = .24$). As in the comparisons of age groups in Experiments 1 and 2, there was also a main effect of Condition, $F(2, 116) = 137.91$, $p < .001$, $\eta_p^2 = .70$, with recognition higher in the self condition than the other person condition, $F(1, 58) = 26.15$, $p < .001$, $\eta_p^2 = .31$, and higher in the other person condition than in the case condition, $F(1, 58) = 140.00$, $p < .001$, $\eta_p^2 = .71$. Unlike the comparisons across age groups, there was a significant interaction of Group $\times$ Condition, $F(2, 116) = 3.42$, $p < .05$, $\eta_p^2 = .06$. Based on 2×2 mixed ANOVAs with Group and only two levels of the Condition variable (Self/Case or Other/Case), high resource older adults exhibited disproportionately higher memory than low

---

[4] A direct comparison of young and high-performing older adults is available from the authors.

resource older adults for other person trials, $F(1, 58) = 5.00$, $p < .05$, $\eta_p^2 = .08$, and marginally higher memory for self trials, $F(1, 58) = 3.54$, $p = .065$, $\eta_p^2 = .06$, relative to the case condition. Results are shown in Figure 1c, and suggest that the availability of cognitive resource contributes to the ability of older adults to achieve enhanced encoding from referencing the self or another person.[5]

The group differences appear to be driven largely by the hit rates, with high-resource older adults making significantly more hits in the self, $t(58) = 2.07$, $p < .05$, and other, $t(58) = 2.25$, $p < .03$, conditions. The false alarm rates for high $(M = .25)$ and low $(M = .28)$ resource older adults do not differ, nor do the hits for the case condition $(ts < 1)$.

Results of Experiment 2 suggest that the availability of cognitive resources plays an important role in the potential to benefit from self-referencing of information. Older adults with higher amounts of resource (as assessed by speed of processing measures) benefited more from referencing the self or another person compared to those older adults with less cognitive resource. The benefits extend across both deep encoding conditions; hence rather than suggesting a unique benefit from self-referencing, it likely reflects the support that high-resource older adults receive from conditions that promote deep, elaborative encoding (see Kausler, 1994).

The equivalent performance in the case condition for older adults with high and low amounts of cognitive resource argues against the influences of resource-based processes in this condition. The pattern also suggests that potential age differences in the case condition do not reflect a tendency for older adults to more selectively allocate encoding resources to the self and other person conditions compared to young adults.

Influence of emotion on group differences. The trend in Experiment 1 for higher corrected recognition scores for negative words $(M = .35)$ than positive words $(M = .32)$ reached significance in Experiment 2, $F(1, 88) = 4.98$, $p < .03$, $\eta_p^2 = .05$. However, valence did not interact with

age or condition $(Fs < 2)$. The availability of cognitive resources across older adults did not affect the magnitude of the positivity bias for older adults. There were no main effect or interactions $(Fs < 2)$ involving valence in a comparison of high and low resource elderly.

These data converge with those of Experiment 1 to suggest that negative adjectives are better remembered than positive ones, but in this experiment with a larger sample, the pattern is the same for self-referencing as for the other person or case conditions. Furthermore, we do not find any differences across the high and low resource groups of older adults in the effects of valence. This pattern contrasts Mather and Knight's (2005) findings that the amount of available cognitive resources contributes to the magnitude of the positivity bias for older adults. It may be that our speed of processing measure is less sensitive to these effects than the cognitive control measures used by Mather and Knight (2005), or that our stimuli are not as strongly valenced as the pictures used in their study.

Experiment 2 establishes that the availability of cognitive resources contributes to mnemonic benefits of self-referencing and, to a lesser degree, other person referencing. The finding of reduced benefits for low resource older adults establishes limits to the strategy of referencing self or other.

EXPERIMENT 3

Because Experiment 2 demonstrated limits to the self-referencing effect for subgroups of older adults, we investigated potential age-related limits to the self-reference effect, while also manipulating the socioemotional nature of the judgements. We propose that subjective judgements that do not require judgements about the self per se could also rely on flexibly referencing the self. In Experiment 3 we investigated the ability of young and older adults to extend self-referencing to subjective judgements about desirability. For young adults, evaluative judgements, such as desirability, can elevate memory to the same level as self judgements in between- (Ferguson et al., 1983), but not within- (McCaul & Maki, 1984), subjects designs. Affective judgements may spontaneously reference the self to some degree (i.e., Do I find this desirable? Is this a trait I would want to display?), and participants may capitalise on the overlap between processes to better encode information when making both

---

[5] This pattern is also present for the smaller samples tested in Experiment 1. The interaction of condition and group is significant, with high resource older adults, but not low resource older adults, exhibiting significantly higher memory for the self-referenced items compared to the other-referenced items. Analyses are available from the authors.

kinds of judgements. Young adults may be more prone than older adults to adopt a strategy that extends self-referencing to evaluative judgements, and socioemotional judgements to self-referencing, which would demonstrate a limit to the self-referencing effect with age.

Method

Participants. A total of 18 young adults (ages 18–26) from Harvard University and 18 older adults (ages 61–79) from the surrounding community participated in the study. Demographic characteristics and performance on measures of cognitive ability are displayed in Table 1.[6] Older adults were significantly more educated than young adults, $t(34) = 5.23$, $p < .001$, but completed fewer items on the speeded digit comparison task, $t(33) = 3.93$, $p < .001$. Although vocabulary scores were in line with those collected from older adult samples in Experiments 1 and 2, older adults did not perform significantly better than young on the vocabulary test ($t < 1$). Older adults scored at least a 27 on the Mini-Mental State Examination (MMSE; Folstein, Folstein, & McHugh, 1975), with an average score of 29.33 ($SD = .98$).[7] The research was approved by the Harvard University Institutional Review Board.

Materials and procedures. The experimental materials and procedures were identical to the previous studies, with two exceptions. The Shipley vocabulary test (Shipley, 1986) was administered during the retention interval in place of the pattern comparison task, which was not administered. The key manipulation change was that participants made desirability judgements instead of judgements about another person. Instructions emphasised the self-referential nature of making desirability judgements, in that they should be based on the participant's personal experience. We verified that the participants' desirability assessments evoked self-referencing through the use of a debriefing questionnaire with a 5-point scale where a rating of "1" denoted "almost all the time", a rating of "3" denoted "about half the time", and a rating of "5" denoted "never". Participants rated that they often thought about

the self while making the desirability judgements (young $M = 2.67$, $SD = .77$; older adults $M = 1.71$, $SD = .92$). Even though older adults reported referencing the self more than did young, $t(33) = 3.36$, $p < .005$, both groups similarly claimed ($t < 1.6$) that what they reflected upon to make the self judgements overlapped with that for the desirability judgements (young $M = 3.50$, $SD = .86$; older adults $M = 3.94$, $SD = .83$ where a rating of "3" reflects "sometimes yes, sometimes no" and rating of "4" reflects "fair amount of overlap"). Desirability judgements had little in common with the case judgements (young $M = 1.94$, $SD = .73$; older adults $M = 1.71$, $SD = 1.05$ where a rating of "1" corresponds to "not at all – very different" and a rating of "2" corresponds to "not particularly"), though both groups again responded similarly, $t < 1$.

Results and discussion

Age differences. In a 2×3 mixed ANOVA with Age (Young/Older adults) as the between-groups variable and Condition (Self/Desirability/Case) as the within-subjects variable, multiple effects emerged, as shown in Figure 1d. Young adults ($M = .45$) remembered significantly more words than older adults ($M = .34$), $F(1, 34) = 7.83$, $p < .01$, $\eta_p^2 = .19$. The main effect of Condition was also significant, $F(2, 68) = 83.36$, $p < .001$, $\eta_p^2 = .71$, and follow-up 2×2 ANOVAs suggested that the self condition resulted in higher levels of memory than the desirability condition, $F(1, 34) = 7.42$, $p < .05$, $\eta_p^2 = .18$, and that the desirability condition resulted in greater memory than the case condition, $F(1, 34) = 93.15$, $p < .001$, $\eta_p^2 = .73$. In contrast to Experiments 1 and 2, the interaction of Age × Condition was significant, $F(2, 68) = 4.29$, $p < .05$, $\eta_p^2 = .11$. To interpret the interaction, we conducted a series of 2×2 ANOVAs with only two levels of the Condition variable (Self/Case or Desirability/Case), and results suggest that young benefited disproportionately more than older adults from making self, $F(1, 34) = 4.77$, $p < .05$, $\eta_p^2 = .12$, and desirability judgements, $F(1, 34) = 5.99$, $p < .05$, $\eta_p^2 = .15$, during encoding, relative to making case judgements. Note that in contrast to the previous experiments, young and older adults are matched on performance in the case condition. This provides an equivalent baseline across age groups from which to compare the benefit from

---

[6] For Experiment 3, one young participant did not complete the digit comparison task, and one older participant did not complete the vocabulary measure. The debriefing questionnaire was also omitted by one older adult.

[7] Current MMSE scores were available for 15 out of 18 older adults.

referencing the self, and thus provides a means of matching performance.

Age influenced both hit and false alarm rates, similar to the pattern that emerged for Experiment 2. Young made significantly more hits for self, $t(34) = 2.09$, $p < .05$, desirability, $t(34) = 2.18$, $p < .05$, but not case trials ($t < 1$), whereas older adults made marginally more false alarms, $t(34) = 1.90$, $p = .07$.

Previous findings in the literature (e.g., May et al., 2005; Rahhal et al., 2002) suggest that attending to socioemotional information can equate memory across young and older adults. In contrast, our results from Experiment 3 show that adding an evaluative social judgement increased the magnitude of age differences, with young adults performing disproportionately better than elderly people in both the self and desirability conditions. Thus, Experiment 3 suggests that the self-reference advantage does not benefit elderly people solely due to the socioemotional nature of the task: When attention is heightened to socioemotional information in this experiment, elderly adults benefit less than young adults and the results diverge from the findings of our initial experiments.

We further argue that our pattern of results suggests that young adults may extend self-referencing to other socioemotional judgements more than older adults. When making desirability judgements, participants were encouraged to reflect on their own personal experiences to make the subjective judgements. Orienting to desirability and self-relevance, in comparison to the case condition, disproportionately improved young adults' memory relative to that of older adults. Perhaps young adults were able to benefit from the overlap between evaluative and self-referential processes and devoted resources to these trials at the expense of case trials. It seems that the desirability condition, rather than the self condition, drove the heightened memory performance of young adults particularly when compared to the pattern for Experiment 2.[8] In contrast to Experiments 1 and 2, desirability judgements required explicit evaluation of the positive or negative connotations of the adjectives. There may be increased awareness of the social desirability of traits when making judgements about oneself, whereas one is less focused on this feature when making judgements about others. When both decisions are jointly presented in one context, desirability judgements may involve consideration of the self to some extent (e.g., "Do *I* consider 'rude' to be a desirable trait?") but self-judgements may also involve consideration of desirability (i.e., "Because it's an undesirable characteristic to exhibit, I'm ashamed to admit that I can be 'rude' sometimes."). This suggests that the extension of self-referencing to the desirability judgements, and vice versa, disproportionately benefits young adults.

Because Experiment 3 sampled from a different population of young and older adults, we cannot definitively rule out sampling differences. However, it is the young adults, not the older adults, who appear to differ on some neuropsychological measures (see Table 1), but memory does not differ for the comparable conditions across experiments.[9]

It also seems unlikely that the effects involving age in Experiment 3 result from different interpretation of the instructions by each age group. If anything, older adults claimed in the debriefing measure that they reflected on themselves to a greater extent for the desirability condition than did young adults. Even so, introducing desirability judgements did not support successful *encoding* of self or desirable trials for older adults as much as it did for young, which we interpret as a limitation in older adults' ability to extend self-referencing as broadly as young adults. The co-occurrence of the self and desirability conditions may be critical; young adults may not benefit disproportionately in a between-subjects design (see McCaul & Maki, 1984, for a similar argument). Further research is needed on this point.

Notably, the age groups are matched on the case condition in Experiment 3. We do not believe that this explains older adults' reduced benefit in the self and desirability conditions relative to the young. When case performance is matched across groups in Experiments 1, we do not replicate the pattern seen here of reduced benefits for older adults.[10]

Influence of emotion on age differences. In a comparison of hit minus false alarm rates using an ANOVA of Age (Young/Older adults) × Condition (Self/Desirability/Case) × Valence (Positive/Negative), there were no significant main effects

---

[8] Analyses are available from the authors.

[9] Analyses are available from the authors.

[10] Analyses are available from the authors.

or interactions involving valence ($Fs < 2.5$). Inclusion of a condition that focuses on the socioemotional aspects of words, as accomplished with the desirability judgements in this experiment, may equate the encoding of positive and negative words.

Even when valence is explicitly referenced in the desirability condition, we do not find a greater enhancement for positive items in the self condition, relative to the other conditions. The pattern of results from Experiment 3 converges with the previous experiments to suggest that the self-reference effect is not attributable solely to the emotional nature of self-judgements. If emotion drove the self-referencing effect, the emphasis on evaluative, emotional encoding processing should lead to equivalent memory enhancement relative to the case condition for both young and older adults. Rather, the pattern of findings suggests that the intact self-reference effect for older adults reported in Experiments 1 and 2 may reflect additional non-emotional properties of the self as a structure that facilitates encoding.

GENERAL DISCUSSION

Over a series of three experiments we demonstrated that under some circumstances, older adults can benefit from self-referencing to the same extent as young adults. Self-referencing similarly enhanced recognition performance for young and older adults relative to familiar others, personally familiar others, and shallow perceptual encoding. Although we predicted that self-referencing could restore older adults' memory to the level of young adults, this finding was not obtained, and the results indicated instead that older adults are more limited in their application of self-referencing. Older adults with fewer cognitive resources benefited less from self-referencing than those with greater cognitive resources. Further, drawing on the self to make desirability judgements did not enhance memory for older adults as much as it did for young adults. Thus, we conclude that older adults may be limited in their application of self-referencing due to its demand on cognitive resources and their diminished ability to apply the strategy flexibly and broadly in other types of evaluative judgements.

In a similar vein, we proposed in the introduction that self-referencing could partially explain effects in the literature that have been attributed to emotion (e.g., May et al., 2005; Rahhal et al., 2002). This possibility seems unlikely because the results of Experiment 3 suggest that self-referencing does not support older adults' memory solely due to its socioemotional features and self-referencing alone does not support equivalent levels of memory performance in young and older adults. Casting information in terms of its emotional significance would likely involve spontaneous extension of self-referencing, which we have demonstrated is difficult for older adults even with explicit instructions. We maintain that it would be a worthwhile venture for future studies to delineate the individual contributions of self and emotion. For example, must an older adult be able to project him or herself into the situation as the target of deception, illness, or risk in order to encode as effectively as young adults?

Our study of self-referencing departs from previous studies of socioemotional processing in a few important ways. The source information presented in previous studies (Rahhal et al., 2002; May et al., 2005) is of a consequential nature, suggesting impending danger or deception. Participants may find the potential outcomes more pertinent to future behaviour, real or imagined, than making simple, quick judgements of the self- or other- relevance of adjectives. Self and other judgements that are more relevant to the future and invoke more deliberative reflection could bolster older adults' memory to the level of the young. A second important departure from prior studies is the presentation of conditions within participants, rather than between. The magnitude of the self-reference effect changes as a function of the other conditions included in the design (McCaul & Maki, 1984). This result could be particularly relevant for our third experiment in which the co-occurrence of self and desirability trials could be critical to the pattern of findings; age differences could be less pronounced in a between-subjects design. The intermixing of trials could be of particular concern in a between-subjects design because it might induce task-switching demands, which impact older adults more than young adults (Kray & Lindenberger, 2000) and could contribute to impoverished encoding with age. In addition, our studies had high memory loads (e.g., 144 items to encode), which may put older adults, particularly those with less cognitive resources, at a disadvantage relative to young adults. Additional empirical investigations, holding all other factors constant, would be necessary to assess the contribution of each of these factors to the present pattern of results.

Although we identify a role for cognitive resources in determining the magnitude of the benefit from self-referencing, our use of a speed of processing measure does not indicate which specific resources are important. While it is possible that speed of processing measures tap directly into processing constraints, such as the speed of neural transmission (Salthouse, 1996), or inhibitory function (Lustig, Hasher, & Tonev, 2006), it may be that the measure reflects the indirect operation of differences due to age or education (low resource samples are both older and less educated than high resource samples), or the availability of additional time to encode stimuli after making an adjective judgement response. More nuanced approaches to assess cognitive control (Mather & Knight, 2005) or executive function (Marquine, Walther, & Glisky, 2006) may ultimately offer greater specificity regarding the locus of the effects of ageing on the self-reference effect, but our results offer initial evidence that the magnitude of the self-reference effect depends on the availability of cognitive resources. It is important to note that while the adjective judgements themselves are performed quickly and perhaps with low effort, the *encoding* of adjectives places demands on cognitive resources.

The limitations in older adults' ability to use self-referencing have implications for the viability of using self-referencing in everyday situations. Real-world applications necessitate flexible and spontaneous application of the strategy to overcome age-related declines in memory. In our paradigm, participants were explicitly instructed to evaluate desirability based on their own personal experiences—even without demands to spontaneously self-initiate use of self-referencing, older adults were constrained in their ability to apply it successfully. Because these limitations exist even for high-functioning older adults, the strategy does not seem to hold much promise as an intervention for clinical ageing populations, such as those with mild cognitive impairment (MCI) or in the early stages of Alzheimer's disease. These qualifications are not intended to discount the improvements in memory that do occur as a result of self-referencing. Self-referencing does appear to be an effective encoding strategy, even compared to other "deep" strategies, and should result in some gains in memory even for cognitively impaired older adults.

However, moving the strategy away from sterile laboratory conditions and explicit task instructions would likely pose significant challenges to successful application of the strategy.

Finally, more work is needed to understand what aspects of items are better encoded through self-referencing. Self-referencing may be prone to memory distortion in that it evokes a schematic representation of oneself. Young adults commit more false alarms for items that are self-descriptive than for those that are not (Rogers et al., 1979). This tendency could be exaggerated with age, as is the case for other types of memory distortion (e.g., Koutstaal & Schacter, 1997). Compounding this possibility, schematic support seems to be intact for older adults, and compared to schema-inconsistent or irrelevant information, it can sometimes support memory performance (Castel, 2005), but also be more difficult to inhibit with age (Malmstrom & LaVoie, 2002). In terms of the self-reference effect, an older adult who considers his/her unselfish nature to be a defining feature essential to his/her self-schema would have heightened activation associated with "unselfish". This activation could be mistaken for familiarity in the task at hand, leading to a false alarm. Alternatively, for words that resonate with one's self-schema, encoding could emphasise the connotation of the word rather than the precise word used to illustrate the concept. This would lead to heightened familiarity for associated words, such as "generous" and perhaps even the antonym, "selfish".

In conclusion, we have provided evidence that self-referencing (1) can enhance memory similarly for young and older adults, (2) depends on the availability of cognitive resources and has more limited effectiveness in older adults, and (3) diverges from socioemotional processing.

Manuscript received 26 February 2007
Manuscript accepted 20 September 2007
First published online 13 November 2007

REFERENCES

Anderson, N. H. (1968). Likeableness ratings of 555 personality-trait words. *Journal of Personality and Social Psychology, 9,* 272–279.

Aron, A., Aron, E. N., Tudor, M., & Nelson, G. (1991). Close relationships as including other in the self. *Journal of Personality and Social Psychology, 60,* 241–253.

Bower, G. H., & Gilligan, S. G. (1979). Remembering information related to one's self. *Journal of Research in Personality, 13,* 420–432.

Castel, A. D. (2005). Memory for grocery prices in younger and older adults: The role of schematic support. *Psychology and Ageing, 20,* 718–721.

Charles, S. T., Mather, M., & Carstensen, L. L. (2003). Focusing on the positive: Age differences in memory for positive, negative, and neutral stimuli. *Journal of Experimental Psychology, 85,* 163–178.

Craik, F. I. M., & Lockhart, R. S. (1972). Levels of processing: A framework for memory research. *Journal of Verbal Learning and Verbal Behavior, 11,* 671–684.

Craik, F. I. M., & McDowd, J. M. (1987). Age differences in recall and recognition. *Journal of Experimental Psychology: Learning, Memory, and Cognition, 13,* 474–479.

Craik, F. I. M., Moroz, T. M., Moscovitch, M., Stuss, D. T., Winocur, G., Tulving, E., et al. (1999). In search of the self: A positron emission tomography study. *Psychological Science, 10,* 26–34.

Craik, F. I. M., & Tulving, E. (1975). Depth of processing and the retention of words in episodic memory. *Journal of Experimental Psychology: General, 104,* 268–294.

Derwinger, A., Neely, A. S., MacDonald, S., & Bäckman, L. (2005). Forgetting numbers in old age: Strategy and learning speed matter. *Gerontology, 51,* 277–284.

Erber, J. T., Herman, T. G., & Botwinick, J. (1980). Age differences in memory as a function of depth of processing. *Experimental Ageing Research, 6,* 341–348.

Eysenck, M. W. (1974). Age differences in incidental learning. *Developmental Psychology, 10,* 936–941

Ferguson, T. J., Rule, B. G., & Carlson, D. (1983). Memory for personally relevant information. *Journal of Personality and Social Psychology, 44,* 251–261.

Folstein, M. F., Folstein, S. E., & McHugh, P. R. (1975). Mini-mental state: A practical method for grading the cognitive state of patients for the clinician. *Journal of Psychiatric Research, 12,* 189–198.

Greenwald, A. G., & Banaji, M. R. (1989). The self as a memory system: Powerful, but ordinary. *Journal of Personality and Social Psychology, 57,* 41–54.

Gutchess, A. H., Kensinger, E. A., & Schacter, D. L. (2007). Ageing, self-referencing, and medial prefrontal cortex. *Social Neuroscience, 2,* 117–133.

Hashtroudi, S., Johnson, M. K., & Chrosniak, L. D. (1989). Ageing and source monitoring. *Psychology and Ageing, 4,* 106–112.

Hedden, T., Park, D. C., Nisbett, R., Ji, L-J., Jing, Q., & Jiao, S. (2002). Cultural variation in verbal versus spatial neuropsychological function across the life span. *Neuropsychology, 16,* 65–73.

Hultsch, D. F. (1969). Adult age differences in the organisation of free recall. *Developmental Psychology, 1,* 673–678.

Kausler, D. H. (1994). *Learning and memory in normal ageing.* San Diego, CA: Academic Press.

Kelley, W. M., Macrae, C. N., Wyland, C. L., Caglar, S., Inati, S., & Heatherton, T. F. (2002). Finding the self? An event-related fMRI study. *Journal of Cognitive Neuroscience, 14,* 785–794.

Klein, S. B., & Kihlstrom, J. F. (1986). Elaboration, organization, and the self-reference effect in memory. *Journal of Experimental Psychology: General, 115,* 26–38.

Klein, S. B., & Loftus, J. (1988). The nature of self-referent encoding: The contribution of elaborative and organisational processes. *Journal of Personality and Social Psychology, 55,* 5–11.

Koutstaal, W., & Schacter, D. L. (1997). Gist-based false recognition of pictures in older and younger adults. *Journal of Memory and Language, 37,* 555–583.

Kray, J., & Lindenberger, U. (2000). Adult age differences in task switching. *Psychology and Ageing, 15,* 126–147.

Lustig, C., Hasher, L., & Tonev, S. T. (2006). Distraction as a determinant of processing speed. *Psychonomic Bulletin & Review, 13,* 619–625.

Macrae, C. N., Moran, J. M., Heatherton, T. F., Banfield, J. F., & Kelley, W. M. (2004). Medial prefrontal activity predicts memory for self. *Cerebral Cortex, 14,* 647–654.

Malmstrom, T., & LaVoie, D. J. (2002). Age differences in inhibition of schema-activated distractors. *Experimental Ageing Research, 28,* 281–298.

Marquine, M. J., Walther, K., & Glisky, E. L. (2006). *Self-referential processing in older age: A neuropsychological approach.* Poster presented at the Cognitive Ageing Conference, Atlanta, GA.

Mather, M., & Carstensen, L. L. (2005). Ageing and motivated cognition: The positivity effect in attention and memory. *Trends in Cognitive Sciences, 9,* 496-502.

Mather, M., & Knight, M. (2005). Goal-directed memory: The role of cognitive control in older adults' emotional memory. *Psychology and Ageing, 20,* 554–570.

May, C. P., Rahhal, T., Berry, E. M., & Leighton, E. A. (2005). Ageing, source memory, and emotion. *Psychology and Ageing, 20,* 571–578.

McCaul, K. D., & Maki, R. H. (1984). Self-reference versus desirability ratings and memory for traits. *Journal of Personality and Social Psychology, 47,* 953–955.

McDaniel, M. A., Lapsley, D. K., & Milstead, M. (1987). Testing the generality and automaticity of self-reference encoding with release from proactive interference. *Journal of Experimental Social Psychology, 23,* 269–284.

Mitchell, J. P., Macrae, C. N., & Banaji, M. R. (2005). Forming impressions of people versus inanimate objects: Social-cognitive processing in the medial prefrontal cortex. *NeuroImage, 26,* 251–257.

Mueller, J. H., & Johnson, W. C. (1990). Trait distinctiveness and age specificity in self-referent information processing. *Bulletin of the Psychonomic Society, 28,* 119–122.

Mueller, J. H., Wonderlich, S., & Dugan, K. (1986). Self-referent processing of age-specific material. *Psychology and Ageing, 1,* 293–299.

Park, D. C., Lautenschlager, G., Hedden, T., Davidson, N. S., Smith, A. D., & Smith, P. (2002). Models of visuospatial and verbal memory across the adult life span. *Psychology and Ageing, 17*, 299–320.

Pullyblank, J., Bisanz, J., Scott, C., & Champion, M. A. (1985). Developmental invariance in the effects of functional self-knowledge on memory. *Child Development, 56*, 1447–1454.

Rahhal, T. A., May, C. P., & Hasher, L. (2002). Truth and character: Sources that older adults can remember. *Psychological Science, 13*, 101–105.

Rogers, T. B., Kuiper, N. A., & Kirker, W. S. (1977). Self-reference and the encoding of personal information. *Journal of Personality and Social Psychology, 35*, 677–688.

Rogers, T. B., Rogers, P. J., & Kuiper, N. A. (1979). Evidence for the self as a cognitive prototype: The "false alarms effect". *Personality and Social Psychology Bulletin, 5*, 53–56.

Salat, D. H., Buckner, R. L., Snyder, A. Z., Greve, D. N., Desikan, R. S. R., Busa, E., et al. (2004). Thinning of the cerebral cortex in ageing. *Cerebral Cortex, 14*, 721–730.

Salthouse, T. A. (1996). The processing-speed theory of adult age differences in cognition. *Psychological Review, 103*, 403–428.

Salthouse, T. A., & Babcock, R. L. (1991). Decomposing adult age differences in working memory. *Developmental Psychology, 27*, 763–776.

Schacter, D. L., Kaszniak, A. W., Kihlstrom, J. F., & Valdiserri, M. (1991). The relation between source memory and ageing. *Psychology and Ageing, 6*, 559–568.

Shipley, W. C. (1986). *Shipley Institute of Living Scale.* Los Angeles: Western Psychological services.

Sui, J., & Zhu, Y. (2005). Five-year-olds can show the self-reference advantage. *International Journal of Behavioral Development, 29*, 382–387.

Symons, C. S., & Johnson, B. T. (1997). The self-reference effect in memory: A meta-analysis. *Psychological Bulletin, 121*, 371–394.

Terracciano, A., McCrae, R. R., Brant, L. J., & Costa, P. T. (2005). Hierarchical linear modeling analyses of the NEO-PI-R scales in the Baltimore longitudinal study of ageing. *Psychology and Ageing, 20*, 493–506.

Subject index

T - #0063 - 270225 - C0 - 270/200/8 [10] - CB - 9781848727083 - Gloss Lamination